+ STIRLING
WILFORD
AMERICAN BUILDINGS

STIRLING + WILFORD
AMERICAN BUILDINGS

EDITED BY ALAN BERMAN

Artifice
books on architecture

Contents

Acknowledgements

The unexpected suggestion that I should assemble this collection of essays has involved collaborating with many people on both sides of the Atlantic whom I did not previously know, some of whom have happily become firm new friends. I am immensely grateful to all of the contributors for their generous work: with them I have engaged in a theatre of words — some delivered exemplars of precise language that I had no need to touch, others challenged the boundaries of English as I know it. All deserve my enormous thanks for their persistence and patience, particularly Amanda Reeser Lawrence who produced her essay very quickly. I owe particular thanks to Gary Wolf who initiated the project, drove me from Harvard to New York to Cornell and back, and has given constant encouragement, while exchanges with Nicholas Ray and Marco Iuliano have taught me a great deal. Michael Wilford has been generous with advice but scrupulous in offering it only when requested. Many others have been generous with their support: Paul Hester gave free use of his photographs, Cate St Hill prepared the bibliography, Renata Guttman and Elspeth Cowell at the CCA Archive were as helpful as ever, Albert Ferre first believed in the book, Kevin Bone and Steven Marks provided board and lodging in the US; also generous with help in a variety of ways were Natalie Belson, Philippa Berman, Peter Daners, the late Michael Spens, and Roger Stretton. I am sure there are others who I hope will forgive me if I fail to mention them. Thanks also to Kenneth Frampton who took considerable persuading before writing his contribution. It is a privilege to have his participation — our breakfast discussions in his favourite New York delis about architecture and the state of the world will remain cherished memories.

The book would not have been possible without financial support for production costs from The Arthur M Sackler Foundation for The Arts, Sciences and Humanities and from three individuals who wish to remain anonymous. To all of these I am immensely grateful.

At the last minute Marco Iuliano and Nicholas Ray subjected the text to detailed scrutiny and excised many errors for which I am enormously grateful. My two daughters Philippa and Zoe persuaded me to do this book, but, no longer living at home, it was Alison, my wife, who had to cope with the disruption it caused to any semblance of sane home life: thanks above all to her.

A note on the practice of James Stirling and Michael Wilford
Michael Wilford joined the practice of James Stirling and James Gowan as a young architect in 1960 to work on the Department of Engineering at Leicester University. Following dissolution of the Stirling and Gowan Partnership in 1964 Michael continued working with Stirling. His contribution increased over the years and was recognised with a full partnership in 1971, when the practice became James Stirling and Michael Wilford.

As Editor I have tried to ensure that these essays properly refer to the practice of Stirling and Wilford, or make the distinction, where appropriate, with James Stirling in his own right — his earlier work, writing, talking, teaching and his ideas. Such distinctions can never be exact, most particularly when it comes to ideas, and there will undoubtedly be instances where a reference to either Stirling or to Stirling and Wilford is only partially correct. But the fact that "Big Jim" made Michael Wilford a full partner in 1971 means that the work discussed in this book is that of James Stirling and Michael Wilford.

Introduction
Alan Berman

James Stirling and Michael Wilford's buildings and unbuilt projects in America warrant consideration because, coming from one of the twentieth century's most admired architects, they were greeted by fiercely differing opinions as to their merits. The controversy which surrounds these buildings, and the revisionism of which Stirling was accused, raise issues about late twentieth century architecture, about modernism, postmodernism, and about American and European sensibilities. When discussing what gives a work of art value Italo Calvino considers that a measure of their importance is the extent to which they generate debate and controversy long after they have been made:[1] it is a characteristic—even possibly a requirement—of important works that they "disrupt the tradition to which their audiences are accustomed".[2] These buildings attracted opprobrium because the "tradition" that Stirling and Wilford were accused of disrupting was one which James Stirling (with James Gowan), in his earlier work, had appeared to so powerfully uphold.

This book about Stirling and Wilford's buildings for the Universities of Rice, Harvard, Cornell and Irvine, and the unbuilt New York projects, was intended to follow the format of my book *Jim Stirling and the Red Trilogy, Three Radical Buildings*, in which architects discussed the importance of Stirling's renowned trio of "red" buildings.[3] The book's structure is similar: a first section has chapters which describe each building, and a second section contains essays which discuss the work. As the book progressed, however, it developed into something with a different slant. Not only did my initial commissioning editor, Albert Ferre, believe that the greater interest would be in a more critical "contextualising" of this work, but architects were reluctant to write about these buildings, whereas critics and theorists were keen to do so. The fact that architects are uncomfortable with Stirling's later work and with Stirling and Wilford's overt historicism, while critics see in it opportunities to discuss architectural fashion, cultural theory, and textual analysis, reflects the controversial nature of the work.

James Stirling was hailed as a guardian of modernism by architects of his generation and their students; a post-war hero, young, ambitious and smart, who produced buildings which were determinedly modernist, which "held the ground for the idea of significant form".[4] It was his early 'Red Trilogy' and other buildings from 1957–1968 (most famously the Engineering Department at Leicester, designed jointly with James Gowan) which won worldwide recognition. But from 1975, the work in Germany and America became different, and appeared to succumb to the then fashionable historicism: Egyptian cornices, Doric columns, keystones, rusticated masonry and other elements were decidedly on-trend. In the fevered world of the architectural lodge Stirling, the third generation modernist, was accused of apostasy, his historicist tendencies considered superficial stylistic games that were the hallmark of much derided postmodernism. He was thought to have sold out, and articles were written such as that which cried "I want the old Jim back."[5]

Notwithstanding the work of recent scholars such as Anthony Vidler in his exhibition and book *Notes from the Archive*[6] and Amanda Reeser Lawrence's *Revisionary Modernist* it persists in the minds of many that Jim Stirling turned his back on the true path of modernism, influenced perhaps by his time in America where he was immersed in the superficial, populist, consumerist, tides of postmodernism.[7] Some who knew him wondered if there wasn't an element of "popular" Jim so enjoying his renown that he played up to the image of the bad boy from the north of England who, with an eye to the gallery, enjoyed his power to shock.[8]

We can now consider this work with the benefit of some 40 years distance, as well as with a sense of urgency because the future of one of them, the Sackler Museum at Harvard, is uncertain. Fear about a notable building's future focuses minds, and it was a similar uncertainty about the Florey Building in Oxford which prompted me to write *The Red Trilogy*. While Stirling and Wilford's German and American work clearly manifests new pre-occupations, it now seems that the accusations of stylistic game-playing were to some extent a superficial readings of Jim Stirling's trajectory. Stirling quite evidently had a grounding in, and a deep understanding of, architectural history which we can identify—although less overtly—in the earliest work. Stirling's "unblinkered eye" and acute gaze allowed him to dip in and out of history, magpie-like, picking and

choosing from the whole of architecture's canvas.[9] He was able to skillfully manipulate these elements and mould them to satisfy and express the requirements of each project's programme and context. But the formal delight in historical references seldom took precedence over the primary place which Stirling and Wilford gave to the demands of their briefs. These American designs, no less than the early work, resolve the complexities of their spatial requirements into masterfully simple arrangements which successfully integrate the buildings' function with the determinants of their site and surroundings.

A criticism levelled at Stirling's earlier buildings was that they ignored their context and were conceived as isolated monuments which failed to respond to neighbours or urban grain. But the buildings at Rice, Harvard, and Cornell, as well as the unbuilt New York projects, not only respond to, but strengthen the fabric of their urban or suburban contexts. While a response to their surroundings is more evident in the German projects, owing to their location in dense historic cities, the American buildings—designed after the projects for Dusseldorf, Cologne, and Stuttgart—display a similar concern to make a positive contribution to the contexts in which they are set.

As a practising architect my interest was stirred by James Stirling's early buildings, potent examples of the practical art and craft of architecture. These buildings manipulate volumes, structure and materials to develop expressive form which is functionalist in the widest sense of the word: this is functionalism not limited to utility, but which includes human sensibility. Stirling's friend Colin St John Wilson put it eloquently when reminding us of what Le Corbusier wrote: buildings work on us through "the physical subjective facts which exist because the human organism is like it is".[10] These buildings, to a degree, display the same understanding of the facts, the elements and the subjective language of architecture which distinguishes buildings such as Lutyens' Little Thakeham, Wright's Robie House and Unity Temple, Le Corbusier's Villa Savoye or Maison La Roche, Aalto's Säynätsalo Town Hall and Viipuri Library. In buildings such as these the architects have "engaged in the whole culture of conventions,

mythical and stylistic, that... transmutes the day-to-day transactions of utility and the prevailing lore of technology" into something magical.[11]

If we look behind the playfulness we find similar kinds of experience in Stirling and Wilford's work from this time. Bob Maxwell describes the entry sequence at the Clore Gallery, Tate Britain, in his chapter in this book where one moves from the front door through the lobby to the entrance of the first floor gallery in a progression which offers a rich experience similar to that at the Sackler Museum. Those who see in the Sackler only its quirky colouring fail to acknowledge the enjoyment of progressing from a wide dark entrance with a strong cross-axis into and through a long, narrow light-filled space, rising to the first and then second floor galleries before turning back to progress through the top gallery to where the bridge was intended to connect to the Fogg Museum. Such a *promenade architecturale* is not simply an enjoyable spatial experience, but gives to the galleries a significance appropriate to the fabulous collection for which they were so carefully designed.

The use of circulation as a principal organising and compositional element is evident in all of the American buildings although it is absent from the interiors at Irvine. The many different spaces in the complex building at Cornell, for example, are connected to each other and to the main street by means of an external promenade, which serves to make the dramatic landscape part of the experience when moving about the building. At Rice, the existing building for which Stirling and Wilford designed an extension was a banal rectangular form containing a central corridor with rooms on either side: the whole of which was transformed by the addition of a circulation spine with a double volume on one side, and two dramatic conical roof lights at each end, thus creating a complex spatial arrangement at the heart of the building that is much more than a link between the old and the new.

These buildings demonstrate no less a masterful manipulation of spatial volumes and routes than Stirling's earlier buildings. They show an understanding of, and interest in, a building's material presence and enjoyment in use. To occupants this is much more significant than whether or not Stirling and Wilford "sold out" to contemporary fashion. Above all, like most of the work Stirling did with his two different partners, they have powerful physical presences.

This effect on the senses stems from the way the buildings are composed, and in this the American buildings are little different from the earlier work. They are all assemblies of distinct volumetric elements, each of which expresses a discrete function of the programme, sometimes only in the interior, as in the Sackler Museum, at other times externally, as at Cornell. So comprehensively do the buildings' spatial requirements determine their form that when one uses a Stirling building it is hard to imagine that it might be other than it is. The Sackler Museum is an obvious example: there seems to be no better way of arranging a building which must accommodate both high gallery spaces and small administrative offices than the Museum's bi-partite section and bi-partite plan: a central stair gives access to and makes visible the high gallery spaces on three levels on the right, and also to the five levels of lower office spaces on the left. Offices which require windows are on the street side of the stair, galleries which do not require windows are to the rear, while the circulation route running between these different spaces acts as a unifying shared element, which is emphasised by the internal windows which look into this space. No simpler arrangement can be imagined, and few museum complexes can be as easy to find one's way around. As Gary Wolf writes in his essay, the museum's first director, Seymour Slive—who acted as Stirling and Wilford's client—considered that the design works exceptionally well. I was saddened to hear of Seymour Slive's death just as this book was going to press.

The American buildings obviously differ from the earlier work in that they do not deploy glass as a malleable, plastic skin, nor are their structural components exposed as expressive sculptural elements—excepting in the bridge supports at the Sackler Museum, and in the unbuilt Columbia project. This suggests that Stirling and Wilford took heed of the statement attributed to James Gowan that each commission should develop a "style for the job".[12] Notwithstanding the fame which followed the "red trilogy" and other early work such as the Olivetti, Derby, and Dorman Long projects, with their consistent architectural language, forms and elements, few of these elements are evident in the American designs. These manifest a design approach which develops appropriate and unique solutions for the requirements of each building's site and functional programme. As Brian Carter reveals in his chapter, this characteristic of the practice's work was recognised by the Professor of Music at Cornell, Don Randall, who was one of the selection committee: "There was no 'house style'... you couldn't be sure what one of Jim and Michael's buildings was going to look like."

This flexible and inventive approach supports the proposition made by Nicholas Ray in his chapter that Stirling had always been part of the tradition of English Eclecticism. This directly counters James Gowan's, description of Stirling as a "classicist" while considering himself to be a "gothicist".[13] Rather than organising a building into a controlled, preconceived conceptual arrangement, Stirling's approach, which he continued with Wilford, was to develop unique, sometimes idiosyncratic and playful solutions in response to the exigencies of each project. The Rice, Sackler, and Cornell buildings demonstrate this 'gothic', eclectic, perhaps even romantic approach to the conception of buildings. The library at Irvine, the least successful of the American buildings, is not this, with its spatial requirements squeezed into a strong preconceived form. This rigid 'Beaux Arts' arrangement appears to

have been developed in order to establish for the building its own context on a site where none existed.

An examination of material in the Stirling and Wilford archive at the Canadian Centre for Architecture suggests that most of the projects gelled quickly into clear and simple strategic arrangements, yet went through endless iterations of facade treatments. These studies explore different historical elements and allusions in a way that certainly suggests Stirling and Wilford's postmodern tendencies and here one can see Stirling—described by Summerson as *Vitruvius Ludens*—at play.[14] But I would suggest that Stirling and Wilford were not applying historic elements gratuitously to their buildings, but seeking in each case a language culled from architectural precedent, which was appropriate to the nature of each project and its context. The building at Rice, described by Peter Papademetriou in his essay, amply demonstrates this. There are endless exploratory sketches of different arrangements of walls, windows and gables that were made in search of an arrangement which would sit comfortably beside the existing florid brick facades: the final design succeeds in producing an addition which is subtly distinct from the original building but which transforms the whole into a coherent and integrated part of the central campus. Here, more visibly than ever, Stirling and Wilford had the courage to do with great success what the old guard—many of their contemporaries—decried as revisionist. As noted by Marco Iuliano in "Stirling under Review" no matter that Philip Johnson laughed and commented that he couldn't see it, the campus is very much the better for Stirling and Wilford's intervention, not something that can be said for many projects whose main aim appears to be to draw attention to themselves. For someone who had become a superstar such a sensitive and modest project was no less an act of courage than were the early works.

After the projects of the late 1970s Stirling and Wilford's star waned. Those who felt that the path of modernist functionalism was the only route to "good" architecture lost their faith in Jim Stirling and his one-time young assistant. But such a progression from young radical to mature historicist is not unusual in the life of artists: the young visionary throws over current norms, proposes new ways of doing things, and proclaims the past to be dead. Acolytes follow their hero in his pursuit of new directions, then to everyone's surprise the past begins to appear and historic elements can be seen in the work. The next generation cries "sell out" and the star's reputation declines, until time permits a clearer analysis, and reappraisal suggests that there are consistencies throughout the *œuvre*. This has been James Stirling's trajectory: the past was never dead: it was sometimes less evident than others, but it was always there.

So while the flag carriers for the Modern Movement saw in Stirling's early work continuity with the Modernist project, today's critics see continuity between the later more overt historicising tendencies and the early work, finding history never far below the surface. Here is the use of architectural history not by virtue of stylistic reference, but reinterpreted and used as the foundation for new work. Nicholas Ray, in an unpublished lecture about Rafael Moneo, eloquently explains Moneo's attitude to history which could describe Stirling's: "It is irresponsible of the architect in the late twentieth century not to be aware of the multiple precedents that architectural history provides for the expression of contemporary building.... Gratuitous formal invention without a sense of architectural precedent, however skilful, should be avoided. While architects have a moral duty to understand their culture, they can be permitted to choose freely from it and acts of invention are possible within... the conventions that have been inherited."[15] In Stirling and Wilford's work the architectural past is called upon both as a source of the fundamental lessons of architectural composition, and also as a source of devices to be overtly referenced for their expressive qualities. From his earliest days Stirling understood and used the lessons of history that he had absorbed so thoroughly from Colin Rowe, first when he was Rowe's student at Liverpool, and then through their long and close friendship. This comprehensive understanding of architectural history afforded him the means to craft a dynamic architecture which has a powerful formal and material presence.

This mastery of architectural form and invention shines even more brightly in some of Stirling and Wilford's later projects, most particularly the Braun factory at Melsungen, 1986–1989, completed just before Stirling's untimely death in 1992. This large complex of buildings shows a return to earlier quite abstract formal invention which eschewed overt stylistic references. The same can be said for other late projects such as the small bookshop at the Venice Biennale, 1989–1991, and the unbuilt Mostra del Cinema, Venice, 1990. Their inventive dynamic sculptural forms would have been as strikingly unusual, as astounding and as exhilarating as the early buildings. It seems appropriate that this work should be in Europe because, as these essays show, in America James Stirling, in partnership with Michael Wilford, demonstrated the extent to which he had, from the very first, absorbed and utilised a deep understanding of European architectural history to create buildings that are much more than examples of contemporary fashion. They may be not as radical nor as exceptional as the earlier work, but if respected and cherished the buildings at Harvard, Rice and Cornell will stand the test of time.

Practice photo, Rice University, with James Stirling on the left and Michael Wilford third from left (with hat). Peter Papademetriou far right.

Four American Buildings

School of Architecture, Rice University

Peter Papademetriou

Career Context and the Commission

By awarding James Stirling the 1980 RIBA Royal Gold Medal for Architecture,[1] and then in 1981 the Pritzker Architecture Prize,[2] the profession recognised the achievement of James Stirling, notwithstanding Sir Nikolaus Pevsner's assessment that his buildings were ugly and that he was rude.[3] The subsequent works in America reflect his by then equal partnership with Michael Wilford, and beg the question of the effect on the design process resulting from their collaboration.[4] As a transition from the projects prior to that partnership, the Rice commission is possibly the most subtle and inventive design work representing new directions.

The raison d'être for the commission was based on a pragmatic evaluation of space needs for the School resulting from the National Architectural Accreditation Board report to the University in late 1978, citing both an increased need for studios, as well as specialised spaces for work that was not a part of the programme at that time. Simply stated, the brief was to "… remodel an existing 28,990 square feet building and extend for total of 45,438 square feet, to include studios, classrooms, offices, jury and exhibition spaces".[5] Space needs were such that several studio spaces (for example those for Freshmen) were not even housed within the existing MD Anderson Hall, which contributed to a level of ennui among students' perception of the School as having no "heart". In September 1978, the then new Dean of the School wrote to the University President of a "critical space shortage", concluding that there was no way to remodel Anderson Hall to accommodate these needs, and an addition was soon decided upon.

Anderson Hall occupies a strategic site within the University, and forms an element of its symbolic centre within the General Plan developed in 1909 by Ralph Adams Cram (Cram, Goodhue & Ferguson). The prominence of its location was among the reasons why the School of Architecture, established in 1912 (with William Ward Watkin, the firm's supervising architect, as Chairman), opted to keep its significant location and remain a part of the central campus.[6] This commitment was based on a philosophical stance by the School Faculty which favoured adaptive reuse and conservation by efficient additions and reintegration of facilities, as opposed to an independent building. For this it was necessary to seek an architect of international significance, whose sympathies

Aerial view of Rice University, 1953, with 'footprints' of future buildings: **1** Lovett Hall/Administration (Cram, Goodhue & Ferguson, 1911); **2** Physics (Cram, Goodhue & Ferguson, 1913); **3** MD Anderson Hall (Staub & Rather, 1947); **4** Fondren Library (Staub & Rather, 1949); **5** Rayzor Hall (Staub, Rather & Howze, 1962); **6** Sewall Hall (Lloyd, Morgan & Jones, 1971); **7** School of Architecture addition and renovations (James Stirling and Michael Wilford, in collaboration with Ambrose and McEnany, 1981).

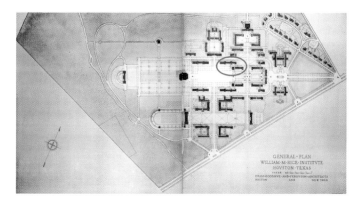

would assure this direction. A "short list" included Venturi, Rauch & Scott Brown, Mitchell/Giurgola, Fumihiko Maki and James Stirling Michael Wilford & Associates, the latter being "matched" with the local Houston firm of Ambrose & McEnany, the former doing design development and the Associate Architects having responsibility for contract documents;[7] the main contractor and principal subcontractors were also lined up when initial schematics were reviewed in early July 1979.[8] Thus for Stirling and Wilford, in scope and process, Rice was a "little job"—a bit of a conundrum perhaps for both the practice and the University, because here were the first architects of international stature to work at Rice, and British at that. "All eyes" would be on the design: on how they developed a creative concept, and how the implicit imperative of "being Jim Stirling" would be handled?

The Programme

The character of the Rice Campus is a curious anomaly in Houston: a coherent visual environment of buildings consciously ordered in their relationship to one another by a collective idea. The composition proposed in the General Plan of 1909 is a clever synthesis, whereby the 233-acre campus comprising an irregular, trapezoidal, nearly triangular, site was organised by a primary east west axis aligned parallel to the northern boundary's longest site dimension. In counterpoint to this axis was a parti of defined courts articulating the major programme areas. As a formal means of underscoring the main axis, building blocks ran parallel to it, while the secondary courts were linked laterally by cross-axes in a north south direction. This arrangement matched symmetries which were freely played off against asymmetrical balance. Thus a pattern was established which ensured that future development would produce a clear sense of evolutionary growth. A primary element to anchor such growth was the core of the General Plan, the "Academic Court". This quadrangle, the first portion to be developed (but in fact not completed until 1971), gave an image of "place" to the campus.[9]

The visual character of the campus architecture was also a constituent part of its definition, as Cram took a regional approach to determining appropriate features, "... the dominating idea was that this was an institution of higher learning and that it must look like a college, and one built in a warm climate".[10] A conscious use of eclecticism was deployed as a means to express uniqueness of programme, academic structure and culture. Yet Cram was clear in making a distinction between pure revivalism and what he regarded as the libertine use of style in the nineteenth century, and inventive eclecticism as a process of stylistic rehabilitation, by using principles which synthesised cultural association, regional expression, response to climate and romantic allusion. The Board, alumnae and other Rice constituents held these attributes to be inviolate.[11]

Considerations of orientation and the use of covered arcades, demonstrate the design's respect for climate. Building masses rose from a base storey of *cloisonné* masonry, characterised by horizontal banding in contrast with the vertical articulation of wall surfaces by modular bays. Pantile-covered roofs were generally hipped, occasionally hidden by an articulated parapet or a flat gable where separate wings were clearly to be seen as appendages to a main block. Even with a clear programme of ornament, Cram's emphasis on planar composition suggested the superiority of massing over decoration.

The Design

As a student at Liverpool University, Stirling absorbed from Colin Rowe an ambivalence toward rhetorical modernism, which, as he characterised it, "... to succeed one had to be good in many styles".[12] His initial reconciliation with Modernism's loss of Utopia in the 1950s was to skirt the issue and turn,

opposite

'Skyline' view of the Rice Campus, illustrating the School of Architecture's conical skylights echoing other vertical elements from the surrounding buildings. © Paul Hester

top

General Plan William Marsh Rice Institute (Cram, Goodhue & Ferguson, 1909); location of the future MD Anderson Hall is circled.

bottom

Detail of Physics Building, south elevation, illustrating Cram's material palette, showing the west "tabernacles". © Paul Hester

rather, to excursions into the "vernacular".[13] This was a wise alternative as it at once contained aspects of abstraction appealing to a modern sensibility, while its formal issues were removed from any didactic position.[14] As his own career enlarged the range of formal interests, including the recognition of a broad spectrum of architectural history, it oscillated as Stirling characterised it, "... between the formal and the informal, between the restrained and the exuberant". The evolution of the design of the Rice School of Architecture—so thoroughly limited as it was by numerous constraints—may therefore be seen as consistent with much of his earlier work and not at all as an "exceptional" work.[15]

As with any commission, a number of choices were dictated by the client, others were conditioned by the exigencies of the budget, and others were conscious refinements to which the architects were philosophically committed.[16] The critical move in Stirling and Wilford's development of the parti was the proposed Z-shape footprint that was formed by the grafting together of two opposing L-shapes, connected by a lateral "spine" containing the special programme elements; this arrangement achieved several important features. Firstly, the theme of the General Plan is continued, as the new wing is parallel to the existing block, thereby maintaining the direction of the east west axis. Second, the configuration allows for separate readings of facades, so that analogous but distinctly different designs could be created, thereby obviating the need for straight replication. Third, as a piece of campus fabric, the building adds a defined courtyard space created by the new wing, in conjunction with the existing arcade which connects Anderson Hall to the Fondren Library, thereby reinforcing a cross-axis terminated by the Chemistry Building. This subsidiary space is clearly related to, and extended from, the main quadrangle of the Academic Court, which enhances the location of Anderson Hall and the School as the symbolic centre of the campus.

MD Anderson Hall, originally built in 1947 to the designs of Houston architects Staub & Rather, reflected the design ambivalence of the late 1940s, created by both a pause in the construction of the Rice Campus in the 1930s, as well as a loss of faith in the formalism of Ralph Adams Cram's General Plan and his original buildings, due to the advances of the aesthetic of "functionalism". Designed as a "general classroom" building, Anderson Hall's internal order, however, was curiously specific, for instead of being a simple loft space, its plan was that of a "programmatic" interior. It was this physical context to which Stirling and Wilford had to respond: classrooms were classified as being of two distinct, differently-sized "functional" types, and arranged on opposing sides of an internal double-loaded corridor. Because of the varied sizes, this corridor was not centred within the symmetrical block, but configured off-centre. The net result was a paradoxically complex asymmetrical structural frame contained in a symmetrical mass, creating an exterior facade expression which, while stripped of much of Cram's ornamental programme, adhered in abstracted form to the character which had become a virtual "Rice style".[17] Additionally, the patterns of window openings reflected this interior arrangement, so that those on the south elevation (fronting on the Academic Court) do not align with those on the north elevation.

It is in this context that the evolution of Stirling and Wilford's design may be seen ultimately as a conscious reformation of the principles and of their role within the context established by Cram. The programme given the architects, to create an addition half again the size of the existing facility, mandated that it should "read" as a whole project, clarifying formal connections between the parts, old and new. The design strategy is, in effect, a didactic synthesis of the opposition of conflicting forces, reflecting the tension between the context, programme and the formal "image" for the School. The "provocative" nature of the visual expression that the architects evolved perplexed critics, who could not reconcile their expectations of Jim Stirling with a solution that was deferential

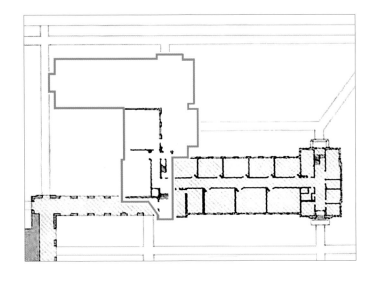

above

Plan of the existing MD Anderson Hall, with an overlay of the future Stirling and Wilford 'footprint' on the projecting L-shaped east wing.

opposite top

"Nolli plan" (spaces in public domain) of the Academic Court articulating Stirling and Wilford's parti strategy with regard to siting, existing campus axes, and the through-linkage of entries within the internal 'spine'.

opposite bottom

North facade of the MD Anderson Hall, 1947, with projecting L-shaped east wing in the distance.

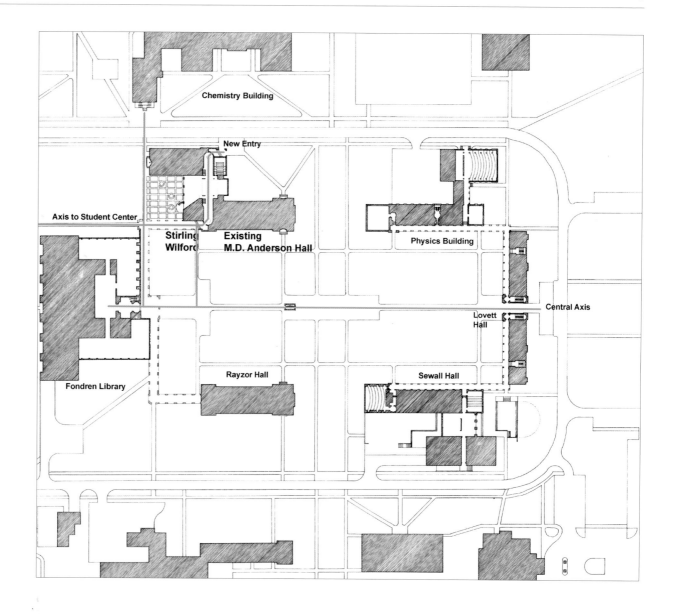

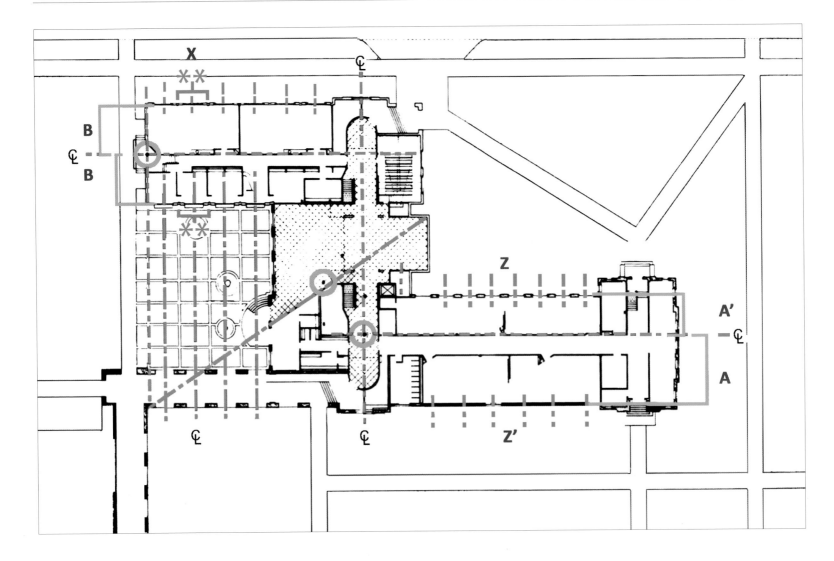

above

Analysis at ground floor of Stirling and Wilford's integration of the renovation of the
existing MD Anderson Hall, insertion and addition of special functions and a "spine" as a
unifying element, also showing the expansion with addition of a "new" wing, completing
the Z-form and defining the newly-created courtyard in relation to the existing arcade.
Major strategies:

• Asymmetrical centreline of the structural bays A and A¹ of existing "old" block.

• Differing windows and facade spacing on the south (Z) and academic court (Z¹).

• Blue circle at the end of the structural grid indicates the existing column incorporated
   within the "spine", which positions the corresponding cross-axial centreline of "spine".

• Oblique gallery wall is rationalised by its alignment with the end of the arcade and
   position of the jury room.

• Blue circle at the "relic" column in the gallery.

• The "new" Stirling and Wilford wing with simple, equal structural bays B and B, on
   cross-axis with the "spine", which results in the perimeter column (blue circle) being
   centred on entry/exit.

• Identical windows on both north (exterior) and south (courtyard interior) of the Stirling
   and Wilford facades, **X, in turn is strategically aligned axially with the centreline of
   the arcade arches.

opposite

Perspective rendering of proposed courtyard, illustrating the historically sensitive
design approach.

in the extreme. Expectations of Stirling and Wilford's first American building in, of all places, Texas where "culture recognition" through "signature" objects is a particular cliché, went unrequited. Could it be that the puzzlement aroused by the design was partially due to its apparent contradictory position relative to the imperatives of "modernism"?[18] The question had to be asked: If such a significant level of anticipation was ascribed to the design, carrying as it did the burden of a Stirling pedigree, to what degree did it represent a *volte-face*?

A portion of the old block's north elevation massing was an L-wing, and is absorbed in forming the Z configuration, creating a "new" east facade, which contrasts with it materially through the collage attachment of the Aalto-like Jury Room.[19] The new Stirling and Wilford wing's entry at the north facade is articulated by a risalit identical to that on the opposite end of the 'spine' at the south Academic Court facade of the old building. A juxtaposition of a full bay of window grouping from the existing north facade with a harbinger of the bays on both north and south facades of the new addition, presents simultaneous aspects of both on opposing sides at the re-entrant corner. On the other re-entrant corner of the newly formed courtyard, the new arched south elevation meets the squared openings on the remaining existing west wall of what became the carved-out two-storey Farish Gallery, opening out onto the exterior courtyard.

The parti evolved from the existing constraints: a cross-section which comprises a clear distinction of studio spaces which are opposite the Faculty Office/Seminar

below
View into the "new" courtyard created around the existing live Oak tree, forming an intimate social space for both the School of Architecture and the campus at large. © Paul Hester

opposite
The "new" entry as "social space", with the old, existing wing seen through the archway. © Paul Hester

top

Stirling and Wilford's "new" wing addition from the north, with the flat end gable west facade and central column. © Paul Hester

bottom

Interior view up into one of the conical lanterns overlooking the entrance atop the two-storey volume. © Paul Hester

top left

Functional diagrams of the floor plans: PINK/'Spine'; RED/secondary circulation; YELLOW/Studios; LIGHT BLUE/Faculty offices; DARK BLUE/Lecture, Seminar; LIGHT GREEN/Administration; BRIGHT GREEN/Farish Gallery & Jury Room; ORANGE/Student Social; TAN/Support Spaces; GREY/Ancillary.

bottom left

The "spine" as social space, with sliding panels being used for a student design "crit", with a view looking toward the south entrance volume beyond. The Farish Gallery is below to the right. © Paul Hester

right

Interior of the Jury Room, being used for a student design review, illustrating the filtered light brought in by clerestory/skylights. © Paul Hester

spaces, aggressively displaced the existing double-loaded corridor, the deliberate asymmetry rendering it more "programmatic". This section was ultimately modified as final adjustments were made to both building costs and programme; the first floor of the old wing retains a double bank of studio spaces, while the second floor and both levels of the new wing clearly manifests the concept.

The heart of the design is the lateral cross-axis "spine", which not only connects both wings, but anchors the building to existing campus pathways. The ends of the "spine" are punctuated by transitional entry thresholds defined as two-storey voids, topped by glass conical lanterns thrusting through the roofline. At the centre of the "spine" are the "special" major collective spaces, the Jury Room and the Farish Gallery, both double-height volumes penetrated by circulation. By means of continuous clerestories on the former and double rank of windows facing west on the latter, natural light is brought deep into the interior. Architecturally the "spine" is read as concourse and bridge, an open connection whose iconic power as a socialising element is a feature of many Stirling buildings, articulated here by contrasting rubber-stud tiles which mark it.[20]

Second Floor

Ground Floor

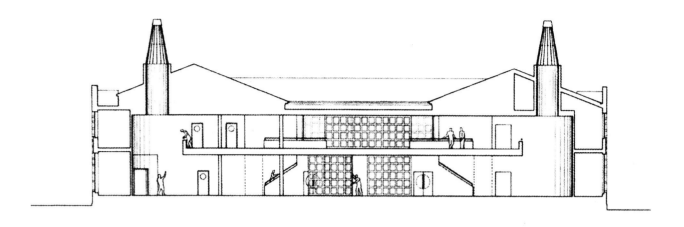

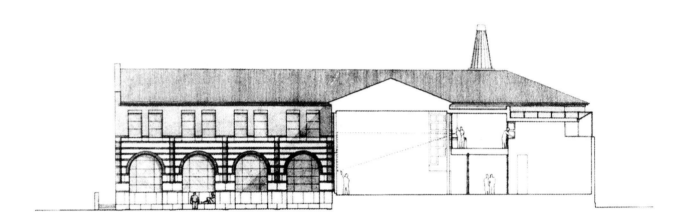

top

Section N-S through the "spine", showing two-storey volumes and overlooks at entries, with the concept of the concourse and bridge serving as socialising space, and the initial design of grille-like gate/panels for the Jury Room and Farish Gallery.

bottom

Section W-E, looking toward the "new" Stirling and Wilford South Courtyard facade, with the Farish Gallery on the left retaining the existing pantile roof. The "spine" is a bridge across the special volumes, with the Jury Room visually "different" in massing, to the right.

opposite

Axonometric of the "spine", articulated as an "object" or piece of furniture inserted within the shell of the building interior. Collection Centre Canadien d'Architecture/ Canadian Centre for Architecture, Montréal © CCA

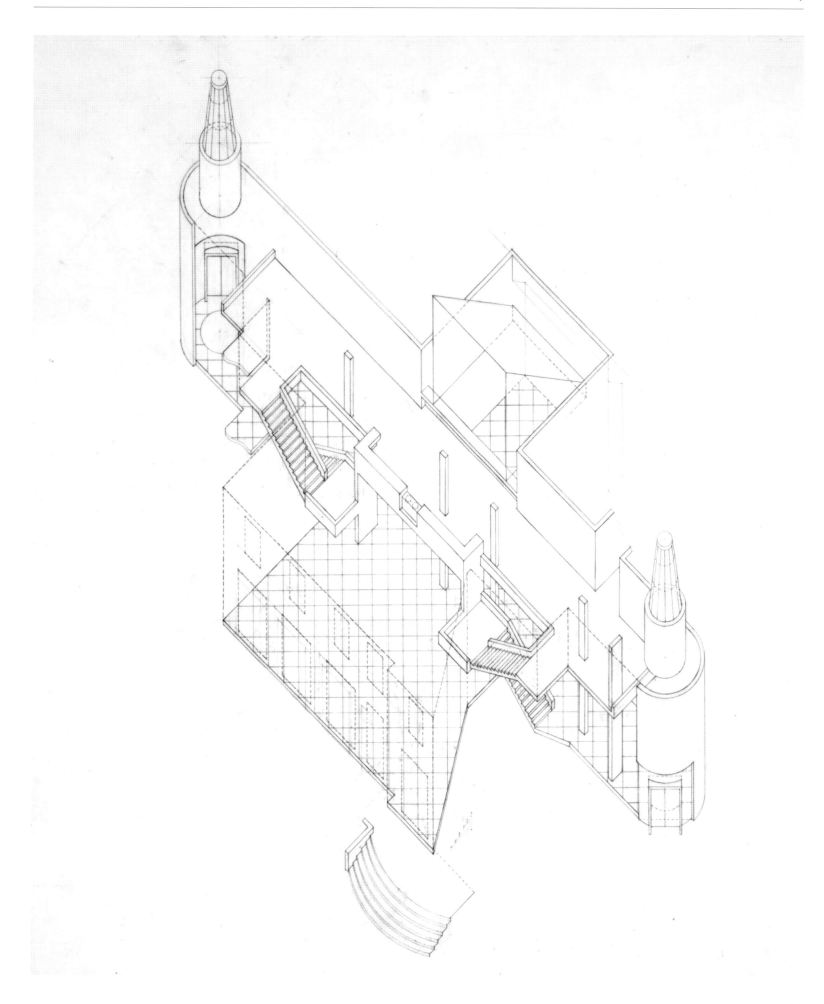

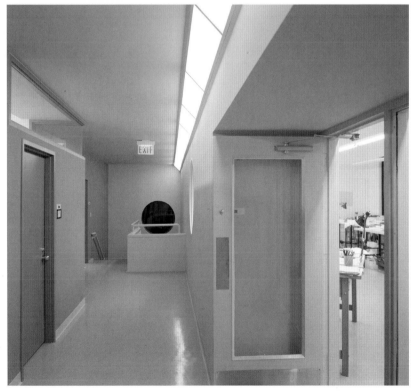

top
Second floor corridor in the "old" wing, with the reconfigured parti showing the relationship of the Studios to the Faculty offices. The distant circular window in the red door echoes other axial alignments. © Paul Hester

bottom
Second floor corridor in the new wing: Faculty offices to the left, typical recessed/articulated Studio entry to the right, exit staircase to the west facade with circular window at the end of the corridor. © Paul Hester

opposite top
The axis of the second floor corridor in Stirling and Wilford's addition terminates directly at the circular window in the west facade: the preferred parti of Faculty offices to the left, Studios to the right, and the "provocative" "Pink-Pansy" original wall colour. © Paul Hester

opposite bottom
Studio interior on the second floor of the new wing: Studios are en suite with "porthole" view windows between them. Note the curved wall and cylindrical form of the "spine" north entry volume within. © Paul Hester

Finishes of the interiors are modest, and slightly indifferent in their detail, reading as "workaday-modern". Studio wings are characterised as work spaces, and the cross-section of the corridor features a canted continuous lighting cove at the wall/ceiling junction, denoting the Faculty side of the section. Recessed entries elaborate the rhythm of the corridor on the studio side and a series of large-scale "porthole" apertures provide visual connection as they also do between studios. Seminar and office spaces have continuous clerestory glazing on the corridor and bright colour was applied on their side of the corridor wall: a "dusky orange" on the first floor administration and initially a fay-"pink" at the second floor on both wings. The "Pink Pansy" infuriated a Senior Faculty, former Director of the School, a devotee of Mies van der Rohe and black, white and grey.[22]

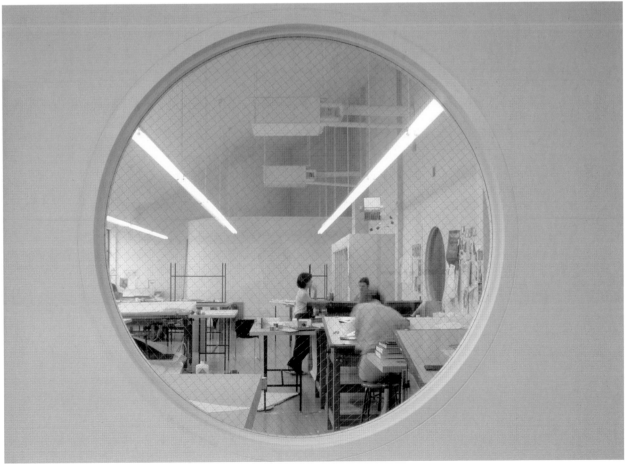

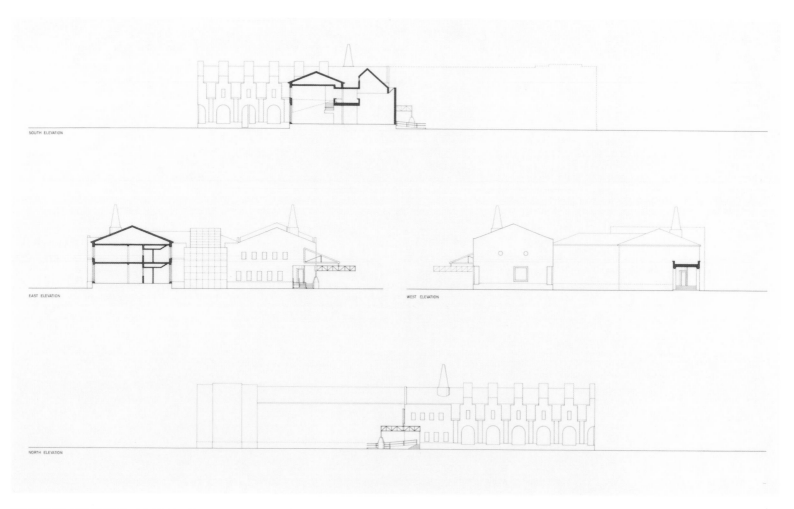

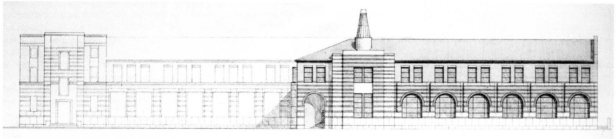

top

Facade studies of Stirling and Wilford's "new" wing,
searching for "being different" and "original"; note
the "Constructivist-like"/Stuttgart Neue Staatsgalerie/
Stuttgart Musikakademie/Berlin Wissenschaftszentrum
(WZB) entry canopy, eventually abandoned with design
of risalit.
Collection Centre Canadien d'Architecture/
Canadian Centre for Architecture, Montréal © CCA

bottom

North elevation: Stirling and Wilford's "new"
wing to the right, existing facade of the "old"
wing to the left, shown in the distance.
Collection Centre Canadien d'Architecture/
Canadian Centre for Architecture, Montréal © CCA

below

Typical Studio interior, at ground floor of the
'old' wing, with the north facade showing
expansive exterior views. © Paul Hester

The exteriors are subtly deferential to those of the existing building and the campus vocabulary as a whole. Certain heights, lines and patterns of banding have been picked up and reference is made to the immediate surroundings, such as the precise alignment of arched openings to the arcade on opposite edges of the courtyard which links Anderson Hall to the Fondren Library. Thus "old" and "new" create a dialogue and a kind of symmetry across the new exterior space. Moreover, the arched windows of the new wing are not a direct reiteration but rather an inventive inversion, since their articulation as pavilion-panels (positive/ projecting versus negative/recessed) is in a manner seen nowhere else on campus.

A series of Stirling and Wilford's design studies illustrates that such simplicity of expression was not a beginning point but rather a difficult process of refinement. In earlier versions, elevations contained elements jarringly "modern" in their origin, particularly a staggered dormer form originally part of a clerestory roof light design and a "constructivist" entry canopy clipped on one end.[23] Gradually, the designs overcame this apparent need to "be Jim Stirling", and these elements were subsumed within a visual rendering that was evocative of the given conditions, less assertively original or creative, and more second-glance architecture.[24]

Fragments of the original fabric exist to suggest that the adaptive redesign accepted deliberate "unresolved" juxtapositions in order to retain a sense of the past in its reformation. For example, the symmetry of the "spine" is broken by the presence of two pre-existing columns in the centre of circulation. The purity of the

above
Incorporation of the existing columns of the 'old' existing wing's structure within the 'spine', looking toward the Gallery, Student Social spaces entry at the left, with the 'new' entry in the distance. © Paul Hester

opposite
View along the oblique wall of the Gallery with exhibition installed, toward the 'spine': on the far right, the 'relic' column, resulting from the demolition of the existing second floor to create the two-storey interior. © Paul Hester

"bridge" and its flanking stairs is marred by the uncomfortable position of what can only be another pre-existing column, a move which underscores what was once something else, a "palimpsest", the acceptance of a condition "as found".[25] Against the splayed oblique wall of the Farish Gallery, a single one-storey 'relic' column holding part of the demolished section of the second floor appears almost as a "found object", reworked as a sculptural element. Existing sets of windows were retained in the resulting two-storey space, although the initial design proposal was to remove a portion of exterior masonry and to represent the interior volume by joining the existing small upper windows and large lower ones into a "bottle" form, suggesting erasure as a visual strategy. This gesture was denied by the Campus Business Manager, but is noted by a slight recessed deformation of wall surface on the interior which implies the connection.

The integration of "givens" with the new extension suggested a proactive design, not a passive imitation. A new order was developed to "anchor" the elements of the "spine" in relation to old and new, to rationalise the oblique Gallery wall, the relationship of the Gallery carved out of the existing interior, and the position of the jury room grafted onto the centre: "Parts to the Whole".

Interior view of the Gallery from the stair landing of the "spine", looking at the oblique wall and free-standing "relic" column. The natural light pattern from the west windows reflects the trees in the Courtyard beyond. © Paul Hester

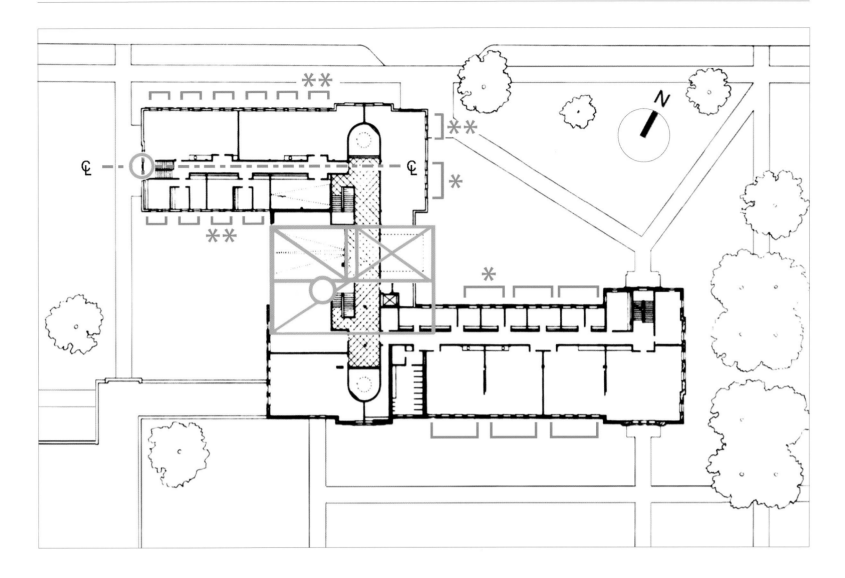

Analysis at second floor of Stirling and Wilford's integration of the "new"
renovation and addition with the 'old' building features.

Major strategies:

• Window pattern of the north facade of the existing MD Anderson Hall,
  represented as *, is incorporated in the transitional end elevation of Stirling and
  Wilford's addition and risalit entry, represented as **, creating a segue from
  "old" to "new".

• Stirling and Wilford's facade window pattern of the "new" block repeats the
  basic window pattern, represented as **, throughout.

• Blue circle at the end of the structural grid indicates the existing column, which
  provoked intense alternatives of "how" to incorporate the internal column within
  the facade, and "how" to resolve the asymmetrical programmatic section of the
  Studios/Faculty spaces.

• The centreline of the corridor aligns with the circular aperture within the west
  elevation, rationalising the discordant position of the facade staircase window.

• Blue overlay of the geometry unifying the form and position of the Farish Gallery
  (left), Jury Room (right), oblique Gallery wall, combining existing "givens" within
  a reformed building fabric.

• Blue circle at the "relic" column in the Gallery.

The west end of the new wing is a flat gable, set perpendicular to a similar form of the adjacent Cram-designed Chemistry Building, creating another, different, dialogue between old and new at the crossing of campus pedestrian pathways. Possibly the most disturbing element is also contained in the west facade: a window which lights the interior stair. The rational, direct structural frame of the Stirling and Wilford wing impacts the west gable end by a central column line which is "expressed" by revealing the column by means of a recessed porch, which compels one to move around it to get at the displaced doorway.[26] Numerous studies were made to position the window, a determined struggle to "do something", but ultimately a deliberately "incorrectly crude" choice, a round window that is discordant with the facade's symmetry. Yet this bothersome aperture is, in fact, centred on the interior hall, is "functional" in the broadest sense, and is a shot at "Being Jim Stirling" after all.

This provocative window reflects the dialectic between context and the specific requirements of the functional programme. Strictly speaking, both the figure and the ground of the west facade are correct, creating a tense relationship true to their separate realities. The symmetrical flat gable end is consistent with other campus features, nearly a "quotation" from the neighbouring Cram-designed Chemistry Building. The round window evokes the functional asymmetrical cross-section; the "pesky" window re-centres the corridor axis.

View through the archway of the existing arcade, deliberately aligned on axis with the Chemistry Building (Cram & Ferguson with William Ward Watkin, 1925), and defined by the position of Stirling and Wilford's west wing end, and Courtyard to the right. © Paul Hester

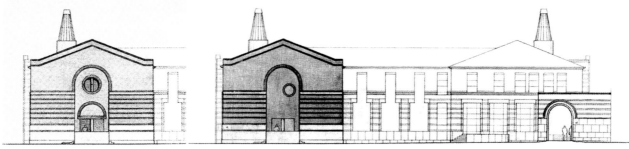

top

Construction photograph of the "new" wing, illustrating simple shed framing with centre column grid (at right, demolished interior of existing Anderson Hall, to create two-storey Farish Gallery). © Paul Hester

bottom

Original published design of the west facade (left), compared with the Final version and "displaced" circular window, reconciling the presence of the centred column within internal parti.

A Generation Later (Pluses and Minuses)

Dean Sarah Whiting commented (February 2013) as an insider having to deal with a 30 plus year-old facility:

> There were several compromises during construction, including reducing the number of air handling coils, building slab-on-grade with no cavity, and others that mean technical matters are in need of some serious work.[28]
>
> In terms of its functionality, the building's pretty great—the Jury Room/ Farish/"bridge"—all work to create a central space that really functions well to bring the school together and to encourage the eavesdropping that makes architecture school what it is: you can listen in to crits, lectures, etc..
>
> The flipside of that openness is that the acoustics are pretty lousy, and we may build an acoustic cloud and replace the lighting in Farish Gallery/ Jury Room in order to make both better spaces for Reviews. Strangely, the seminar rooms all have lousy acoustics as well, even though they are small, closed spaces. Additional issue: they are too small. Most seminars are 15 and under, but with a group of 20, the seminar rooms really don't work.
>
> The Studio spaces continue to be the best part of the building: they are big (even too big for our small numbers) and have such terrific window views out to the campus. I know that it was a conscious decision to move from an open Studio to the separate Studios, but in today's environment, where everyone is glued to his/her screen with her/his earphones on, the problems that existed previously in big open spaces have been lessened. Consequently, we have to really encourage the students to make an effort to interact.
>
> Finally, the auditorium, which only seats 54 students, doesn't accommodate lectures, so lectures are in the Farish Gallery. I actually like that because of the overlapping spaces created by the 'spine', and because it is really the heart of the school. Yet, the auditorium is a bit wasted space, 'though used for lecture classes, mostly not over 40–50 students. However, the Gallery can't be used for exhibitions (also true because it's not a secure space).
>
> The Administration was rearranged in 2012, as the Staff space was really subpar. We incorporated the Reception desk area with the Staff space, one big room, and created a glass wall with locking glass door to the hallway. That was our only move that really affected Stirling's work; it worked when Stirling did the design, but not for how we work now: more "Staff" and more "Stuff", so while Reception as Open Space Idea was great, the Staff office behind it was short-shrift by not having adequate windows.
>
> I feel like a complaining administrator. I wish the building had been built better and had been better cared for over the past 30 years. But for the most part, it actually works pretty damn well.

"Postmodern" or Post-Mortem?

Deference to context, that the building might be seen not as object but as fabric, has been a continuing theme in Stirling's work. It may be seen in the Selwyn College project, 1959, where the building form functioned as a "wall"; or the Derby Town Centre project, 1970, as a piece of urban fabric; or St Andrew's Art Centre scheme, 1971, where the edge condition of the enclosing volume has as a primary purpose the development of a coherent exterior space.

So, what about that label "postmodern"?[29]

Adherence to programme was a fact in all of the firm's work, and its expression meant the reconciliation of inherent contradictions. More obvious motifs, such as porthole windows, recall Modernism's rhetorical nautical references, while being a somewhat whimsical self-indulgence but also suggests that the modern

top
Original Administration Office Reception desk lobby, aligned on the centre with the existing arcade arches. © Paul Hester

bottom
Reconfigured Administration Offices, designed by Dean Sarah Whiting (WW Architects) to meet new performance standards; the lobby remains aligned with the axis to the arcade arches. © Paul Hester

opposite
Isometric drawing by Hans Söder for a "Kurhaus at Bad Mergentheim", as published in Gustav Platz's 1927 canonical edition of *Die Baukunst der Neuesten Zeit*.

experience is itself a resource, and that a knowledgeable architect is aware of that legacy while deferential to tradition.[30] Stirling rewards those who know their architectural history and who probe deepest. Such is shown in Gustav Platz's 1927 canonical edition of the *Die Baukunst der Neuesten Zeit*, for the formal quality of the lateral "spine" at Rice bears a literal kinship to Hans Söder's designs for a "Kurhaus at Bad Mergentheim": not only in plan form, but there is a virtual quotation of the central element, with paired dog-leg stairs, also the grille-panels, and the conical lanterns punctuating each end. The Past and the Future, and even the Past-Future, are all part of a deliberate dialectical tension.[31]

In the early 1960s, Henry-Russell Hitchcock observed, "... a sort of modernism in architecture that should be in its every aspect as different as possible... had diminished. Architects today are less afraid of continuity and partial identity in theory, in materials and in emotional content with buildings of the past.... But it chiefly creates confusion, I believe, to call these tendencies "postmodern"... however badly some generic name for them has evidently come to be needed."[32]

Peter Collins in *Changing Ideals in Modern Architecture* concludes "... to discipline their architectural forms to harmonize with earlier forms without sacrificing any of the principles of the modern age... works deliberately intended to be banal, if one uses the word in its strict etymological sense as meaning 'common to all'... for as Perret once remarked, 'He who, without betraying the modern conditions of a programme, or the use of modern materials, produces a work which seems to have always existed, which, in a word, is banal, can rest satisfied.'"[33]

Ultimately James Stirling and Michael Wilford have been faithful to site context, to predetermined 'givens' inherent in a renovation, and to a rewriting of these that is grounded in the programme, suggesting that actual reality requires comprehension of its deepest meanings. On the occasion of being awarded the Rice commission, Stirling speculated, "So, freed from the burden of utopia... we look to a more liberal future producing work perhaps richer in memory and association in the continuing evolution of a radical Architecture."[34]

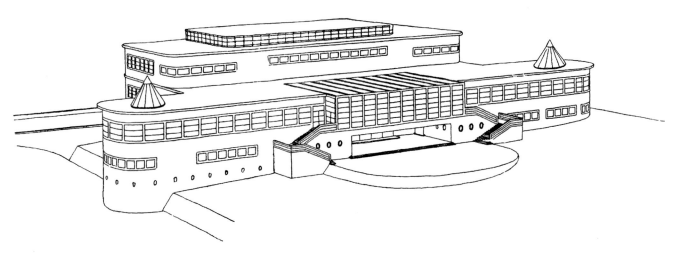

The Arthur M Sackler Museum, Harvard University

Gary Wolf

The Original Fogg Museum: A Fine Arts Laboratory

Stirling and Wilford's Sackler Museum was initially intended to extend the facilities of Harvard University's Fogg Museum of Art, a legendary and influential teaching museum that was "the first purpose-built structure for the specialised training of art historians and museum professionals in North America".[1] Unlike the typical museum that is designed as a "treasure house" to preserve and display great art for an appreciative audience, the original Fogg had been conceived as an experimental educational facility—"a well-fitted art laboratory", in the words of long-time University President Charles Elliot, a chemist. Classrooms, professors' offices, and conservation labs were interspersed alongside the art collection and reference resources. The building's design "gave architectural expression to the concept that scholarship in the field of art was ideally shaped by the interactive study of objects, techniques, images, and texts".

The 1927 Georgian Revival Fogg building placed every room around a gracious three-storey skylit courtyard that was, in both type and derivation, an internalisation of an exterior space and facade. Its first two floors of ashlar masonry were modelled after a Renaissance facade by Antonio da Sangallo the Elder, while the upper level was finished with rough plaster. The teaching museum's mixed uses were discovered around the perimeter and by tucked-away stairs leading up to offices, studios and classrooms and down to a basement lecture hall and storage. This juxtaposition of interrelated functions facilitated the Fogg's hands-on pedagogical programme, hailed as "The Fine Arts in a Laboratory".

These features of the Fogg—this little-remarked variation on the familiar museum type, the old building's internalised outside space, and its hidden stairs—all provide insight to the design of the new museum.

Programme and Origins

By the 1970s, despite two expansions, the Fogg needed more space of every sort. While the museum administration initially considered taking over an academic lecture hall across the street while shoe-horning yet another small wing behind the building, Arthur M Sackler, a benefactor of major art and science institutions around the world, challenged Fogg director Seymour Slive: "Why not build a museum with spacious exhibition galleries and storage-study areas, and gain

below

James Stirling, Michael Wilford, and
Associates Perry, Dean, Stahl & Rogers
Arthur M Sackler Museum, Harvard University,
Cambridge, Massachusetts: entrance facade,
1979–1985. © Timothy Hursley, photographer

opposite

Coolidge, Shepley, Bulfinch and Abbott
Fogg Museum of Art, Harvard University, Cambridge,
Massachusetts: view of central courtyard.
Robert Kahn, photographer
James Stirling/Michael Wilford fonds
Collection Centre Canadien d'Architecture/
Canadian Centre for Architecture, Montréal © CCA

improved facilities for museum support services, lecture and seminar rooms?"[2] A significant gift from Sackler—which eventually reached 10.3 million dollars, the largest cash donation that Harvard had ever received for the Arts—spurred the Museum to embark on what would be a lengthy, challenging and often frustrated path toward realising this vision. Over ten years, this initiative would at times encounter something less than enthusiasm from University President Derek Bok and the University's governing four-person Corporation, who, during this period, found themselves deep in disastrous cost overruns on a medical school co-generation plant.

Despite what would be a University-set construction budget and a net-to-gross ratio that were more appropriate for an office building, the Fogg had produced an ambitious 234 pages of detailed programme goals for expansion in all programme areas: galleries for ancient and oriental art; a temporary exhibition gallery; a conservation lab; a lecture hall; seminar rooms; collection storage; library with stacks and a reading room; curatorial, faculty, and museum membership offices; a registrar's department; and a loading dock and delivery area.

A new 60,000 square foot building, was to house this, squeezed on the tight site 150 feet north of the Fogg across busy Broadway, on Quincy Street, the "arts" avenue that runs north and south at the edge of Harvard's campus, crowded with such cultural landmarks as Le Corbusier's Carpenter Center for the Visual Arts, HH Richardson's Sever Hall, and the Fogg to the south, and John Andrew's Graduate School of Design, the High Victorian Gothic Memorial Hall, and the hand-crafted Busch-Reisinger Museum to the north. The expansion site's city block—set behind a fire station—is shared with a large brick apartment building and a Victorian house. Amidst an array of challenges, the programme threw down a gauntlet to the architect when it called for an enclosed pedestrian bridge to connect the new structure to the old Fogg across Broadway, but acknowledged the uncertainty of approval in a city where town/gown relationships can be acrimonious. Thus, while the new building would ideally have a permanent umbilical connection to the existing museum for a smooth flow of students, faculty, visitors and art between the two, it also must function—and appear—as a free-standing building, if the linking bridge were not possible. To some, this built-in ambiguity suggested that the new edifice should be designed to read as only a piece, while, at the same time, it should be designed to read as a whole.

Architect Selection and Process

A huge initial field of 84 architects was narrowed to a short list of Aldo van Eyck, Frank Gehry, IM Pei and Partners; Kevin Roche, John Dinkaloo and Associates; Richard Meier, Stirling and Wilford, Venturi and Rauch, and the local firm of Crissman and Solomon, recent winners of the Charleston Museum of Art competition in South Carolina. In vetting the candidates, Slive instantly bonded with Stirling, and visited nearly every Stirling building, where he even interviewed the buildings' custodians to ascertain operational problems. He strongly advocated for Stirling and Wilford, despite his awareness of what he termed the "disasters with a few buildings".[3] Without having completed a single museum building, Stirling and Wilford became the unanimous choice for the high-visibility project.

If desirable for its institution's stature, the new museum had a budget that was, in Stirling's frank assessment, "rather lean", particularly in a period of double-digit inflation, along with a low fee, typical of Harvard, which had to be split with local architect of record, Perry, Dean, Rogers and Partners (who had recently finished two new museum buildings). To add to the challenges, midway through the design process Bok and the Corporation cancelled the project, after earlier proposing that the Fogg sell some of its collection in order to create an endowment for future maintenance costs. As the cancellation became an art-world scandal, the Corporation treasurer publicly criticised Stirling (unjustifiably, according to insiders who saw the architect responsibly grappling with a difficult client and project); Stirling felt snubbed and bullied. Yet Slive and the Fogg's supporters—buoyed by the public condemnation of the University's decision—managed to raise an additional three million dollars and pushed the project back on track.

Mark Girouard, in his biography *Big Jim*, briskly summarised the entire process: "… the Sackler Museum presents what one is tempted to call a typical Jim story: comic and tragic, mixed success and failure, not enough money, too many rows; and

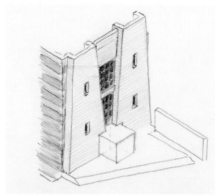

top and middle
James Stirling, Michael Wilford, and
Associates Perry, Dean, Stahl & Rogers
Arthur M Sackler Museum, Harvard University, Cambridge,
Massachusetts: axonometric sketches of the facade, 1979–1985.
James Stirling/Michael Wilford fonds
Collection Centre Canadien d'Architecture/
Canadian Centre for Architecture, Montréal © CCA

bottom
James Stirling, Michael Wilford, and
Associates Perry, Dean, Stahl & Rogers
Arthur M Sackler Museum, Harvard University, Cambridge,
Massachusetts: view of the facade, 1979–1985.
© Timothy Hursley, photographer
James Stirling/Michael Wilford fonds
Collection Centre Canadien d'Architecture/
Canadian Centre for Architecture, Montréal

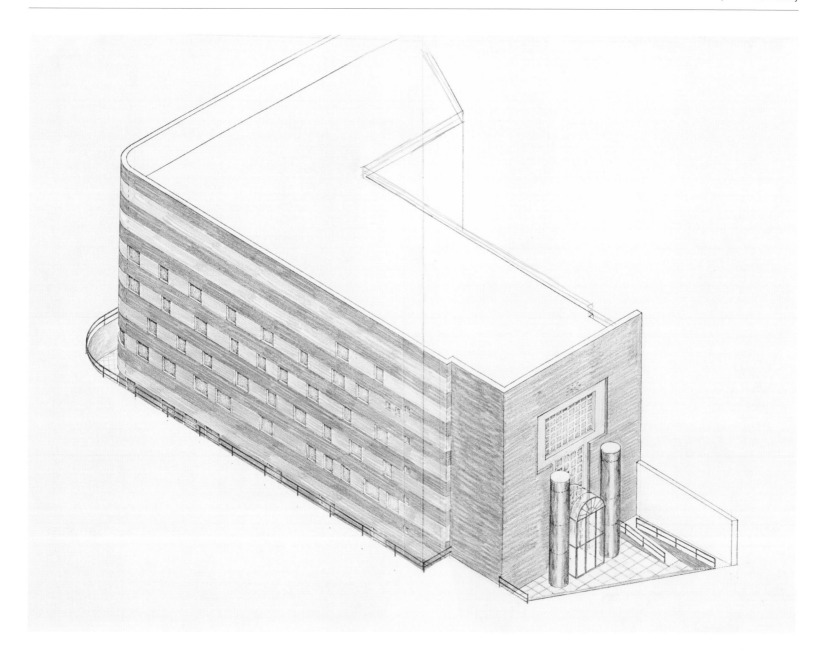

James Stirling, Michael Wilford, and
Associates Perry, Dean, Stahl & Rogers
Arthur M Sackler Museum, Harvard University, Cambridge,
Massachusetts: axonometric sketch of the facade, 1979–1985.
James Stirling/Michael Wilford fonds
Collection Centre Canadien d'Architecture/
Canadian Centre for Architecture, Montréal © CCA

an imbroglio in University politics, with which Jim was not well qualified to deal".[4]
As an ironic conclusion, by the end of the building's construction the University had
reorganised its art museums' institutional structure. The project had begun as an
extension of the venerable Fogg Museum, and Harvard exhibited the drawings as
Stirling's "Design to Expand the Fogg Museum". (Stirling assigned the programme
and site to his Yale students as the "Fogg Museum Expansion".) Now the building
was reconceived as a separate and equal entity, the Sackler Museum. What began
programmatically as a part, was clearly now, in institutional terms, a whole.

The Building

Despite these less than ideal conditions, Stirling and Wilford inventively responded
to the demands of the programme and the site, were true to the concept of the
Fogg as an "art laboratory", and produced what has generally been regarded in the
field as a sound, functional, and well-detailed art museum which still managed to
project the creative shock of those problematic 1960s buildings. Walking through
the building, and studying the drawings, one senses deliberate, considered
attention being paid to the programme requirements, spatial limitations, and
exterior envelope. Every square foot in the structure is allocated for use, with

neither the wide corridors nor the lavish lobbies more typical of treasure house museums. A dramatic collection of small and larger spaces provides the stimulating adjacencies that made the old Fogg so successful a teaching museum, but without its security weaknesses and its woefully inadequate mechanical systems. The top-lit galleries receive indirect light from roof-top monitors, not skylights; there are no window walls to threaten the art through leakage, uncontrolled temperature fluctuations or excessive daylight. Harvard's official publication for the opening of the Sackler proudly recounts that "The designers have… chosen to continue the intimate scale and atmosphere of the Fogg gallery spaces."

Morphology

The Sackler sits firmly and simply on its odd site, part of an urban wedge that penetrates this edge of campus between Cambridge Street and Broadway — busy thoroughfares that run through a neighbourhood jumble of apartments, groceries, civic institutions, and residences. The end (or top) of its L-shaped block faces the flank of the Fogg across the street, as an entrance pavilion of monochromatic iron-spotted orange brick that is taller, but slightly narrower than the rest of the building behind it. The frontal nature of this volume is emphasised by its being on the orthogonal, parallel to the Fogg, rather than following the angled street. This creates a small triangular entrance plaza, dropped three steps lower than the sidewalk in order to align the top floor more closely to that of the Fogg across Broadway. Behind this entry block, the main body of the L stretches down Quincy Street and around the corner onto Cambridge Street in alternating bands of orange and charcoal grey brick.

That the Sackler, to the Fogg's north, is one of only four US buildings by Stirling and Wilford, while, to the south, Carpenter Center for the Visual Arts is the only US building by Le Corbusier, makes this a unique ensemble of architecture for the arts. And although the Sackler's rounded corner at the Quincy/Cambridge Street end clearly echoes the apsidal form of Memorial Hall's Sanders Theater diagonally across the way, it is perhaps not coincidental that bold curves are also found at the concrete assemblage at the other end of the Fogg, the Carpenter Center. The quiet, symmetrical Fogg is bracketed on both sides by shocking, abstract, asymmetrical, curving bookends — landmark structures that share a defiance of the sometimes staid local architectural traditions. The implied rotation at the Sackler's banded brick radius would have been much more evident had the tall, conical skylight designed for the top-floor library — as both a source of light and a highly visible "pivot" — not been cut from the project.

At the entrance, two free-standing, cylindrical concrete columns straddle a glass entry extruded from a slot in the masonry wall; they function as intake and exhaust stacks for the mechanical room located below the entrance court, a solution which recalls the inventiveness of Stirling's double-functioning ventilator at Queens College, 1966. These columnar air shafts' first purpose was to support the pedestrian bridge. Together with what can be seen as a cyclopean "Gibbs' surround" framing the entry, this monumental, symmetrical, frontal facade is in strong contrast to the side elevations of sweeping brick stripes and random window spacing that deny any focus along Quincy and Cambridge Streets.

On Cambridge Street, the architects simply excised a mass of the striped brick building to create a truck tunnel through to a service courtyard between the Sackler and the apartment building to the east. They called upon neither outsized cantilevers nor structural exhibitionism to span the opening. The elevations of the service court are carefully detailed and proportioned, clad with an economical, neutral grey oversized utility brick, in contrast to the colourful street facades, in the same way that the service court of the adjacent red brick apartment house is faced with a functional, off-white brick. Judiciously placed windows and a projecting bay facing the service court introduce controlled light to interior gallery spaces.

top

James Stirling, Michael Wilford, and
Associates Perry, Dean, Stahl & Rogers
Arthur M Sackler Museum, Harvard University, Cambridge,
Massachusetts: view of the facade, 1979–1985.
© Timothy Hursley, photographer
James Stirling/Michael Wilford fonds
Collection Centre Canadien d'Architecture/
Canadian Centre for Architecture, Montréal

bottom

James Stirling, Michael Wilford, and
Associates Perry, Dean, Stahl & Rogers
Arthur M Sackler Museum, Harvard University,
Cambridge, Massachusetts: corner detail, 1979–1985.
© Alan Berman

opposite

James Stirling, Michael Wilford, and
Associates Perry, Dean, Stahl & Rogers
Arthur M Sackler Museum, Harvard University, Cambridge,
Massachusetts: view of the entrance facade, 1979–1985.
© Timothy Hursley, photographer
James Stirling/Michael Wilford fonds
Collection Centre Canadien d'Architecture/
Canadian Centre for Architecture, Montréal © CCA

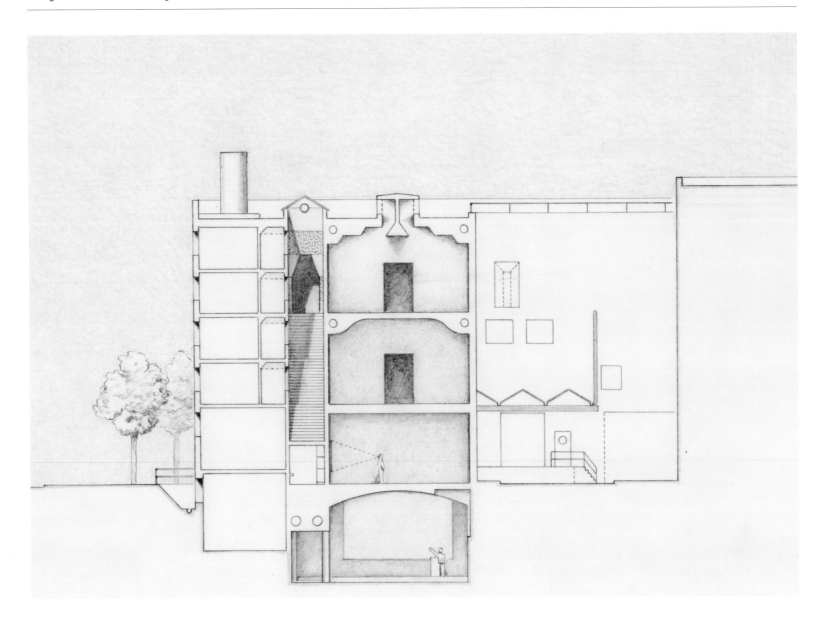

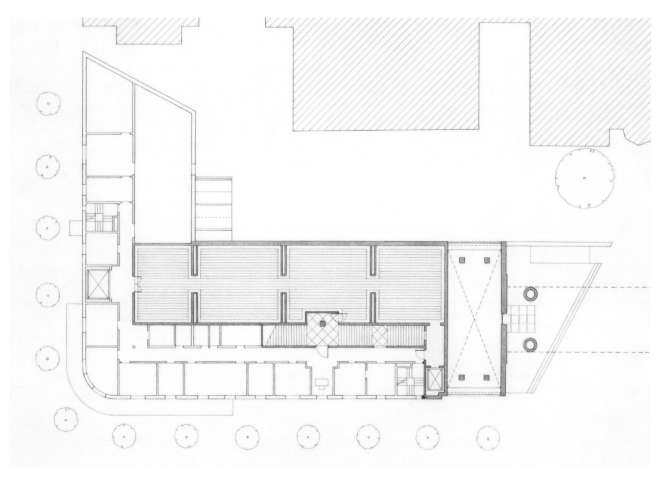

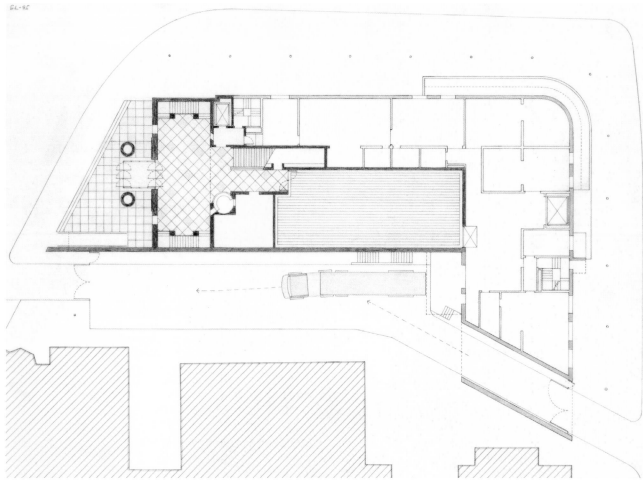

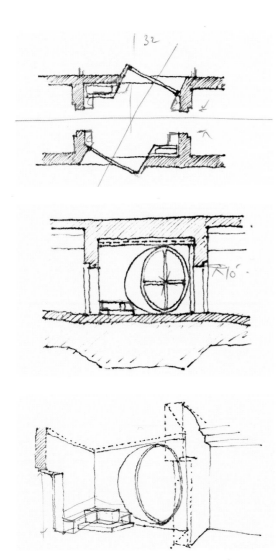

Approximately 11,000 square feet of exhibition space is contained in the 60,000 square feet building, arranged as double-height galleries along the east side (giving them twice the volume of the single-storey academic and service spaces). An attenuated, shallow lobby three-storeys high provides a surprising, dramatic and light-filled entry hall, its ashlar stucco glowing. On each side are pairs of full-height back-lit columns, behind which are tucked stairs to the basement lecture hall (recalling the Fogg's arrangement). Ribbon windows high in both side walls emphasise the volume's width and height, while v-grooves in the white stucco walls (now inexcusably defaced with a mural) envelop the hall with coursing related to that of the giant entry quoins outside—an internalisation of the facade. Collaged to the right of the passage to the temporary exhibit gallery is a circular, space-age information kiosk and shop, clad with illuminated Corian panels.

Across this imposing space, a grand stair—shifted slightly off centre—rises through the whole of the building in a narrow chasm, lit by a long skylight high above. It is this stair that organises the building around it, in place of the courtyard at the Fogg (with its stairs hidden away). On the left are five low floors of offices and study facilities, with windows and doors to the stair; to the right are the three floors of double-height galleries. This split section—recalling historic urban types such as palazzi and hotels, with their service mezzanines and entresols—is a masterly solution that balances the need to mix numerous small pedagogical spaces alongside grand galleries, in a building whose height was limited by zoning regulations.

The top-lit stair "chasm" repeats the exterior's theme of coloured stripes in banding of lavender and ochre stucco, into which are embedded fragments of Coptic sculptures. Again, an internal suggestion of an exterior space, this unusual long stair elicits a sense of joy and wonder, and recalls both high and low references: the Scala Regia; an Italian hill town path; Sir John Soane's museum. This narrow architectural form is at once a memorable, evocative and functional device which brings together students, professors, curators and the public, all the while being an extremely economical gesture in terms of how little space it occupies. (Stirling and Wilford "stole" a portion of the full-height stair shaft to provide two side alcoves for the top-level gallery—a violation of the section that is one of the few faults that Colin Rowe would find with the finished building.) The architect described the stair as "a steeply inclined bazaar with overlooking windows, people talking and flanking activities... a sort of mini-bazaar".

In fact, this building is planned so tightly that it omits any large public gathering space such as a courtyard, for which there wasn't either the room or the budget. But Stirling and Wilford can be seen as taking advantage of this limitation to emphasise the structure's deferential inflection toward the Fogg, where, with the construction of proposed bridge, the grand internal courtyard of the Fogg Museum could be seen as "completing" the whole.

Bridge

Early studies of the bridge show a minimal functionalist tube with exposed steel structure, but, as the building's design evolved, the bridge assumes the architectural character of the museum itself, to become a massive linking form hailed by some local residents as "a marker at the gateway to our neighbourhood". The bridge houses two formal "long galleries" (presumably adopted from a British country house), in order to carry the visitor seamlessly between the exhibit halls of the Fogg and the new museum.

To be supported by pairs of concrete columns at both ends, the connector was to be striped like the main block of the Sackler, though with buff and white stucco. At the centre, between the two gently sloping galleries, a seating area is shifted off the orthogonal, and sports enormous circular windows offering diagonal views up and down Broadway. Local project architect Donald Tellalian recalls Stirling being fascinated by the rotating, circular air vents in the dashboard of Tellalian's 1974 Alfa Romeo GTV, and believes that these were the source of the distinctive pivoting oculus windows. In making what might have been merely a "passage" into a "place", this bridge asserts an architectural presence comparable to that of Michael Graves' widely published, and also unrealised, Fargo-Morehead Cultural Center Bridge proposal that preceded it by a short time.

Although the neighbourhood voted in favour of the bridge, it fell short of the two-thirds majority required to get a sympathetic appraisal from the city. In the face of a challenging and uncertain City Council approval process, the University decided not to submit the design proposal, and abandoned the connector—initially, only temporarily—without a fight. As a result, a building that always was hoped to be connected became a free-standing fragment. In retrospect, the failure to commit to this connection may have been the seed for what became, under a more recent and less appreciative museum administration, the official opinion that the Sackler does not perform well as a free-standing facility.

Shock of the Old: Continuities of Design and Context

The new design was widely reported—and widely controversial—starting with Harvard's major exhibition of Stirling and Wilford's design studies in 1981, at a time when each new design of the architects was scrutinised worldwide. (The exhibit opened the day before Stirling received the Pritzker Prize!) This proposed building was either virtuoso play at the cutting edge of design, or post modernist heresy, coming as it did from an architect lauded for his astounding, light and fragile modernist assemblages of the 1960s. Unlike those works, here was a massive building with small punched windows—more akin to the Preston Housing, 1957, than to the Cambridge History Faculty, 1964. The Sackler is no structural *tour-de-force*: load-bearing exterior walls of concrete units are faced with brick veneer; poured concrete shear walls are buried inside the building; and steel beams spanning the large openings of the galleries are concealed by wallboard and plaster. The only instances of exposed structure are the free-standing support columns at the entrance—with no bridge to support—and the precast concrete planking of the office ceiling slabs, which is surely more indebted to a brutal construction budget than to Brutalist ethics. Even the proposed bridge—the one element that demands engineering ingenuity—hides its 150 foot long structure. Local principal architect Tad Stahl jokes that "In terms of construction, the building is basically a motel." (But, it's worth noting, it is a very well-built one.)

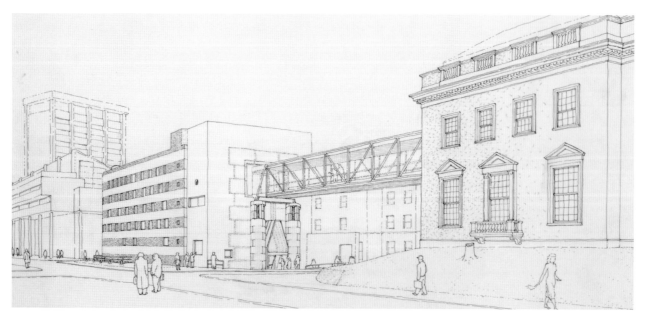

opposite top

James Stirling, Michael Wilford, and
Associates Perry, Dean, Stahl & Rogers
Arthur M Sackler Museum, Harvard University,
Cambridge, Massachusetts: bridge model,
1979–1985.

opposite bottom

James Stirling, Michael Wilford, and
Associates Perry, Dean, Stahl & Rogers
Arthur M Sackler Museum, Harvard University,
Cambridge, Massachusetts: early perspective
for bridge, 1979–1985.
Collection Centre Canadien d'Architecture/
Canadian Centre for Architecture, Montréal © CCA

below

James Stirling, Michael Wilford, and
Associates Perry, Dean, Stahl & Rogers
Arthur M Sackler Museum, Harvard University,
Cambridge, Massachusetts: elevation for the
bridge, 1979–1985.
Collection Centre Canadien d'Architecture/
Canadian Centre for Architecture, Montréal © CCA

The building was seen as a continuation of Stirling's foray into "postmodernism", notwithstanding Stirling's own disparagement of this "movement": "I think it's absolute junk and I think it's journalism." "As far back as 1957, we were using historical precedents." An open-minded observer, attuned to the American architectural world, and also interested in inventive urban architecture, *New York Times* architectural critic Ada Louise Huxtable proclaimed the design to be "the architectural event of the 1980s, which parallels Le Corbusier's Carpenter Hall as the architectural event of the 1960s".[5]

Upon examination, the sheer range of the Sackler's "connexions" and continuities confounds any simple characterisation of the building as "postmodern": there are historical forms, transformed; typological and programmatic elements, revisited and adapted without any particular stylistic bent; a commitment to modernist abstraction and machine-like imagery; and continuities with the architects' earlier work. The shock of Stirling and Wilford's design seems to have obscured the fact that while this building may exhibit wide ranging references, few of these, by themselves, truly appear as "postmodern" in style. It is the entrance ornament, recalling neoclassical devices in exaggerated form, that is the primary application of a historic element here, representative of a sense of humour shared with Robert Venturi and Michael Graves, but also evidence of a grander sense of play, as explored by John Summerson in *Vitruvius Ludens* (where the Sackler cut-away axonometric is the frontispiece). (Is it relevant that the Gibbs surround evoked by the Sackler's quoining is named after James Gibbs 1682–1754, also a learned Scottish architect, whose neoclassicism preceded Stirling's by two centuries?) This decorative device is also a clear reference to details found elsewhere on campus and on the adjacent apartment and fire station. Looking down Broadway today, one sees these three neighbouring brick structures, all featuring flat, buff classical decoration.

This oversized quoining, truncated glass entrance form, and quadripartite window above are all the more scandalous because the elements together can be seen as being suggestive of a figure and a face. When asked about this, Stirling acknowledged that "there's a head with a face, a visage overlooking the campus." One cannot help but put the architect's willing reading of this frontal end facade in the context of a negative comment by Stirling's teacher and friend, Colin Rowe, about the Stuttgart Staatsgalerie, 1984, expressed in an otherwise favourable review (and perhaps shared with the architect in person). Rowe described the German museum as "a building with no face", and then asked, "... could there not be something slightly crumbly about the absence of facade?"

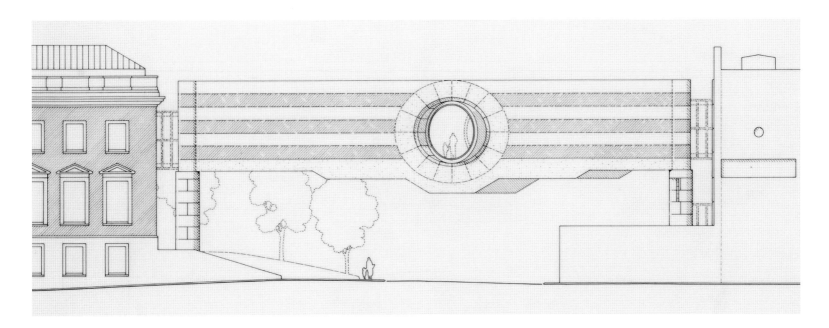

"Face, except for Le Corbusier from time to time, was never a preoccupation of modern architecture."[6]

In this same essay Rowe also observed the fact that axonometric drawings — the most characteristic drawing type used by Stirling and Wilford — "will, never, yield a prime face". Only a one-point perspective allows the architect to focus on an elevation, Rowe argued. He then extended this discussion to observe that, "so far as I know — Stirling has never used one point perspective". One must wonder whether the perspective drawing of the Sackler's frontal south facade tailed by the striped mass, as seen from Sever Hall — a two-point perspective that presents both the front elevation and the side — might be the architects' rejoinder to Rowe's search for face in modern architecture.

The Sackler facade's apparent embrace of representation accompanied its jolting side elevations which were, at heart, abstract, despite any reference to Memorial Hall's polychromatic roofscape and brickwork. Not only does the unfamiliar polychromy of orange and grey clash with the traditional red brick of Harvard and Boston, but its patterning runs continuously from ground to roof, with the uppermost band cut off partway, as though the repeating stripes could continue upward forever. The way that the banding flows smoothly around the northwest corner works with its unrelenting repetition to produce a strident, mechanical appearance. Rather than appearing as postmodern — in which case, the banding might be expected to demonstrate an interest in distinguishing top from bottom, sky from ground, as at the Berlin Science Center, 1981 — the connotation of the Sackler stripes is instead machine-like or industrial. It suggests a manufactured object, or a 1930s warehouse; it references the ribbon windows of modernist Gund Hall across Cambridge Street and of Yamasaki's nearby 1963 William James Hall tower. As Stirling noted, "Well, nowadays one can draw equally, without guilt, from the abstract style of modern design and the multiple layers of historical precedent. Here we are combining the abstract repetitiveness of the long facade with the more representational character of the entrance facade...."

With windows floating with apparent random in the grey bands — windows varied in size, type and placement — the striping perhaps appears as a somewhat gimmicky device. In a published postcard to the architect, Kenneth Frampton objected to the "no doubt deliberately 'shocking' disorder of the facade" seen in the design drawings. Yet the irregular spacing and shapes derive from the decision to locate the windows always in the centre of rooms of varying sizes and uses — Stirling's deliberate play on a "functionalist" external expression of interior spaces. More importantly, in terms of the museum's public expression, the small windows manifest the placement of offices and teaching rooms on Quincy Street, and deny this "arts" avenue the grand scale of double-height spaces and giant orders traditionally associated with art museums. In this way, the fenestration clearly expresses the Fogg's unique type of the teaching museum/laboratory: the regularly occupied rooms for teaching, study and work are given views to the street, while the adjacent galleries, preferably without windows, are placed on the service court. Stirling certainly was familiar with one precedent for such a displacement of a building's grand spaces away from the street in order to privilege its "secondary" functions located in small single-storey rooms: William Butterfield's polychromatic All Saints, Margaret Street in London.

The Sackler Museum also presents continuities within the architects' own oeuvre. While the cast-concrete columns heroically marking the entrance relate contextually to the concrete piloti of both the Carpenter Center and Gund Hall, after the abandonment of the bridge and of the need to support any load, they assume a rhetorical monumentality comparable to that of the vestigial columns of an ancient portico. Thus they belong on the same page of a Stirling encyclopedia of paired entrance markers, with the double towers at the History Faculty in Cambridge, 1964, and at Oxford's Florey Building, 1966. Stirling's "Connexions" lecture and article illustrate the architect's model for this arrangement, Trinity

opposite

James Stirling, Michael Wilford, and Associates Perry, Dean, Stahl & Rogers Arthur M. Sackler Museum, Harvard University, Cambridge, Massachusetts: interior view, 1979–1985.
© Timothy Hursley
James Stirling/Michael Wilford fonds
Collection Centre Canadien d'Architecture/
Canadian Centre for Architecture, Montréal

above

James Stirling, Michael Wilford, and Associates Perry, Dean, Stahl & Rogers Arthur M. Sackler Museum, Harvard University, Cambridge, Massachusetts: looking down main staircase, 1979–1985.
© Alan Berman

College's gate in Cambridge, 1520, where projecting stair towers flank the entrance archway. (Were the painted rebars that extended from the tops of the Sackler's columns for many years an abstract recollection of Trinity's crenellations?) A photo of paired obelisks on the mantel in Stirling and Wilford's office suggests that such twin vertical markers captivated the architects at varied scales.

The boldly coloured banding of the Sackler similarly continues Stirling's interest in stripes colouration, seen as early as 1957 in the dark blue brick bands on the red-brick Old People's housing in Preston; in the brightly coloured vertical stripes, alternating green, blue, yellow and orange, at Runcorn, 1967; and in similar vertical banding at the Olivetti Training School, 1969, for which Stirling is reported to have tried 17 different colour schemes for the external glass-reinforced polyester panels. (His unrealised first choice for this polychromy merited a colour reproduction in the 'Black Notebook'.) Anthony Vidler's exhibit, *James Frazer Stirling: Notes from the Archive*, includes travel photos that document the architect's long-abiding attention to multicoloured banding, at San Miniato al Monte, at the Baptistery and Church in Pisa, and at Porto Venere. Stirling had also expressed admiration for the "stripey brick and tile of the Victorian architects" of nineteenth-century Britain.

Continuity with Stirling and Wilford's earlier work also appears in the Sackler Museum's assemblage of isolated architectural components, where forms brashly abut one another, each piece clearly articulated, including the long diagonal path of the stair cutting through the full-height section. Instead of the "controlled bricolage" that has been seen in the architects' expansive designs for Dusseldorf, 1975, and Cologne, 1975, here one discovers an internalised collage, fixed in an enclosing L-shaped container. Yet its juxtapositions clearly relate to the earlier assemblages. The ornamented entry mass behind two abstract concrete columns fronts the wider, banded, machine-like main block. Inside, the distinctively proportioned vertical entrance volume, without any visual connections to surrounding spaces, "misses" its alignment with the narrow, grand stair shaft, which splits the low teaching spaces from high galleries, and with the sci-fi kiosk as well. Abruptly entered, these galleries—generally admired suites of well-designed rooms—are like found objects, hidden within the building, where, somewhat remarkably in the sometimes strange world of museum design, they are intelligently planned, offering generous wall space for art display, reflected natural light from overhead for light-tolerant ancient sculpture on the top floor, and warm oak floors, baseboards and portals.

All in all, it is a *tout ensemble* of juxtapositions contained, of expansion— and—compression, of exaggerated proportions, a "succession of minor shocks or jolts" that has the effect of spatial tension that can be compared to that of Michelangelo's Laurentian Library (also missing its intended concluding space). The discontinuities, together with the play with typological forms, the treatment of the street elevations, and the (minimal) historic detail, combine to make this tightly sited urban fragment Stirling's mannerist palazzo.

Consequences

It was only the omission of the gallery-bridge that assured that the Sackler's boldly frontal facade would remain a face, uncompromised by being turned into a bridge abutment. Yet the architectural promenade that the architects favoured remains, if truncated: the visitor passes through the expansive tall vestibule, up the joyful stair, and then turns to march back to the front of the top-floor's Oriental gallery, to arrive at the oversized, glazed central opening with its dramatic view (now blocked off) to the empty flank of the Fogg Museum and, beyond, to Harvard's campus and Sever Hall. Stirling said that "When you arrive at the big window, having gone through all the galleries, you're confronted with the Fogg and with the desire to make the crossing, as it were, ideally, of course, through a long gallery connecting

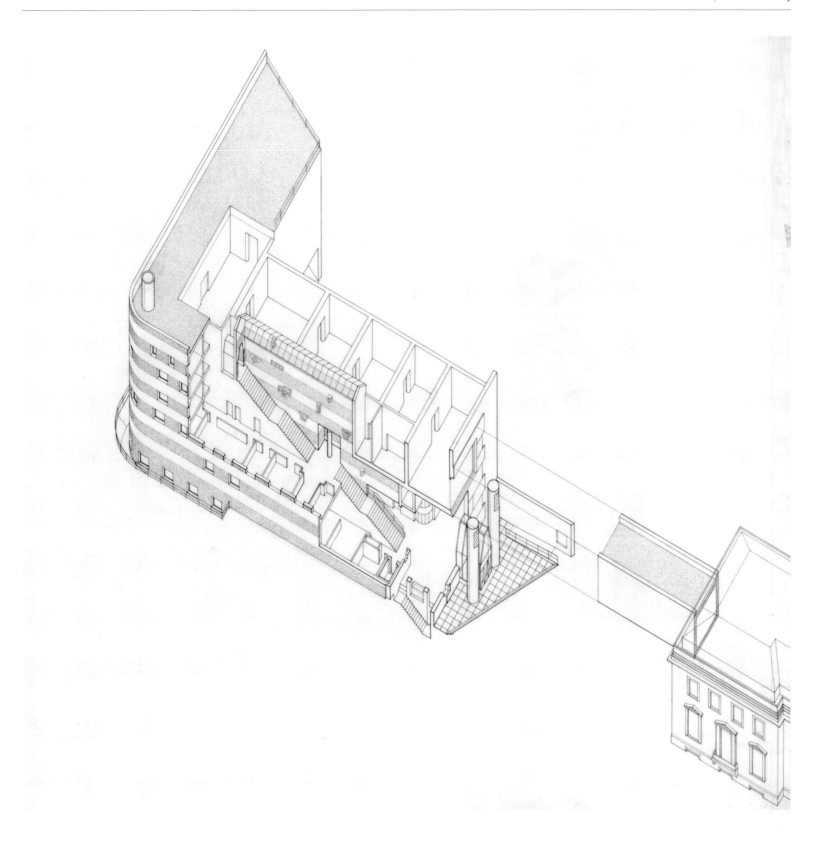

James Stirling, Michael Wilford, and
Associates Perry, Dean, Stahl & Rogers
Arthur M Sackler Museum, Harvard University,
Cambridge, Massachusetts: cutaway
axonometric, 1979–1985.
James Stirling/Michael Wilford fonds
Collection Centre Canadien d'Architecture/
Canadian Centre for Architecture, Montréal © CCA

the two museums." He continued: "The big window suggests in the mind where you would make the leap, and I think the termination of the galleries at that window is how you connect back, not only to the Fogg, but to Harvard itself."

Reception, Success and Failure

Given its inflection toward the Fogg in so many ways, Stirling and Wilford's Sackler Museum, though free-standing and independent, can be seen as the most deliberate and considered example of a building as a fragment. With its own brash identity, it oscillates between dependence and independence. As a whole, it is not so much the sum as a collection of its parts, but this collection is calculatedly incomplete. Major decisions express the design's deference to the existing, legendary Fogg Museum. Stirling's Sackler Museum could not have created a sharper contrast with the old, while still respecting it.

In the face of a new generation's plan to abandon the Sackler Museum because of its alleged failings, it is instructive to revisit former Fogg Museum director John Coolidge's avid admiration and defence of the Stirling and Wilford design in his publication, *Patrons and Architects: Designing Art Museums in the Twentieth Century*.[7] In this volume, published four years after the Sackler's debut, Coolidge evaluates museum buildings in black and white terms. The results are bad, Coolidge argues, "when the architect has his way". Frank Lloyd Wright's Guggenheim and Mies van der Rohe's National Gallery are his two offending examples of architectural dogmatism at the expense of a museum's purpose. In contrast, good buildings result "when the architect and the professional staff collaborate". Coolidge concludes his review of successful museum buildings with Stirling and Wilford's Sackler. "Stirling's brilliant parti has produced a building at once striking, convenient, and—above all—a sympathetic setting for works of art." Agreeing with Coolidge's assessment, Stirling's original client, Slive, remains adamant today: "I can't believe anyone saying that the building doesn't work." Whatever the reputation of the earlier "Red Trilogy" structures in terms of the architects' sense of responsibility to clients and users, for Harvard Stirling and Wilford clearly shaped a building that was respectful of its occupants' goals, while at the same time being an unexpected, brash, and playful work of architecture.

In his positive evaluation of the Sackler, Colin Rowe takes exception to what he sees as a "received critical litany" of disappointment with the Stirling and Wilford building. Instead, he praises the correctness, the "compact, logical and elegant corollary" of Stirling's planning. "All this is ingenious", he proclaims. The notoriously stingy Rowe then concludes his evaluation of the Sackler in understated, yet unmistakably favourable language: "Not only a versatile solution to an almost incompatible array of problems, not in any trivial sense a shocking building, it is a major and tragic statement of physiognomic intensity; and, as if all this were not enough, its urbanistic performance is exemplary." His final judgment: "... *Not quite the Neue Staatsgalerie at Stuttgart; but, for all that, one of the best Stirling realisations to date.*"[8]

Today, the fate of the Sackler Museum building by Stirling and Wilford is uncertain, as the Art Museums plan to abandon it and to transfer its collections and activities to a gargantuan rebuilding and expansion of the Fogg, designed with none of the constraints that helped inspire Stirling and Wilford's imaginative creation. In celebrating the opening of the Sackler in 1985, director John Rosenfield had written that, "Given the vicissitudes of the project, the Sackler Museum is a tribute to James Stirling's clarity of vision, to Arthur Sackler's generosity and loyalty, to Harvard University's commitment to the visual arts, and to Seymour Slive's fiery and single-minded devotion to the project." To now remove from this unique and provocative teaching museum the functions and the art which it so inventively houses, and to abandon it to an uncertain fate less than 30 years after its completion, is surely a tragedy.

James Stirling, Michael Wilford, and
Associates Perry, Dean, Stahl & Rogers
Arthur M Sackler Museum, Harvard
University, Cambridge, Massachusetts:
view of the galleries, 1979–1985.
© Alaistair Hunter, photographer
James Stirling/Michael Wilford fonds
Collection Centre Canadien d'Architecture/
Canadian Centre for Architecture, Montréal © CCA

Center for the Performing Arts, Cornell University

Brian Carter

James Stirling and Michael Wilford were commissioned to design a new building at Cornell University to house the performing arts in 1982. The appointment of the architects followed an interview and, according to Don Randall, a Professor of Music who served on the architect selection committee and was subsequently involved throughout the design and construction of the project, "it was clear in everybody's view that Jim was one of the great talents of his day, extraordinarily important and imaginative. There was no "house style". Jim and Michael's approach to building was to understand the client's problem and try to solve it in a creative way. You couldn't be sure of what one of their buildings was going to look like, because it would be made to order for your particular purposes."[1]

Prior to receiving the commission at Cornell University the architects had been preoccupied with the design of new cultural buildings in historic European cities. And although many of those proposals were to remain un-built Stirling and Wilford's successful competition entry for an extension to the Neue Staatsgalerie in Stuttgart, prepared in 1977, was under construction. It was to be completed in 1983 and although the design was clearly shaped by their earlier plans for buildings in Dusseldorf, Cologne and Marburg, the proposal was also influenced by conversations in America. In particular it reflected ideas outlined by Colin Rowe, Vincent Scully, Robert Venturi, Louis Kahn and Fred Koetter—influential critics and designers who focused on mannerism and modernism while advocating for an architecture of collage, complexity and inclusion. These ideas were in stark contrast to many that were embedded in the buildings being designed by architects in America at that time—a period when increasingly influential corporate practices were promoting a second International Style of glass box modernism while others enthusiastically referenced the work of Giuseppe Terragni.

Although Stirling had been a regular visitor to America since 1958 he did not have an opportunity to design a building there until Stirling and Wilford were invited to make a proposal for a new museum at Harvard University in 1979. In that same year, James Stirling and Michael Wilford were awarded another commission in America when they were asked to design an extension to the School of Architecture at Rice University in Houston. This was followed by a request to prepare a proposal for a new building for the Chemistry Department at Columbia University in New York.

opposite top

James Stirling, Michael Wilford, and Associates, Wank Adams Slavin Associates Center for Theatre Arts, Cornell University, Ithaca, New York: site plan, September 1983. James Stirling/Michael Wilford fonds Collection Centre Canadien d'Architecture/ Canadian Centre for Architecture, Montréal © CCA

opposite bottom

James Stirling, Michael Wilford, and Associates, Wank Adams Slavin Associates Center for Theatre Arts, Cornell University, Ithaca, New York: topographic survey of study area and axonometrics of building types for the Collegetown urban design study, 1982–1989. James Stirling/Michael Wilford fonds Collection Centre Canadien d'Architecture/ Canadian Centre for Architecture, Montréal © CCA

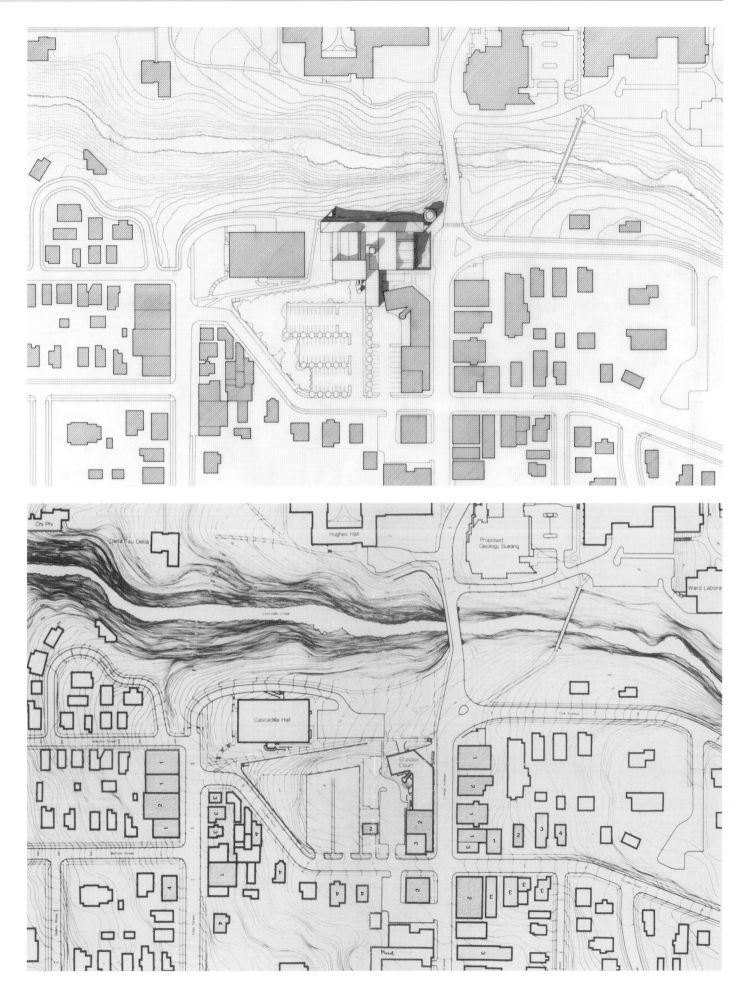

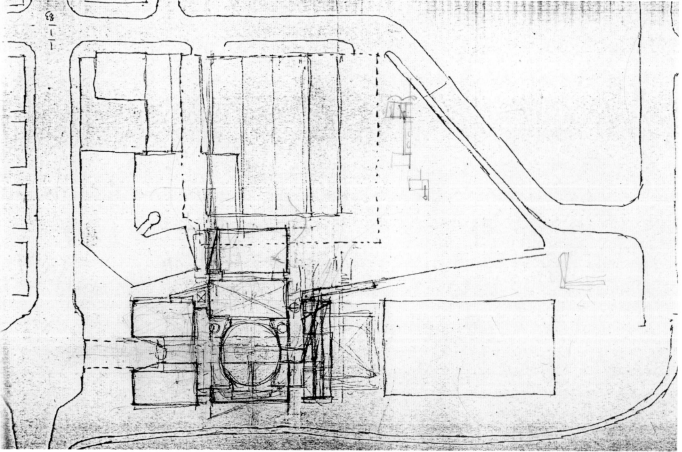

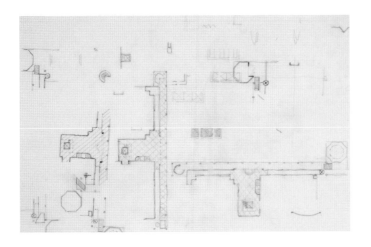

The commission from Cornell University presented Stirling and Wilford with problems that were radically different. Situated in the hilly, wooded landscapes that characterise upstate New York Cornell University, with a population of about 20,000, is in Ithaca—a small city of about 30,000 people. And, while both city and campus share the same expansive landscape it is also a landscape that dramatically separates them. Ithaca is located on Cayuga Lake—a body of water contained within a gorge—while Cornell University, established in 1865, is situated high up on a ridge that is defined by two other gorges. One of those, Cascadilla Gorge, a cleft in the land that drops almost 300 feet, dramatically separates the campus from the city.

The site that was designated for the new Performing Arts Center fronts onto Cascadilla Gorge and is alongside a bridge that spans the gorge and forms the main entrance to the campus of Cornell University. Collegetown, a discrete neighbourhood of housing, shops, offices and restaurants that line College Avenue, is, as its name suggests, a focus for students. Situated at the threshold to the campus, and with views across the gorge, the site that was presented to the architects consisted of a rectangular strip of land with a narrow frontage onto College Avenue along its eastern edge and large but relatively undistinguished buildings to the south and west. It was a site which, according to Stirling, required a building with "a front side, side side and two back sides".[2]

The choice of this site underlined Cornell University's interest in forging a new connection between the campus and the city. The creation of a Performing Arts Center in this location provided an opportunity to both advance the university's academic programmes and bring together students, faculty and the public around ambitious programmes involving theatre, film, music and dance. Initially the design for the new Performing Arts Center was part of a more comprehensive plan to develop land in Collegetown for housing as well as academic facilities. Stirling and Wilford's early proposals suggested new residential buildings to the west of the site designated for the Performing Arts Center. Although these particular plans were to remain on paper, a detailed brief was prepared for the academic building. That brief outlined a need for a new educational facility to accommodate the university's Department of Theatre Arts. It was an ambitious plan that envisaged four large principle spaces: a proscenium theatre to seat 450 people, a flexible performance space for up to 175 people, a dance performance studio with removable seating for 130 and a cinema for film studies to seat 100 people. These were to be supported by a full range of backstage facilities including a scenery shop with vehicular access, costume shop, dressing rooms, control booths, production spaces as well as classrooms and offices for students, staff and faculty.

The requirements to accommodate a range of different academic uses that could also serve the public on this long narrow site wedged into a lively mixed-use neighbourhood and defined by a dramatic gorge that separated the university campus from the city, presented an intricate planning puzzle.

Earlier designs for cultural buildings in Europe that were developed by James Stirling and Michael Wilford had proposed collections of buildings where each represented a distinctive type and consequently took on a particular form. These projects had also been organised to define routes that integrated new development with the existing city. However, the site for this new building in Ithaca was distinctly different. Defined by a deep rocky cleft, dense foliage, the sound of rushing water and extreme weather—hot summers and icy cold winters—it was a place characterised by wild nature.

The plan that Stirling and Wilford developed for the new Performing Arts Center consisted of a series of buildings, each of which housed a different activity, which were arranged *enfilade* and connected by a loggia aligned with Cascadilla Gorge. It was a plan that created a distinct boundary between building and

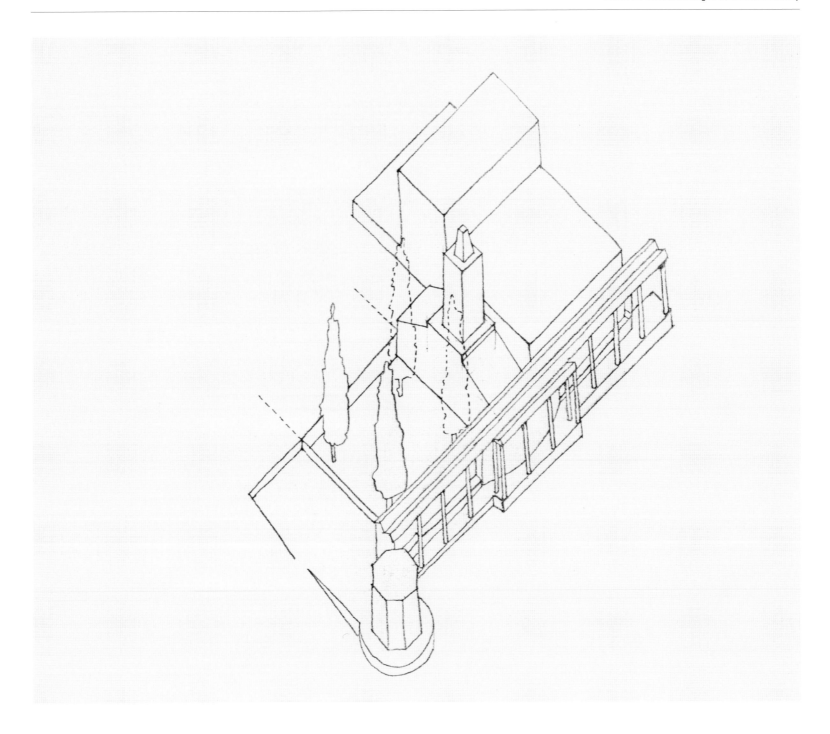

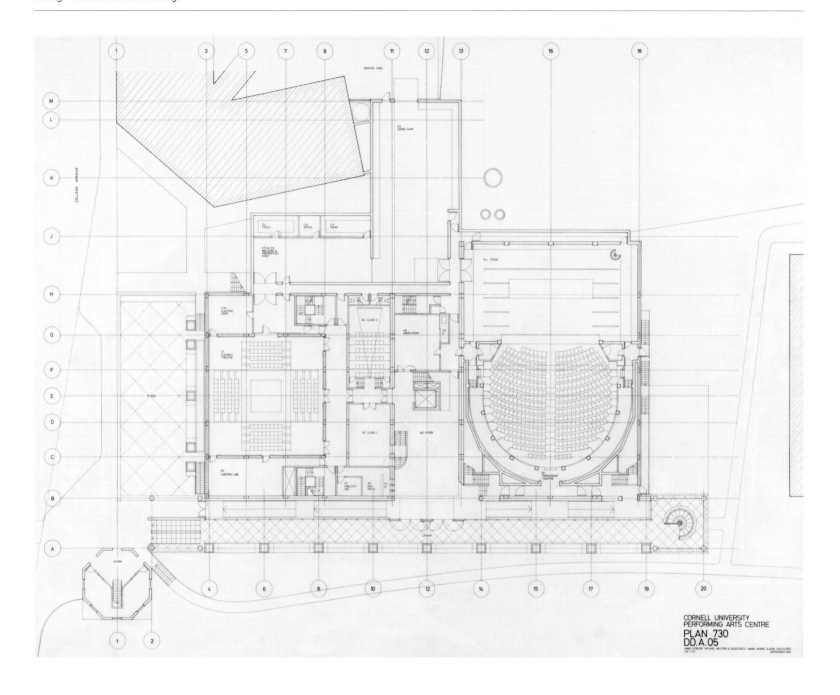

CORNELL UNIVERSITY
PERFORMING ARTS CENTRE
PLAN 730
DD.A.05

James Stirling, Michael Wilford, and
Associates, Wank Adams Slavin Associates
Center for Theatre Arts, Cornell University,
Ithaca, New York: entrance level plan.
James Stirling/Michael Wilford fonds
Collection Centre Canadien d'Architecture/
Canadian Centre for Architecture, Montréal © CCA

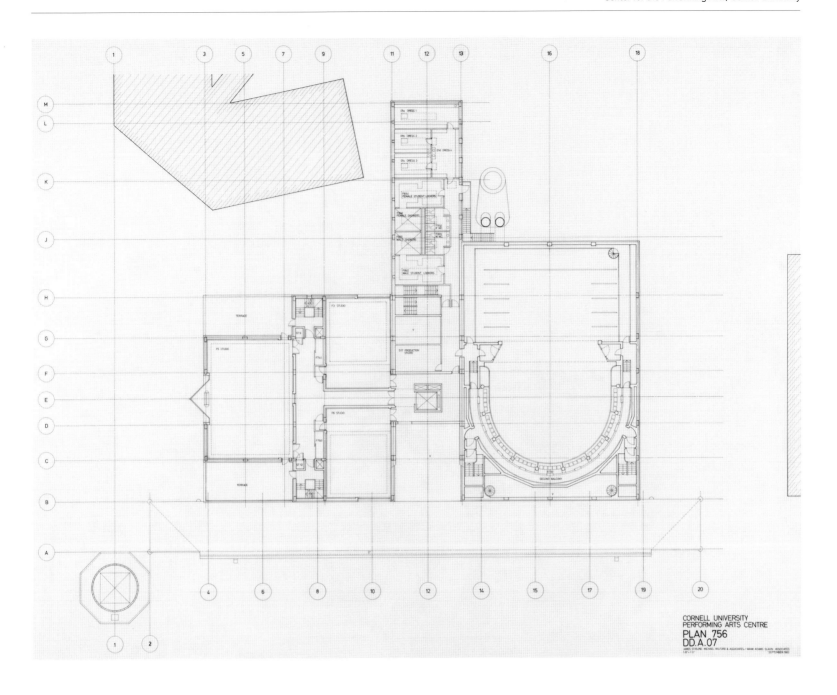

James Stirling, Michael Wilford, and
Associates, Wank Adams Slavin Associates
Center for Theatre Arts, Cornell University,
Ithaca, New York: upper level plan.
James Stirling/Michael Wilford fonds
Collection Centre Canadien d'Architecture/
Canadian Centre for Architecture, Montréal © CCA

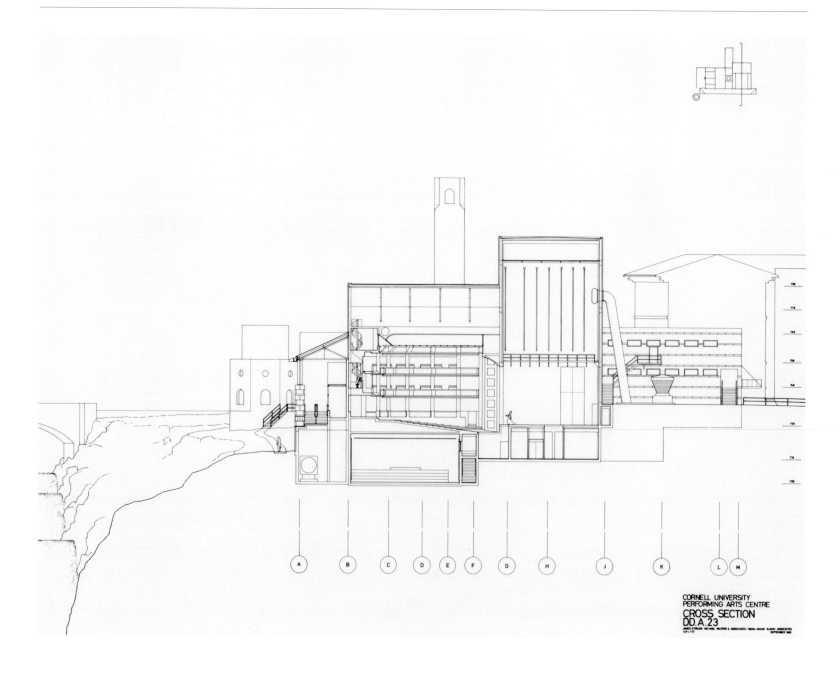

CORNELL UNIVERSITY
PERFORMING ARTS CENTRE
CROSS SECTION
DD.A.23

James Stirling, Michael Wilford, and
Associates, Wank Adams Slavin Associates
Center for Theatre Arts, Cornell University,
Ithaca, New York: cross-section.
James Stirling/Michael Wilford fonds
Collection Centre Canadien d'Architecture/
Canadian Centre for Architecture, Montréal © CCA

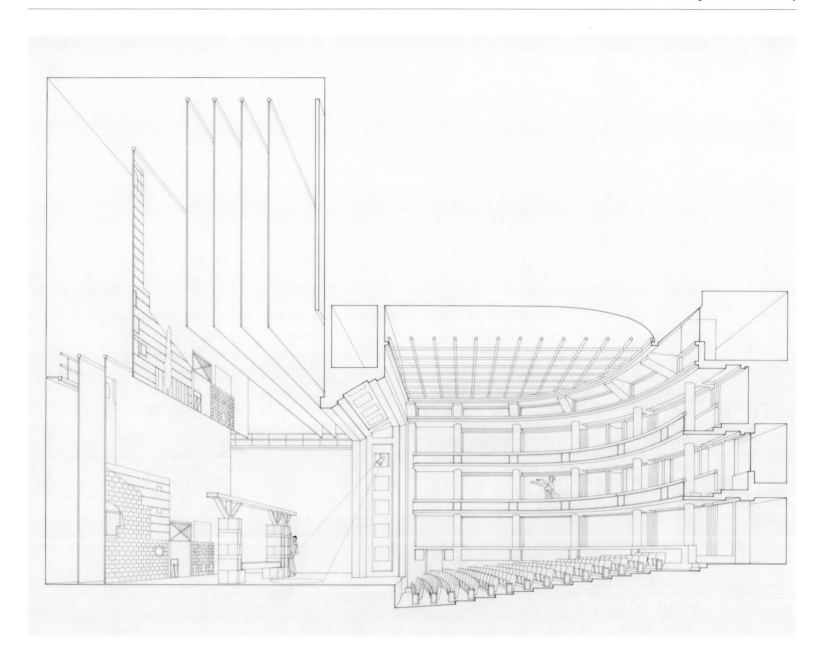

James Stirling, Michael Wilford, and
Associates, Wank Adams Slavin Associates
Center for Theatre Arts, Cornell University, Ithaca,
New York: cutaway perspective of the theatre.
James Stirling/Michael Wilford fonds
Collection Centre Canadien d'Architecture/
Canadian Centre for Architecture, Montréal © CCA

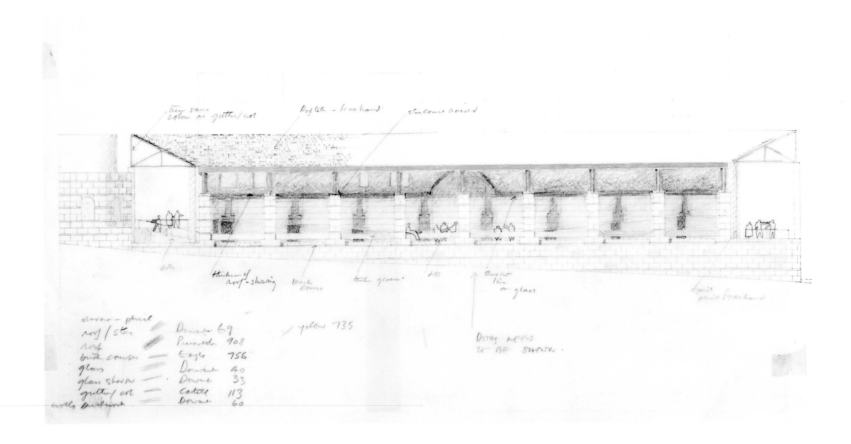

nature while, at the same time, proposing the creation of a new civic space that would connect College Avenue at the eastern end and residential developments to the west.

The loggia was a familiar and arguably an appropriate traditional building type. Fundamental to the organisation of the world's oldest university in Bologna and a vital part of that city it was a form that had been enthusiastically adopted by Stirling and Wilford and was an integral part of their successful design for the Wissenschaftszentrum in Berlin, prepared in 1979. And while the loggia may have seemed an unlikely form in the informal setting of Collegetown, it offered particular benefits. Not only did it provide a sheltered civic space for this new public building that overlooked the Cascadilla Gorge and the campus beyond, and a route through the site to adjacent buildings, it also enabled the connection of the different parts of the new Performing Arts Center and, critically, its phased construction should that be necessary.

At about the time that this building was being designed, Stirling's drawings were changing. The precise, black and white diagrams that registered buildings as machines and characterised much of his earlier work transformed to equally precise yet atmospheric section drawings and perspectives that suggested buildings in use. Sometimes rendered in colour, they were also increasingly populated by people. "A drawing has to be designed", Stirling commented before going on to suggest that "What is left on the image is the minimum required to convey the maximum information with the greatest clarity—related to how we understand the building as distinct from the way it might in reality look."[3]

The drawings that Stirling and Wilford prepared for the Performing Arts Center at Cornell provide insights into how the architects "understood" that building (see pp. 67–71). For example one drawing shows several people in the loggia who are engaged in conversation while a solitary man, wrapped up in hat, scarf and raincoat, walks purposefully along a footpath in the Cascadilla Gorge. Another perspective section cut through the proscenium theatre shows an actor

above
James Stirling, Michael Wilford, and
Associates, Wank Adams Slavin Associates
Center for Theatre Arts, Cornell University,
Ithaca, New York: study for loggia, 1982–1989.
James Stirling/Michael Wilford fonds
Collection Centre Canadien d'Architecture/
Canadian Centre for Architecture, Montréal © CCA

opposite top
James Stirling, Michael Wilford, and
Associates, Wank Adams Slavin Associates
Center for Theatre Arts, Cornell University, Ithaca,
New York: interior view of the main entrance, 1989.
© Richard Bryant, photographer
James Stirling/Michael Wilford fonds
Collection Centre Canadien d'Architecture/
Canadian Centre for Architecture, Montréal © CCA

opposite bottom
James Stirling, Michael Wilford, and
Associates, Wank Adams Slavin Associates
Center for Theatre Arts, Cornell University,
Ithaca, New York: model.
James Stirling/Michael Wilford fonds
Collection Centre Canadien d'Architecture/
Canadian Centre for Architecture, Montréal © CCA

on the stage with a single beckoning figure in the first balcony presumably smitten either by the actor or a set design which was based on the new building. Another drawing suggests a moment in the life of that building with groups of admirers in the foyer, people about to collect tickets and a man with a roll of drawings heading for the exit while a lone ballet dancer pirouettes, surprisingly, outside the elevator on an upper floor. Another view from the gorge shows the man with the drawings about to re-enter the building while two workmen struggle to lift heavy timbers, presumably freshly cut (hence the stump of the tree alongside), into an almost completed loggia as if to record the transformation of wild nature into civic space.

Stirling and Wilford also presented their ideas to the client using models. Built in balsa wood, cork and plywood, these precisely constructed models clearly showed the collection of different buildings that combined to make up the Performing Arts Center. Models were also used to outline options for the potential phased development. In all of these models it was clear that the loggia could not only link together the different buildings but also establish a distinctive identity for the Center.

above

James Stirling, Michael Wilford, and
Associates, Wank Adams Slavin Associates
Center for Theatre Arts, Cornell University,
Ithaca, New York: sectional perspective
through the foyer and loggia, 1982–1989.
James Stirling/Michael Wilford fonds
Collection Centre Canadien d'Architecture/
Canadian Centre for Architecture, Montréal © CCA

opposite

James Stirling, Michael Wilford, and
Associates, Wank Adams Slavin Associates
Center for Theatre Arts, Cornell University,
Ithaca, New York: perspective of the main
entrance, 1982–1989.
James Stirling/Michael Wilford fonds
Collection Centre Canadien d'Architecture/
Canadian Centre for Architecture, Montréal © CCA

However this particular loggia, derived from a distinctly urban model based on a horizontal flat floor, sits uneasily on a site with such a marked slope. While the architects were able to use the form to create a distinct character for the building and a boundary between city and nature that limited costly excavation, the result is that the connections to different ground levels that exist at either end of the loggia are cumbersome.

And, in designing the structural frame, the architects were also able to establish a network of varying grids that worked effectively for the different buildings. That frame, a mix of steel and concrete, was concealed within a masonry skin. Early drawings show the external wall as a mix of stone and brick— presumably to relate the new to the existing buildings around the site. However, that was to change.

Considerations of a phased construction for the project were prompted by uncertainties about funding and, after the project was sent out to tender, the lowest bid submitted exceeded the budget by almost 40 per cent. Inevitably, questions were asked, discussions followed and alternatives were considered. The project became a focus of attention for administrators, faculty and staff. As a result of a successful fundraising campaign, the phasing of the construction was avoided. However changes were made that have affected the long-term use of the building. While the range of facilities that was eventually constructed reflected the diverse requirements of the client's original brief, the sizes of some of those spaces were reduced. Consequently the Performing Arts Center appears cramped and public areas modest.

Other cuts brought about changes in materials and finishes. Internally, finishes consist predominantly of inexpensive materials. Externally the alternating courses of brick and stone proposed by the architects had already attracted the attention of the President of Cornell University, and subsequently those materials were replaced by two different types of Vermont marble. That marble cladding was also limited and in less prominent places it was replaced by rendered panels.[4] Eventually the design was agreed, construction went ahead and the new Performing Arts Center at Cornell was completed in 1988.

The loggia remains a major component in the design. This important architectural element offers fine views over Cascadilla Gorge, to the campus and the landscape beyond. However, perhaps due to extremely cold weather during the academic year, anxieties about security, the awkward changes of level that necessitate a spiral stair on the western end as well as stairs and a ramp onto College Avenue, or perhaps a lack of creative initiatives by the University regarding the use of this new urban space, today the loggia is surprisingly empty.

On College Avenue the loggia terminates at a small open "plaza" and alongside a free standing pavilion. Designed by Stirling and Wilford as an emblematic sign, this octagonal stone-clad pavilion was planned to provide a ticket office and a commercial space on the street and a sheltered space for a bus stop with meeting rooms above. The architects also envisaged prominent signage on a rooftop drum. The potential of this roadside pavilion to generate activity is underlined today when a bus arrives. Whether bound for Ithaca, New York City or beyond, each one that stops here brings with it lively activity and impromptu theatre acted out by passengers, greeters, bag carriers, bleary eyed travellers and tearful friends. Obviously conceived as a marker for the Center, located in a strategic place and planned with clearly visible and changing signage this new pavilion on College Avenue has obvious potential to attract interest and audiences for bringing together town and gown. However currently the building is underused and appears more as a folly than a sign.

Nearby a small square is framed by the gabled end wall of the Arts Center and an existing five-storey apartment building on College Avenue. This paved square is the setting for a free standing structure that has been built with stone faced

top

James Stirling, Michael Wilford, and Associates, Wank Adams Slavin Associates Center for Theatre Arts, Cornell University, Ithaca, New York: Theatre interior, 1982–1989. James Stirling/Michael Wilford fonds Collection Centre Canadien d'Architecture/ Canadian Centre for Architecture, Montréal © CCA

bottom

James Stirling, Michael Wilford, and Associates, Wank Adams Slavin Associates Center for Theatre Arts, Cornell University, Ithaca, New York: facade detail showing plaster panels. © Alan Berman

James Stirling, Michael Wilford, and
Associates, Wank Adams Slavin Associates
Center for Theatre Arts, Cornell University, Ithaca,
New York: view of the loggia from street, 1989.
© Richard Bryant, photographer
James Stirling/Michael Wilford fonds
Collection Centre Canadien d'Architecture/
Canadian Centre for Architecture, Montréal

columns and heavy timber. It provides a conspicuous seat and a hint of Tuscany. However while this space appears logical on plan, it is partially below the level of its surroundings as a result of the slope across the site and consequently isolated from the street.

In contrast, the large bay window that projects out from the dance rehearsal studio over this square and the street emphatically announces the Center with a generous overlook on College Avenue. It was vividly described by James Stirling who, in his address at the formal opening of the Performing Arts Center, described how "a topless gogo dancer will appear in the bay window of the dance studio".[5]

The university campus is like a city and Stirling's provocative description of the Performing Arts Center at Cornell University as an "Italianate hill village" arguably sought to underline that connection.[6] Certainly this particular group of emblematic buildings designed by Stirling and Wilford—a loggia, the pavilion, a series of marble clad blocks, the tiny square overlooked by a projecting bay window on College Avenue and a tall campanile formed from the Center's main elevator shaft—set high above the Cascadilla Gorge, projects the campus into the city while at the same time transforming a particular fragment of Cornell University into a tiny city on a hill for all to see.

previous pages

James Stirling, Michael Wilford, and Associates, Wank Adams Slavin Associates Center for Theatre Arts, Cornell University, Ithaca, New York: exterior view, 1982–1989.
© Richard Bryant, photographer
James Stirling/Michael Wilford fonds
Collection Centre Canadien d'Architecture/
Canadian Centre for Architecture, Montréal © CCA

opposite

James Stirling, Michael Wilford, and Associates, Wank Adams Slavin Associates Center for Theatre Arts, Cornell University, Ithaca, New York: exterior view, 1989.
© Richard Bryant, photographer
James Stirling/Michael Wilford fonds
Collection Centre Canadien d'Architecture/
Canadian Centre for Architecture, Montréal © CCA

Science Library,
University of California at Irvine

Craig Hodgetts

Descriptive summary of the building

The Science Library at the University of California, Irvine, was designed in 1988 for the campus that was laid out together with the city of Irvine by William Pereira in 1959. The intention was to develop a complementary "town and gown". The campus has two concentric rings with a park in the centre allowing the halls of residence to be close to the academic buildings, and encouraging a centralised pedestrian community by means of a network of radial routes.

The early buildings were banal heavy concrete structures set in Irvine's open landscape, until the 1980s and 1990s when David Neumann, responsible for the college estate, determined to bring diversity to this monotonous campus by commissioning high-profile designers such as Frank Gehry, Robert Venturi, Charles Moore, and Robert Stern. Stirling and Wilford were commissioned to design the new Science Library, working with a local firm of executive architects. But when David Neumann left his successor summarily terminated Stirling and Wilford's contract in order to "save money" but before much of the detail design had been completed. He also imposed stringent cost reductions which required extensive value engineering and changes to the specification.

The 30 million dollar Science Library was intended to anchor the western quadrant of the UCI campus circle. It had to accommodate some 2,000 readers, exhibitions spaces, stack areas, reference library, catalogue, loan and reserve counters and administrative offices. To create a meaningful context for the building Stirling and Wilford prepared a masterplan for the biological sciences based on a pedestrian axis radiating from the centre of the campus and terminating in the medical school. This axis runs through the building's three linked but geometrically distinct forms which make up the large six-storey building: a U-shaped linear block facing towards the medical school defines what was to be the central courtyard envisaged in the masterplan; a circular "doughnut" form makes a courtyard for the Library around which are the entrances, stacks, reference desks and study carrels; and a pair of 'pincer arms' contain reading areas.

It was Stirling and Wilford who proposed the building be located astride the axis, intending it to create a safe "mall like", active space running through the campus. The building faces two ways, and its two entrances, equidistant from all departments, are in the central circular court which brings light into the middle of this large building.

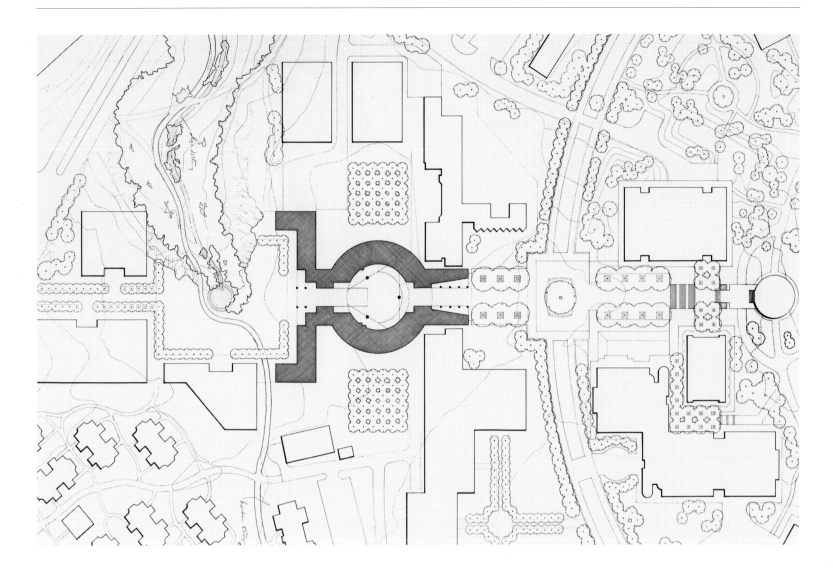

James Stirling, Michael Wilford, and
Associates Michael Wilford and Partners
IBI Group
Science Library, University of California
at Irvine, California: site plan, 1988–1994.
James Stirling/Michael Wilford fonds
Collection Centre Canadien d'Architecture/
Canadian Centre for Architecture, Montréal © CCA

Inward and outward facades are distinctly different: the outer have regular patterns of many small windows and large blank areas, while the inner facades are largely glazed: some of the glazing in the central rotunda is translucent. The walls have a dark red Indian sandstone base with string course, above which the upper levels are faced in light pink stucco; these are surmounted by a deep low pitched metal overhang that shades the facades and hides rooftop services equipment.

The six floors of the building are packed tightly, with few lobbies or gathering spaces normal in a building of this enormous scale—nor is there the *promenade architecturale* that orders so many Stirling and Wilford buildings which is suggested by the big formal gesture of the rotunda: instead there are two utilitarian stairs cramped in the corners—evidence, like so much else, of cost cutting and of Stirling and Wilford's dismissal after the design stage.

Irvine Interrupted

Let's face it. Irvine California is a far cry from Classical Rome. Its presence on Flicker features sophomoric revellers, sterilised byways, and franchise restaurants like MacDonalds limited to the display of shrunken little signs, since officials have banned the "vulgar" ones seen around the world. Irvine the city and Irvine the university campus are twins in more ways than one, since both were carved simultaneously from one of California's largest Spanish land grants. When, in 1968, William Pereira laid down the plans for each, he was inspired to create a "new kind of urban campus" which, in practice devolved to a radial plan centred on a circular park redolent of Ebenezer Howard and the utopian ideals of Campanella and Gillette. Nevermind that California was then sprawling its way to notoriety as the anti-pedestrian nexus of automobile culture. Designed as a bulwark against unplanned suburban cul-de-sacs and the home to the Ayn Rand Institute, Pereira's plan envisioned a kind of necklace, from which the campus would dangle, like a pendant.

To contemporary eyes, that plan, given the failure of grand plans from Brasilia to Dubai was hopelessly naïve, but it is significant that, a mere 20 years after its beginnings, James Stirling and Michael Wilford were approached by David Newman, the highly regarded campus architect, to design what was to serve as the symbolic keystone in the city/campus identity game.

The site itself was symbolic. Marking an ordinate onto the circumference of Pereira's ring road, and flanked by a moat of parking, the site could, metaphorically, be seen as a battlement, with the as yet to be defined Library a stand-in for the fortifications. At least, one imagines, that thought must have been going on in the Stirling and Wilford camp. Here, after all, was an immaculate, nearly virginal "first-growth" city-state, with grand plan ambitions faintly reminiscent of Thomas More's Utopia, Kahn's Bangladesh, or even Chandigargh. All right, an American version of those, but still one with geometry, coordinated road layouts and overall architectural pretensions. It must have seemed like the perfect commission. Especially after all those brilliant, but unbuilt, competition schemes for the bombed-out centres of German cities. But what they failed to understand was that, although the campus plan certainly had imperial overtones, the substance was pre-ordained to reflect the lack of a vital urban culture in Southern California. Above all, it was designed to be a synthetic mix that dictated uniformity and conformity. A pall of mediocrity that promised health and happiness, but left out the challenges that energise a real city's inhabitants.

Enter Piranesi. The Rome he depicts is a near-chaotic jumble of Imperial follies. Oriented with seeming abandon, their pristine, Platonic plan forms jostle ponderously with one another to create an inadvertent froth of exciting interstitial spaces. And that's the game Stirling and Wilford had began to make their own, first with Kaiserplatz, then Cornell, the Berlin Science Center, and the competition entries for Walt Disney Hall and the Bibliothèque Nationale. Each plan depends on the negative space generated by geometrically straightforward building masses, which are then adorned with various accessories, which intrude into and violate the otherwise defined space. But to be effective the strategy demands a grouping, a cluster of buildings which, like those in Piranesi's engravings, or later in Stirling's contribution to Roma Interrotta, create a field of opposites which, like magnets, energize the intervening spaces.

But on the Irvine campus, the would-be surrounding magnets have lost their charge. Stirling's library is encircled by only the most affable campus denizens. Campus buildings which aspire to anonymity. Campus buildings which have garnered laurels for being on time and on budget, rather than engaging. The hoped-for energy field isn't palpable, much less energised, and the building sits, rises, or simply is in a space which might as well be a ghost town.

Were Stirling and Wilford simply misguided in their effort to exploit the nascent imperialism of the Pereira Plan? Or did this project, coming as it did as the only scheme to be realised among the half-dozen or so lofted during the 1980s, simply belong to a gene pool from which much more satisfying schemes might have emerged, had they been realised? This, I believe, would be an entirely plausible explanation for the building that was to be their fourth, and final, expedition to the Americas.

Each of the four suffers from what can only be explained as the American Disease. One remembers Stirling's incredulity at being unable to incorporate a window configuration of his choice at the Rice School of Architecture: his puzzled amazement when he realised that in the United States you have to beg for those

above

James Stirling, Michael Wilford, and
Associates Michael Wilford and Partners
IBI Group
Science Library, University of
California at Irvine, California.
© Richard Bryant, photographer
Courtesy of arcadiimages

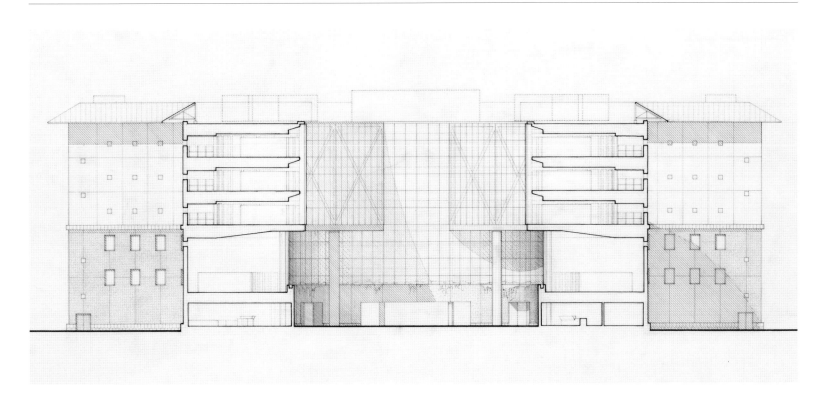

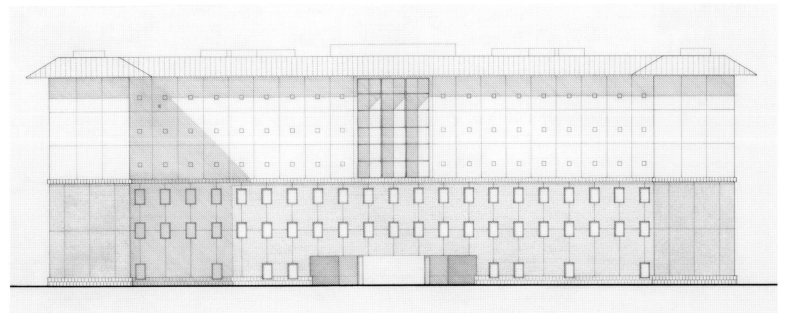

top

James Stirling, Michael Wilford, and
Associates Michael Wilford and Partners
IBI Group
Science Library, University of California at
Irvine, California: cross-section, 1988–1994.
James Stirling/Michael Wilford fonds
Collection Centre Canadien d'Architecture/
Canadian Centre for Architecture, Montréal © CCA

bottom

James Stirling, Michael Wilford, and
Associates Michael Wilford and Partners
IBI Group
Science Library, University of California at
Irvine, California: elevation, 1988–1994.
James Stirling/Michael Wilford fonds
Collection Centre Canadien d'Architecture/
Canadian Centre for Architecture, Montréal © CCA

things which are considered to be the architect's responsibility throughout the rest of the globe.

And so what began as a formal response to the Pereira Imperial plan may have simply collapsed with the realisation that the... er... mercantile forces that lurked behind the academic facade were pulling the strings. This is evidenced by the departure of David Neuman, their defender, and the remaining bureaucrat's conclusion that the local architects should go it alone, thus saving, at one stroke, both expenses and the bother of dealing with a famously idiosyncratic foreigner. One can only guess, but from the desultory details, the painfully inhibited sequence of interior public spaces, and the tight, even restrictive circulation, it is clear that the heroic, spatially complex, and flagrantly open designs characteristic of the pair's early work, had sadly been replaced by a rigidly orthodox, manifestly defensive, and unrelenting formality which seems more appropriate to internecine tensions than collegial discourse.

The resulting hermetic geometry is out of synch with the flayed, even melodramatic posture of earlier projects, which invited the visitor to witness an orgy of pipes, railings, furtive glimpses and vertiginous perspectives before—whew!—depositing him or her at their destination of choice. The formality of the plan, the opacity of the envelope, and the sheer planar expanse of the floors dictate a strict adherence to prescribed routes. One longs for a criss-cross of catwalks across the central, triangular void, or to be gifted with the dexterity of Spiderman to truly exploit its potential as a launching silo, but of course, these are the frustrations of a twenty-first century being—one who has witnessed the coming-of-age of a gilded Era of information.... One who has felt the texture of ink and paper glide away onto the glassy surface of the Kindle, and with it, the massive volume of the volumes housed within the walls of a traditional library.

There is a certain poignancy in the visible mutation of recent libraries—the tension between service and storage, the proliferation—viral spread, really—of the workstation vs the reading table, of the laptop vs the stacks; in fact, of the very proposition put forth by Alexander many continents and centuries ago. But libraries, as surely as banks and movie houses, have reached the end of the line. The ranks of terminals have, to all intents and purposes, eclipsed ritual visits to the stacks and purged all that Post-it clutter from the reference books in PhD carrels. The adventure of sorting through Dewey's decimals on dimly-lit shelves has largely disappeared, and has yet to find a suitable replacement. Lumbered by now-eclipsed technologies, and possessed of a progressive, if spatially humble research brief, the library at Irvine is neither fish nor fowl.

The question is whether you consider the library to be the core of a dynamic information interchange, or see it as a spiritual centre for the intellectual development of a vested scholarly class. At Irvine, it would seem that Stirling and Wilford took refuge in the latter view. Over-reacting, perhaps, to the surfboards and bikinis lurking in every boot, the footprint of the building, its axial gesture, even its introverted bow to Asplund, all suggest residency in a village of forms modelled on classical European universities. There is a suggestion in the Project Brief that the real subject of the Library is student life. This is particularly striking in the effort to frame individual students going about their normal activities—crystalline glass study carrels are thrust out onto the main axis of the campus, hovering above it like observation pods—but other activities are reduced to ant-like scale against the imposing mass of the building itself. There is simply no intermediate scale. Nor is there an effort, as there was at Cambridge, to frame the faculty and administration. Both are relegated to the block which forms the building's outermost flank, and elaborately protected from incursion by mere students.

And so a building which was to be the incarnation of "Library"—which is to all appearances a gigantic vault in which to secure knowledge in the form

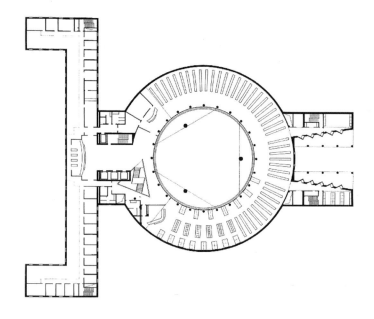

above

James Stirling, Michael Wilford, and Associates Michael Wilford and Partners IBI Group Science Library, University of California at Irvine, California: reference/periodical library and main lending desk.

opposite

James Stirling, Michael Wilford, and Associates Michael Wilford and Partners IBI Group Science Library, University of California at Irvine, California: upper floor plan. James Stirling/Michael Wilford fonds Collection Centre Canadien d'Architecture/ Canadian Centre for Architecture, Montréal © CCA

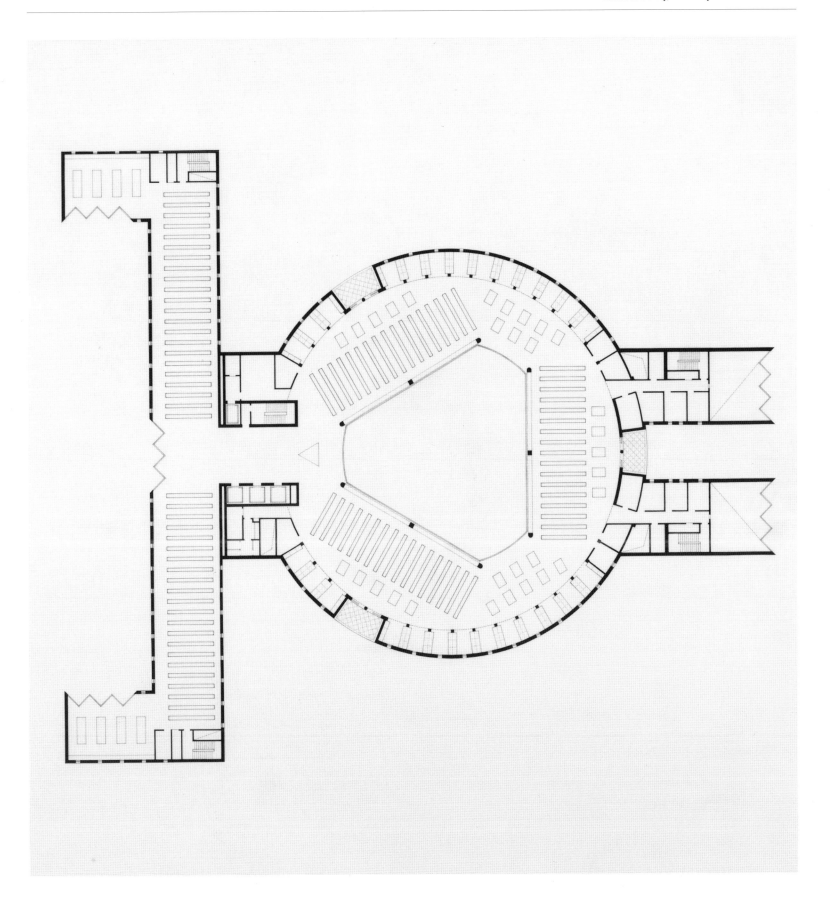

of books—in which the careful delineation of functions has created a kind of Platonic diagram—has, by reason of its rational scheme, become, some 30 years on, a relic whose very presence serves as a kind of cautionary techno-millstone.

Pure, even distilled, that diagram seems oddly out of sync with the immense scale of the building. A bifurcated drum, with stout appendages framing an axial approach, it is perhaps best understood as a much magnified functional appliance. Stripped-down references to antiquity clothe that shape, fleetingly reminding one of a modern-day incarnation of the Castel Sant'Angelo, complete with tiny apertures once suited to the narrow gaze of archers, now given over to study carrels, and a veneer-thin rusticated base. A Nero-like halo, fabricated of stainless steel, rings the top, assuring us of the twentieth century origins of the whole. Entering the rotunda is like disappearing into a great toothy maw as the zig-zagging balconies pass overhead. It's here that you get it. The building is a machine. A vast, forbidden planet kind of machine organised with impeccable, even alien logic. The building simply sits its huge mass at the centre of this most arcadian campus and doesn't even try to look comfortable

Unlike Stirling's other library at Cambridge the library at Irvine rejected the idea of a grand, common reading room in favour of smaller, more "congenial" rooms distributed throughout the "doughnut", above which a circumferential ring of individual carrels girdles an equilateral triangle of book stacks and reference desks. It's a heroic picture, in plan, which immediately puts one in mind of a magnified microchip. Lacking conventional reference points, a strong narrative, or spatial indexes, the plan seems to refer to the multiple layers of an integrated circuitboard rather than formal composition and deftly packages them, one or two to a shelf, within the conceptual envelope. This is not what we expect from Stirling, whose rambunctious miscegenations taunted us with a radical resourcing of history; all the time cloaked in a formal dexterity that led the eye, the mind, and the body through a cocksure ramble of functions. Surprising encounters were the norm. Yet, I must concede that a tendency towards a self-aggrandising majesty underlies the schemes for corporate clients, where Stirling's gremlin wit and subversive insights inexplicitly give way to a nearly suffocating geometry.

This dedication to geometric precision pervades the sectional organisation of the Library as well. Each layer has a particular configuration as well as a specific purpose, so that, leafing through the floor plans of the building is not unlike rifling the pages of an animator's flipbook which, one imagines, is the apotheosis of the serial plans first devised by Stirling for the Siemens AG project (which famously climaxed with the image of a Luger lying on an executive desk on the topmost floor.) There, one was seduced by the parade of gigantic drums, the great criss-crossed solar screens, and the Soleri-like mega-section. Or was that delirious reaction simply tied to the majestic graphic, which was so persuasive that one's impulse for critical analysis was temporarily on hold?

We'll never know. But if the Library at Irvine is taken as a premier example of late Stirling, in which the formal premise is taken straight, with no chaser, then it's fair to question the premise itself. If, on the other hand, we acknowledge the invisible hand of the budgetmeister, the *sui generis* approach of the associated architects, the Irvine Company's totalising influence, and the drive-through mind-set of Southern California, it's a given that the scheme was doomed from the start. Even as what Vidler describes as a "machine in the garden"—a vision reinforced by the up-angle axonometrics which define that premise—the Library, shorn of any manifestation of industrial origins, is more readily interpreted as a hollow, featherweight icon. That impression is reinforced by the client's mandate to follow the Irvine campus design vocabulary, with materials and finishes limited to a specific palette of earth-tone Mediterranean colours, stucco, concrete, and terra-cotta-coloured roofing that echo that of the Big Box stores crowding the parking areas surrounding the campus.

above
James Stirling, Michael Wilford, and
Associates Michael Wilford and Partners
IBI Group
Science Library, University of California at Irvine,
California: view of the central courtyard, 1984.
© Richard Bryant, photographer
James Stirling/Michael Wilford fonds
Collection Centre Canadien d'Architecture/
Canadian Centre for Architecture, Montréal

opposite
James Stirling, Michael Wilford, and
Associates Michael Wilford and Partners
IBI Group
Science Library, University of California
at Irvine, California: exterior view, 1984.
© Richard Bryant, photographer
James Stirling/Michael Wilford fonds
Collection Centre Canadien d'Architecture/
Canadian Centre for Architecture, Montréal

Siemens, of course, was neither the first nor the last in Stirling's chorus line of drums, doughnuts, naughts and cylinders, which he seems to have seized upon as a penance for the geometric abandon that enlivened earlier works. The thread leading back to Stirling's German dalliances—the rotund tower of the Bayer proposition, for instance, with its obtuse cornices, or the sheared off eviscerated cylinders of the housing estate for Canary Wharf, share a visual girth which lends intellectual as well as physical mass to their presence as objects.

The drum became for Stirling what the golden section represented for many others. Here was a form which, in its perfection, could lend an aura of significance to nearly any configuration. It was also possible to pierce it, filet it and otherwise operate on it without compromising its essence, and this, for Stirling, was catnip.

Three decades on, nothing seems to have changed since the Library was first lodged into the ring of buildings at the core of the campus. The sea of parking lots melting imperceptibly into the surrounding shopping malls, the determined gait of students, the absence of "grit", and the hygienic road signs add to what one student admiringly terms a "microclean" campus. Access along the well-travelled central axis of the Library, arguably the most "contextural" gesture possible in an equivalent form, is disappointing. One end dangles impotently at the curb of a parking lot—the other gestures vaguely towards a drab campus building.

Opportunities to employ the syntax so evident in the Staatsgalerie, such as the sweeping energy of the circular ramp, abound, and yet the building is packed with might-have-beens. What the project description terms a "fancy stair" incised into a triangle, which might have bored its way to the sky, wanders into a corner before it peters out after a single storey. The paired entry doors are barely visible at six and nine o'clock, unmarked save for a massive column supporting the triangular mass of the stacks above, and the solemn entry portico offers only a blank stucco wall. All that monumental geometry finally comes to naught, which cannot have escaped Stirling and Wilford, and one can only speculate on everyone's disappointment that what could have been truly great was so eviscerated.

James Stirling, Michael Wilford, and
Associates Michael Wilford and Partners
IBI Group
Science Library, University of California at Irvine,
California: worm's eye view of the model, 1984.
© Chris Edgcombe, photographer
James Stirling/Michael Wilford fonds
Collection Centre Canadien d'Architecture/
Canadian Centre for Architecture, Montréal

A Transatlantic Journey

American Dreams?

Brian Carter

Six months 'practical experience' in an architect's office was required in fourth year at Liverpool School of Architecture and it was on the occasion of informing my mother—a very reserved Scots/Irish school teacher—I had the opportunity to do this in New York, that she uncharacteristically and without warning told me I should know then—I had been conceived in New York during a voyage on my father's ship, he was the archetypal Scottish chief engineer.[1]

James Stirling's preoccupation with America, highlighted by his enthusiastic reporting of creative activities in New York in the roaring 1920s, was reinforced as he grew up in Liverpool. The regular comings and goings of ships from the docks there provided conspicuous reminders of the New World and projected America into the life of the city, connected people and fostered ideas.

Architecture in Liverpool was influenced by those exchanges and it, in turn, shaped American modernism. John Wellborn Root travelled to Liverpool from Atlanta in 1864 before returning to the mid west where he became a founder of the Chicago School, and Louis Sullivan followed. At about the same time the architect Peter Ellis designed two notable office buildings in Liverpool—Oriel Chambers and 16 Cork Street—which were to inspire the development of architecture in New York, Chicago, Buffalo and St Louis. Later Charles Reilly, an influential figure in architectural education in England and head of the School of Architecture at the University of Liverpool from 1904 to 1933, travelled to America where he established other links that connected architects and students on both sides of the Atlantic.

"American Liverpool" continued to provide an influential backdrop for James Stirling after he enrolled as a student at the Liverpool School of Art. He drew enthusiastically, was subsequently admitted into the architecture programme at Liverpool University and, in 1948, selected for the exchange programme in America that had been initiated by Reilly. He left England with two other students on 28 July aboard the *Marine Jumper*, arrived in New York and went to work in the office of O'Connor and Kilham. It was an established practice designing substantial buildings for significant clients and, during that period, Stirling "came to spend time detailing the book-shelving for a new Gothic library in Princeton".[2]

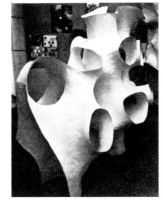

The architecture student's six month stay in New York City and his experience working in an office there was at a time when America, still recovering from the Great Depression and the impact of World War Two, was defined by scarcity and promise. Architectural practices were slowly re-establishing themselves with a workforce made up of an influential yet diminished older generation that had been trained in the Beaux Arts and an influx of younger people recently returned from active service who had studied architecture with the support of the GI Bill. And, when Stirling arrived in New York, the leading professional journals featured articles about large-scale residential developments planned to accommodate growing families alongside details of prefabricated building systems devised to speed up construction and reviews of modest built projects illustrated with predominantly black and white photographs. Together they projected stark images of a remarkably pragmatic architecture.

Stirling was not inspired by the places or the people that he discovered. New York City was, he suggested, "a ghastly monstrosity"[3] and Americans "deadly serious, frightfully hard-working, sober and moral to the point of perversion".[4] He also reacted against the strident commercialism that predominated and which was increasingly shaping attitudes to design—"of course I knew this before I came here—particularly as applied to American cars, but I had no idea that it was so completely all-embracing—everything, from the largest building to the smallest cigarette lighter".[5]

However Stirling also travelled and saw several significant buildings on the east coast including the PSFS tower in Philadelphia by Howe and Lescaze, individual houses designed by Walter Gropius, Marcel Breuer, Hugh Stubbins and Carl Koch and the recently completed Baker House at MIT by Alvar Aalto. However it was a weekend visit to a house on Long Island designed by Frank Lloyd Wright that was to prove particularly memorable. Likely the Rebhuhn residence, a house commissioned by a publisher and mentor of Wright's publisher at Horizon Press, it represented a reworking of Wright's Usonian ideas. Completed in 1937 the house was modest yet, Stirling noted, "really magnificent, the finest building I have ever been in".[6]

This early enthusiasm for the work of Wright was to persist. Between 1953 and 1956, Stirling noted 13 schemes designed by Wright in his 'Black Notebook' alongside ten by Mies van der Rohe and 20 by Le Corbusier.[7] Later he was to travel to the mid west to visit several of those projects including the offices and laboratory tower for Johnson Wax in Racine, Unity Temple and houses in Oak Park, Chicago. He was also to visit the Guggenheim Museum in New York on several occasions, studied other buildings including the Wright's Temple Beth Sholom and, in 1979, presented the Larkin Building as a typological model in his studies for the design of the Wissenschaftszentrum in Berlin.

Stirling also became increasingly enthusiastic about drawing and, in New York, he discovered "Zipatone". This proprietary adhesive film, overprinted with different patterns and densities of linework, was available in sheets and, when applied to tracing paper, introduced an extraordinary precision. Transforming the act of drawing into a mechanical task, designed to save time, increase production and introduce instant style "Zipatone", a uniquely American product, was only available in the United States at that time. However when the young architecture student left New York he packed a supply into his suitcase!

More than 40 years later, Stirling reconfirmed his enthusiasm for drawing. Describing an exhibition of his work at the Venice Biennale, he noted that drawing was a fundamental part of his design process and, in describing the 61 drawings on display, confirmed that "none... are computer graphics and all are hand drawn, mostly in black ink line on tracing paper, although the exhibition does include pencil drawings with colour crayon, "Zipatone" and coloured prints".[8] Perhaps as a result of what he had seen, done and discovered on his first visit to America, Stirling had changed his views about the place by the time that he arrived back in England. The young architecture student spoke positively about New York City, was particularly enthusiastic about the Chrysler Building, and apparently raved about America's "largeness of scale".[9]

After completing his studies at Liverpool University and graduating with a distinction in 1950. Stirling moved to London to work. He also became acquainted with other New World enthusiasts. The Independent Group, which met at the house of Reyner and Mary Banham and later at the Institute of Contemporary Art, included the artists Richard Hamilton, Eduardo Paolozzi, Magda Cordell and John McHale as well as the photographer Nigel Henderson, architects, musicians and graphic designers. Described by John McHale as a "small, cohesive, quarrelsome, abusive group" it also organised lectures and discussions which focused on design, the impact of technology, consumerism and popular culture that, in the aftermath of World War Two, frequently made reference to life in America.[10]

This is Tomorrow, an exhibition initiated by the Independent Group, opened at the Whitechapel Art Gallery in London on 9 August, 1956. An event that "might appear to be setting up a programme for the future" the exhibition consisted of 12 installations, each created by a team of artists, designers and architects. Stirling, one of more than ten architects in the group, participated.[11]

The exhibition was characterised by images from American popular culture. However Stirling's contribution, developed in collaboration with Michael Pine and Richard Matthews, literally stood apart. The installation, a free-standing, three-dimensional screen, was a stark contrast to much of the Pop imagery alongside.

top
Alvar Aalto
Baker House Dormitory, Massachusetts
Institute of Technology, Cambridge
Massachusetts, 1946. © Alan Berman

middle
Frank Lloyd Wright
Solomon R Guggenheim Museum,
New York, 1959. © Alan Berman

bottom
Rear view, Louis L Kahn, Yale University
Art Gallery and Design Center, 1953
Photograph ca 1954.
Courtesy of Yale University Art
Gallery Archives.

Constructed out of chicken wire and papier-mâché the white perforate wall recalled natural forms and the speculations of D'Arcy Wentworth Thompson that related to organic growth.

In 1957 *The Architectural Review* published a special issue entitled *The Functional Tradition* which was followed by a book of the same title. Together they made reference to organic growth, highlighted vernacular buildings in England and drew attention to the development of monumental forms. In America Sibyl Moholy-Nagy published *Native Genius in Anonymous Architecture* at about the same time—a book that also focused on vernacular buildings and suggested they formed an important link in the formulation of a particularly American modernism. These ideas influenced James Stirling.

At this time the young architect was, like many of his contemporaries, also actively seeking out commissions and entering competitions in the hope of establishing his own practice. James Stirling met James Gowan while they were working for Lyons, Israel and Ellis and, after he had been invited to design new housing at Ham Common, suggested that they work together. Stirling and Gowan opened their office in 1956 and, over a period of seven years, designed several residential projects, saw some buildings built and advanced their ideas through drawings. These drawings attracted attention, were widely published and prompted Stirling's return to America.

In 1958, Paul Rudolph invited James Stirling to serve as a visiting critic at Yale University. He followed in the footsteps of Ian McCallum, an editor of *The Architectural Review*, who suggested that "for the young European architect an American Grand Tour is becoming as important as the Italian was to the eighteenth-century English gentleman".[12] When Stirling arrived in New Haven he was also to be immersed in the culture of an outstanding university and join the faculty of one of the most notable architecture schools in the world.

America had changed significantly since Stirling's departure from New York in 1949. Scarcity was less obvious and much of the promise was being realised. Large-scale industrialisation had been infused by the commercialisation of ingenious technical inventions, production methods and capacity developed during World War Two. When combined with the increasing influence and power of corporate business, these factors created a confidence and prosperity that was in stark contrast to attitudes in Europe. Provoked by Russia's successful launch of Sputnik 1 in 1957, America was preparing to join a Space Race and also confronting the Cold War. These developments provided a remarkable stimulus for change.

That change was reflected in a new architecture. Gordon Bunshaft's proposal for Lever House, commissioned as Stirling sailed out of New York in 1949, was completed in the year that he returned. It introduced a scale and transparency that was strikingly different. The glass box modernism celebrated technological innovation and production while at the same time aggressively transforming practice and commercialising ideas imported from Europe—ideas that were made obvious on Park Avenue by a second headquarters tower, designed for Seagram by Mies van der Rohe, and the PanAm building by Walter Gropius. These conspicuous additions signalled sweeping changes in business, society, architecture, professional practice and the city. Park Avenue changed from a collection of stony Italianate palazzos to a cluster of glassy towers and public plazas while the rapid development of vast tracts of readily available land—fuelled by a burgeoning middle class, cheap petrol and access to networks of new freeways—created expansive suburbs around changing cities. Commercial air travel made the vast spaces of North America more accessible and its extreme climates were increasingly 'controlled'. All of this created landscapes and lifestyles that were radically different from the historic cities and social traditions in Europe.

Differentiating between attitudes towards architecture in Europe and North America, Stirling suggested that "to deliberately design a building which is imperfect is surely a romantic attitude, and it is certainly a European phenomenon". By contrast he was enthusiastic about American architecture which he suggested was "natural in its planning and choice and use of materials, and logical in its structural systems" and went on to reference a house designed by Paul Rudolph.[13]

Stirling's appointment as a visiting critic at Yale University placed him in extraordinary company. He was working alongside Rudolph, an internationally renowned architect and a remarkable draughtsman whose work Stirling admired, and sharing an office with Craig Ellwood—a former contractor and the cost estimator for the Eames House turned architect who was an assertive advocate for a Miesian architecture of steel and glass. Ellwood, who had advanced the use of those materials to create a remarkable lightness in the buildings that he had designed on the West Coast, had been appointed as a visiting critic at Yale at about the same time as Stirling and they became close friends. Referred to as "Mr Thick" and "Mr Thin", Stirling and Ellwood spent time together at Yale while Stirling travelled to California where he stayed with Craig and Gloria Ellwood and visited buildings that Ellwood had designed. Vincent Scully, a prolific scholar and notable art historian at Yale who had particular interests in architecture, became another of Stirling's faculty colleagues. In 1955 Scully had published *Shingle Style*—a book which drew attention to the significance of a uniquely American vernacular architecture and suggested that it informed the development of modernism in the New World.

During the time that Stirling was visiting critic in New Haven, he taught his studio on the top floor of the Yale Art Gallery. Designed by Louis Kahn this building, and that space in particular, was defined by a tetrahedral concrete ceiling orientated on a 45 degree axis which integrated structural and environmental servicing systems. Completed in 1953 it was already recognised as one of the most significant new buildings to be constructed in America since the end of World War Two. The Yale Art Gallery vividly represented Kahn's ideas of "hollow stones" and his concept of served and servant spaces. Stirling met Kahn in 1959, subsequently visited him in Philadelphia, saw the Richards Laboratories under construction and when they were completed. The building "is marvelous" he noted and the "best recent thing I have seen here—and also very English".

At about this time, Stirling also noted that "on both sides of the Atlantic the current dilemma of modern architecture seems to be that top architects are absorbed in becoming either stylists or structural exhibitionists" before going on to suggest that "in America, 'styling'" appears as the application of frills and grilles, the introduction of historical fragments, and the indiscriminate use of glass curtain walls. Structural exhibitionism appears as the over-articulation of columns and floors. Both are obsessed with the outer building skin and both are equally effective in masking the volumetric dimensions of the spaces behind the facade."[15]

Robert Venturi was also teaching at Yale at this time. Influenced by Scully's writings and Kahn's work, designing and building himself, and inspired by European traditions, he spent 1962 writing. "Complexity and Contradiction in Architecture: selections from a forthcoming book" was published in *Perspecta 09/10* in 1965 and the book was subsequently published by the Museum of Modern Art in the following year. Five years earlier *Perspecta 06, 1960*, had included an article by James Stirling entitled "'The Functional Tradition' and Expression"—a treatise that also argued for an inclusive view of architecture which embraced vernacular building and history in an effort to articulate an alternative to the International Style of "glass box" modernism that was increasingly pervasive.

In addition to being surrounded by notable scholars who were dedicated to the formulation of ideas related to the advancement of modernism Stirling met

James Frazer Stirling
Lecture notes.
James Stirling/Michael Wilford fonds
Collection Centre Canadien d'Architecture/
Canadian Centre for Architecture, Montréal © CCA
Bequest of the Stirling family

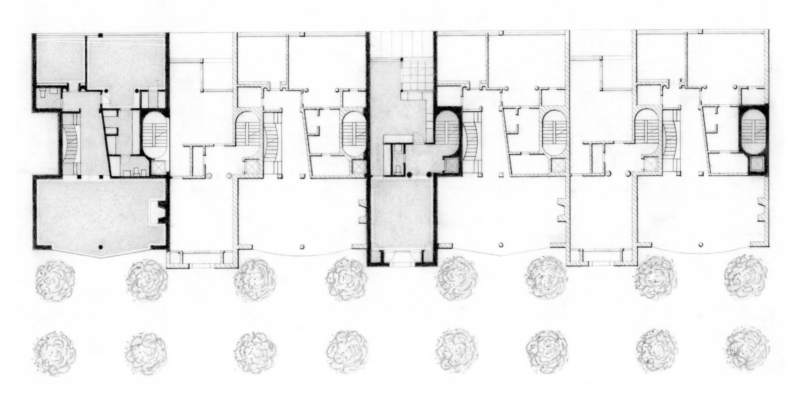

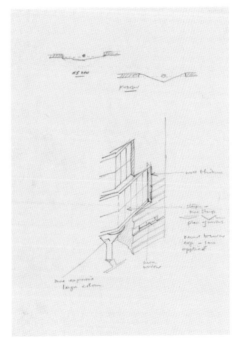

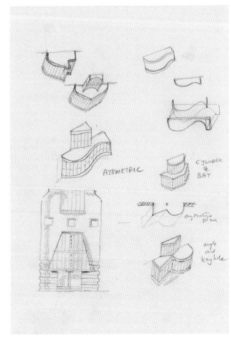

top

James Frazer Stirling

Eleven Townhouses Competition,

New York, New York: plan, 1978.

Collection Centre Canadien d'Architecture/

Canadian Centre for Architecture, Montréal © CCA

bottom left and right

James Frazer Stirling

Eleven Townhouses Competition,

New York, New York: sketches, 1978.

Collection Centre Canadien d'Architecture/

Canadian Centre for Architecture, Montréal © CCA

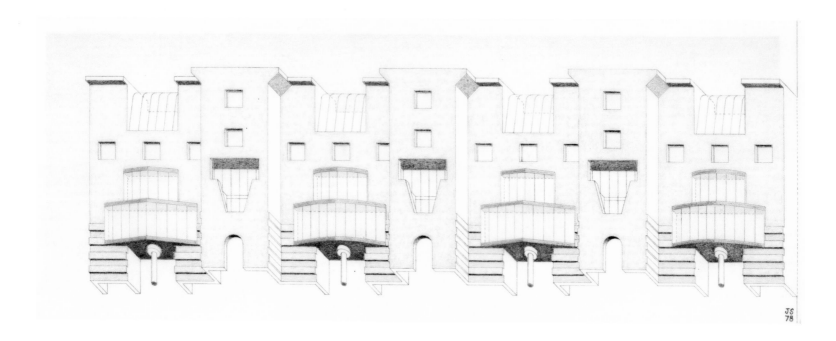

others who were designing new buildings. At this time when enrolment in higher education in America was growing rapidly Yale University was not only Stirling's newly adopted home-away-from-home but an historic campus that was being increasingly transformed by significant new buildings. Those buildings were being commissioned by enthusiastic clients who searched out a new generation of architects. They were architects who had been trained in the Beaux Arts, graduated in the Great Depression, survived World War Two and attracted to architecture at a time when modernism was defined almost exclusively by the work of Le Corbusier, Mies van der Rohe and Frank Lloyd Wright. At the same time prosperity and the need to build in America, together with the availability of new materials and sophisticated constructional techniques ensured that, once designed, buildings were constructed quickly and efficiently. Ingalls Hockey Rink at Yale, designed by Eero Saarinen, opened in 1958 and was followed by proposals for the new Morse and Stiles Colleges that were built alongside existing Collegiate gothic towers there in 1962. A year later the Beinecke Library, designed by Gordon Bunshaft, opened, the Kline Science Tower, designed by Philip Johnson, was under construction and new Schools of Forestry and Architecture designed by Paul Rudolph were completed.

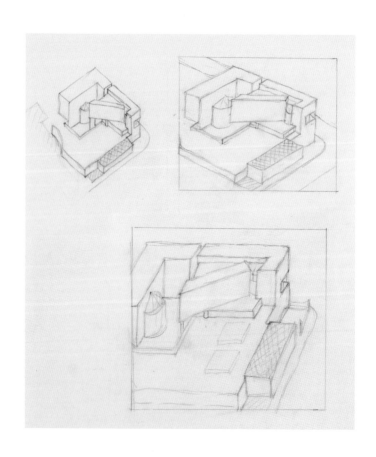

Seeing this work, discovering remarkable technologies and sensing the enthusiasm of clients who were actively searching out modern design, Stirling became increasingly enthusiastic about working in America. Yet back in England, he and James Gowan were designing what was to be their most significant project. The design for the new Engineering Building at Leicester University was developed during the time that Stirling was teaching at Yale and becoming more aware of new ideas and architecture in America. James Gowan presented their proposal to the client and subsequently received approval from Leicester, and it was at this time, in 1960, that Michael Wilford was hired as their first full-time paid assistant, eventually leading the team responsible for the construction documents. Stirling was travelling back and forth between New Haven and London, and perhaps as a consequence the design of the building in Leicester reflected his enthusiasm for the work of Wright and the research of Scully, conversations about lightness with Craig Ellwood, Paul Rudolph's drawings and time spent in the studio under the sculpted roof of Kahn's Yale Art Gallery? Stirling and Gowan produced a series of talismanic drawings of the project and, when the Engineering Building opened in 1963, it attracted international interest.

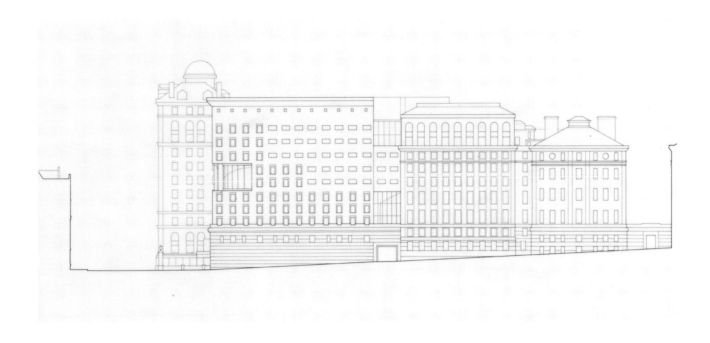

In 1965 Stirling received a letter from Charles Moore. A former teaching assistant for Louis Kahn at Princeton, Moore had gone on to establish a successful practice in California and teach on the West Coast. However, following his appointment as Dean of the School of Architecture at Yale University earlier in 1965, he had moved 3,000 miles. Consequently in his letter, Moore noted that he understood "all too well the problems of exchanging a known practice for an unknown one. I can find or even imagine no way of guaranteeing a practice here in advance." However, he went on to ask, "But I wonder whether the following arrangements wouldn't be the best procedure: would you come as a Visiting Professor (we could stick a fancy name on that) for say ten to 12 weeks each year (more if you like) for the next five years (or more or fewer if you would like) so that we and you could advertise the connection? If the period were not so long that it disturbed your existing practice but long enough so that it gave you the opportunity here to nail down the available jobs, then we would seem to have achieved some modest measure of simultaneous cake-eating and -having."[16]

In 1966 James Stirling was appointed Davenport Professor of Architecture at Yale University after Stirling and Gowan had dissolved their partnership. Consequently when Stirling arrived in New Haven in the autumn to take up his new appointment it not only marked recognition of his growing international reputation but the beginning of a new period in his professional career. Stirling took up his appointment at a time soon after the Yale School of Architecture had recently moved into a new building designed by Paul Rudolph.

As Moore had suggested, Yale University broadcast the news of Stirling's appointment and he taught there as the Davenport Professor until 1984. During that period Stirling became a figurehead for the new School of Architecture and Yale University and was in America regularly. This enabled him to continue teaching, travel extensively and to present his work widely: on occasion, when Stirling couldn't be at Yale Michael Wilford deputised for him.

Stirling was a frequent visitor to New York and, in 1968, was invited to prepare a proposal for a site on the city's waterfront. This commission, to develop a phased masterplan for the redevelopment of a site alongside Riverside Drive that was occupied at that time by a series of existing piers, was spurred by the interest of the Mayor of New York City. John Lindsay envisaged the site being transformed to create a new entrance to the city, and Stirling worked on the project with a group of colleagues anticipating that it might also lead to the design of specific new buildings in the context of the development plan that they proposed. Unfortunately, this work was to remain on paper and no commissions for new buildings followed.

Ten years later Stirling was invited to prepare a proposal for new housing to fill an entire block in New York City. Although a regular visitor to America he and Michael Wilford had also developed a significant practice in Europe during that time. It was a practice built on a series of design proposals and international competition submissions for new civic buildings. And, though relatively few of those proposals were built, it was a period defined by his winning design for the new Staatsgalerie in Stuttgart. These projects provided a basis for Stirling to advance his interest in the reconstruction of cities that had, in turn, been shaped by ideas prompted by his colleagues in America.

Conversations with Colin Rowe, Stirling's former teacher in Liverpool who had subsequently moved to America, focused on the potential offered by traditional buildings in the development of modern cities while Scully's suggestions that a modern architecture could embrace historical forms, the buildings designed by Kahn and writings of Venturi provided additional inspiration.

The scheme that Stirling developed for the new housing in New York City proposed the reconstruction of an entire block in the city with the creation of a five-storey building, made up of 11 new luxury townhouses. The scheme was designed to use existing structural beams over an underground parking garage and created a terrace of houses with frontages of 18 and 36 feet. It was a design proposal that also systematically examined and built on the planning, organisation and external forms of traditional housing in this part of the city. Taking clues from the surroundings the accompanying design report noted "the movement backwards and forwards of the street facade expresses the house within the terrace" and confirmed that "bay windows, studio glazing, balconies, etc., indicate the more important spaces within. This is similar to the surface projections—windows, entrances—on traditional New York townhouses which exist around the site and give the streets on the upper East Side their particular quality."[17] However albeit that this project was distinctly different from the earlier urban design study it was also to remain on paper.

In 1980, following a series of other commissions which had included requests to design new academic buildings at Rice and Harvard, Stirling and Wilford were invited to design a new building to expand the Chemistry Department at Columbia University. The building, to house academic offices, teaching spaces and laboratories, was to be located on a significant site on the corner of the campus bounded by Broadway and 120th Street.

Planned by McKim, Mead and White, the campus of Columbia University consisted of classical buildings that defined a series of axial routes and outdoor spaces. It was also a plan which sought to ensure that the campus would not become an enclave. Consequently Stirling and Wilford proposed a design for a nine-storey block of offices and academic spaces that fronted onto Broadway and defined the western boundary of the site. This building was to be connected to four levels of laboratories housed within an elevated wing that fronted the eastern side of the site. The plan also ensured that the corner of the campus at the junction of Broadway and 120th Street remained open and at the same time created an entrance to the Chemistry Department from the campus. It utilised the existing structure to develop "an air rights possibility" created by buildings that had been constructed on an adjacent site. The design combined these two distinctly different buildings. One, a formal response to the adjacent streets and existing buildings, linked to the other which was signalled on Broadway by a single conspicuous cutout and curving glass wall in the northern corner of the office building. The laboratory building was defined by a four-storey high external trussed structure that spanned over an existing gymnasium and was supported

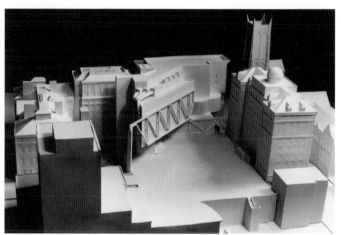

top and bottom
James Stirling, Michael Wilford, and
Associates, Wank Adams Slavin Associates
Chandler North building, Department of
Chemistry, Columbia University, New York,
New York: model views, 1978–1983.
© John Donat, photographer
James Stirling/Michael Wilford fonds
Collection Centre Canadien d'Architecture/
Canadian Centre for Architecture, Montréal

opposite
James Stirling, Michael Wilford, and
Associates, Wank Adams Slavin Associates
Chandler North building, Department of
Chemistry, Columbia University, New York,
New York: elevation, October 1981.
James Stirling/Michael Wilford fonds
Collection Centre Canadien d'Architecture/
Canadian Centre for Architecture, Montréal

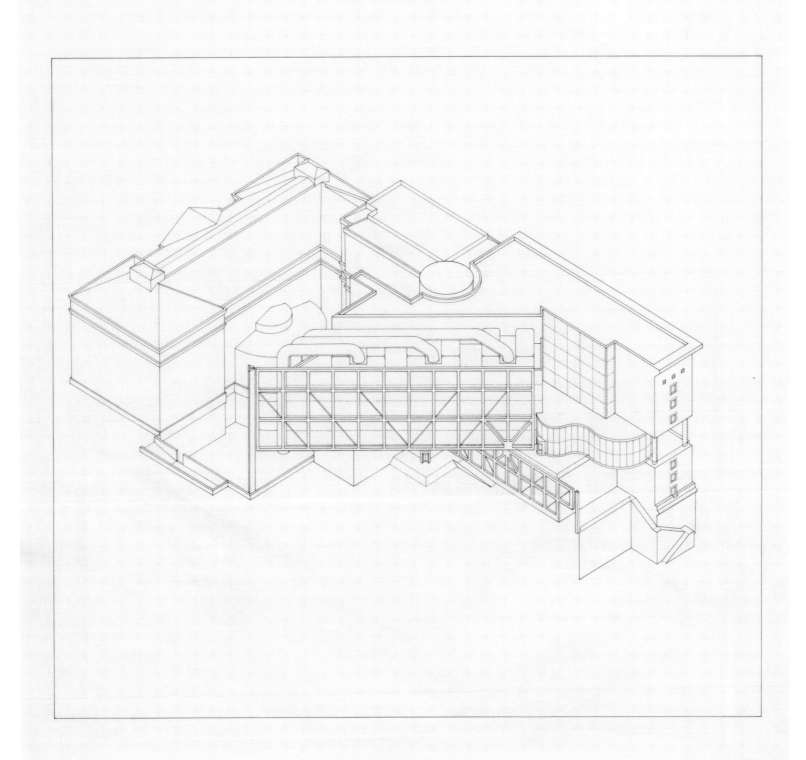

COLUMBIA UNIVERSITY
CHANDLER NORTH PROJECT
AERIAL VIEW FROM 120 TH STREET

JAMES STIRLING MICHAEL WILFORD & ASSOCIATES / WANK ADAMS SLAVIN ASSOCIATES
OCTOBER 1981
1/32"=1'

at one end by a free-standing ten-storey high column. A second two-storey high trussed structure provided a second support. The design integrated contextual references reflected in the massing, rustication and a conspicuously new cornice on the proposed building fronting Broadway while the assertive structural expressionism of the laboratories was to face into the campus. Prepared 20 years after Stirling's scathing commentary on the "styling" of new architecture in America, the design of this project adopted "structural expressionism" and the addition of "historic fragments" with enthusiasm!

The proposal was presented to Columbia University in 1980 but, following changes in the administration, the project was shelved. A perspective of the proposed scheme, viewed from the campus, prepared by the office, showed the building crumbling spectacularly. The drawing was titled "In Memoriam".

While the moment of conception in New York Harbour in the roaring 1920s may be contested, the subsequent impact of America on the life and work of James Stirling is beyond question. He spent a sustained period of time living and working in the United States and that, in turn, coincided with significant societal and political changes which prompted a redefinition of modern architecture. In addition, over a period of almost 40 years, he also became a friend and colleague of outstanding scholars and notable practitioners who were developing ideas and influencing the design of buildings worldwide.

Stirling's enthusiasm for the work of Wright persisted and its influence can be readily detected in buildings that he designed in Leicester, Berlin and elsewhere. And he was undeniably inspired by Louis Kahn and the buildings that he designed. The two architects met on numerous occasions and while Kahn referenced Stirling's design for the History Library at Cambridge when he was developing his own proposal for the Graduate Theological Union Library in California[18] so, when deconstructivist postmodernism was at its height, Stirling was to comment that "It is appalling what students talk about in American architecture schools today—Derrida, indeed! Why doesn't anyone study Kahn?"[19]

America had a profound effect on James Stirling. The work of Wright, with its connections back to Sullivan, Root, Liverpool and the Chicago School, was significant as were the words, ideas and work of Moholy-Nagy, Scully, Venturi and Moore. Enthusiastic clients dedicated to the creation of a new modernism and contractors keen to use new materials and techniques to realise those ideas made a lasting impression. "Zipatone", the remarkable drawings prompted by the Beaux Arts in America and those made by Wright and Rudolph were tantalising while buildings designed by Kahn were inspirational. At the same time the constructed lightness of Bunshaft and Ellwood, together with the discussions of ideas related to the historic city and typologies in New Haven and elsewhere, influenced Stirling significantly as he designed buildings on both sides of the Atlantic.

However perhaps it is the resonance between James Stirling and Louis Kahn which is most potent? Both were preoccupied with time, monumentality and the nature of institutions at a time when the instigation of instant change was uppermost and each designed buildings that presented a stubborn resistance to the oncoming tides of commercialised international modernism that were increasingly powerful. Yet, at a time when those tides continue to gather strength, it is all the more surprising that Stirling and Kahn have only a shadowy presence in the development of modern architecture today.

Richard Portchmouth, draughtsman
James Stirling, Michael Wilford, and Associates
Wank Adams Slavin Associates
Chandler North building, Department of Chemistry,
Columbia University, New York, New York:
perspective of building in decay, 1978–1983.
James Stirling/Michael Wilford fonds
Collection Centre Canadien d'Architecture/
Canadian Centre for Architecture, Montréal © CCA

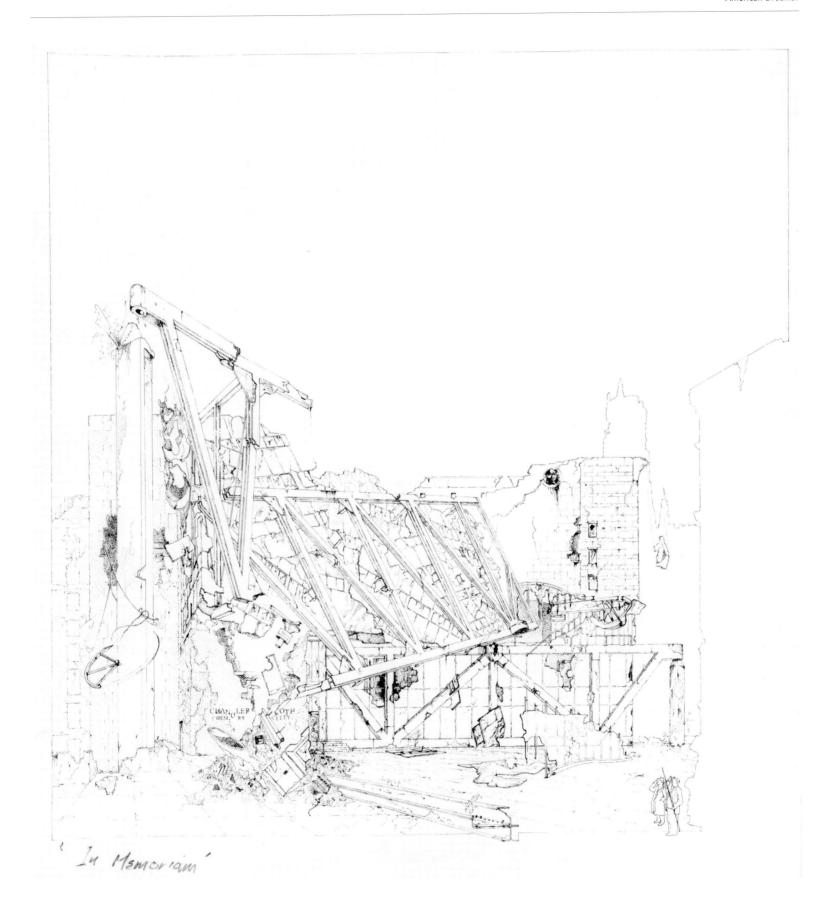

'In Memoriam'

Jim Stirling
Synchrony and Diachrony
Emmanuel Petit

The most provocative double aspect of Jim Stirling's later architecture is that, on the one hand, he was interested in the metaphysics of the building-as-object, while, on the other, his contribution was directed at the urban texture his architecture participated in. While the former interest focuses on a matter that is internal to the object, the latter deals with a more historical, diachronic, and episodic notion of time in architecture. His critics and acolytes alike divided into two camps over this divide of sensibility, and labelled him either a "late-modern" or "postmodern" architect. Choosing sides in this discussion conventionally meant that one had to pick either the Leicester, Oxford and Cambridge buildings as the epitomes of Stirling's legacy, or else, one would side with his more narrative German, French, and American projects—from the Düsseldorf, Cologne, and Stuttgart museums to the Wissenschaftszentrum in Berlin, the Grande Bibliothèque de France in Paris, and finally, the Sackler Museum and the Performing Arts Center at the Harvard and Cornell University campuses, respectively.

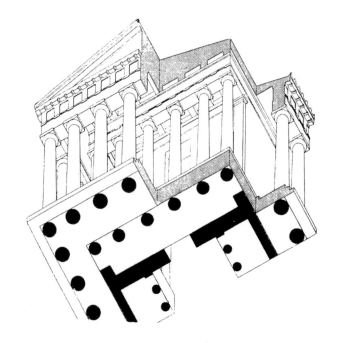

Iconic precedents for both these methods can be found in both Auguste Choisy with his abstract analyses of ancient architecture in the second half of the nineteenth century, and in Giambattista Nolli's transcription of the texture of Rome in the mid-eighteenth century. Choisy had codified the worm's eye axonometric as carrying the code of Hellenic ideality in architecture when he used it to convey his analyses of the Athenian Acropolis, which showed the strong link between the compositional grammar of the plan and the visual effect of the volumes and elevations in space.[1] Certainly, Choisy also analysed the promenades that lead from one such space to the next (famously when he mapped out the Acropolis), but that path too was described in terms of the intrinsic order of the architectural objects along the promenade. Le Corbusier famously referenced Choisy in *Vers une architecture*, and explained in the caption of Choisy's diagram that "the seeming disorder of the plan [of the Acropolis], will fool only the profane". On the other hand, the Nolli map of Rome does not stress ideality, but brings out the factuality of the public urban spaces, and illustrates that they are, in fact, already part of an urban network of relationships in existence. The difference can be expressed in very simple terms: Choisy is looking up into the metaphysical realm of the object (the intrinsic), while Nolli is looking down onto the physical spaces of the actual city.

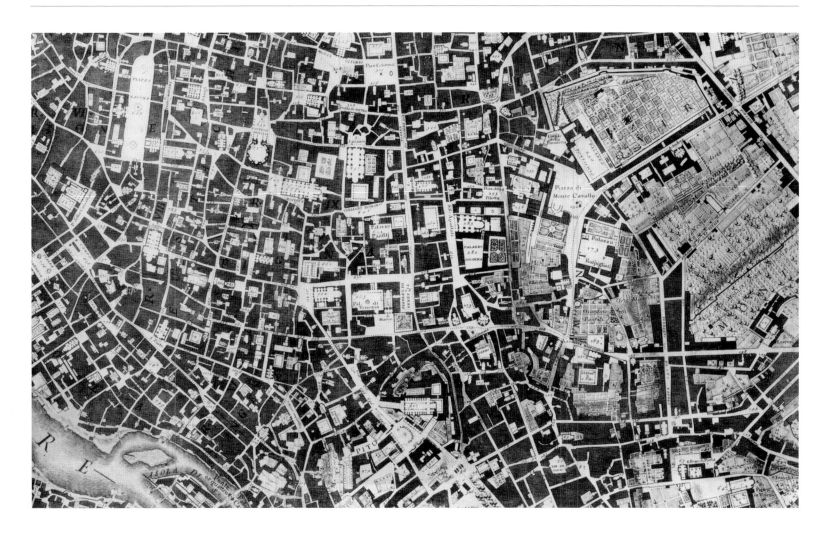

Stirling's architecture hinges on such a double consciousness in architecture: he was no doubt interested in the Corbusian ideality of Choisy—Choisy as an example of the "masterly, correct and magnificent play of masses brought together in light". As such Stirling liked to use the worm's eye view, which he claimed makes architecture "fly off into space".[2] Yet, at the same time, the down-to-earth Stirling, the son of an engineer, appropriates other aspects from Choisy: the interest in the materiality of the brick, the tectonic assemblage of physical elements, the joints between them, and the analytical mindset that discerns the elemental and finite ingredients of an architectural "thing"—as opposed to the infinite and Absolute of an architectural "idea". Both types of documents (the ones that look up, literally and metaphorically, and those that look down) coexist in Stirling, not least in Stirling and Wilford's Düsseldorf museum competition—one of the practice's pivotal and defining projects. In them, the framed, blue sky plays a central role as the signifier of the infinite and of the ideal, the detached, and the Absolute. This notion is further amplified by the circular form of the frame, which geometrically symbolises the idea of the "centre" and the "autonomous". A second axonometric view of the Düsseldorf project looks down and makes the context and reality of the city reappear. (the historic houses (some in ruin)... the materiality of the pavement, trees, sidewalks, and even the tables and chairs of the museum cafe...). In this context, Stirling's friend, the scholar and theorist Colin Rowe was instrumental in introducing Stirling to Nolli, and the idea of the weaving of inside and outside spaces into the continuum of the public surfaces of the city. While the view up distills a sort of architectural DNA, the view down shows the building in its entirety and in its actual appearance as a phenomenon of fact.

Russian literary theorist and formalist Mikhail Bakhtin had coined an expression which I want to invoke as a useful way to conceptualise Stirling's paradoxical interest in these two aspects of architecture that might seem mutually exclusive: Bakhtin coined the expression "synchronous diachrony" to designate those linguistic structures that hinge on a certain density and multiplicity of contradictory meanings: when a conglomeration of languages (both high and low) "mean" in heterogeneous ways simultaneously and condense all the different meanings that can normally only succeed one another in time in one, "thick", present moment, the "spatialised time" (or "vertical time") of Bakthin's mode of reading appears.[3] I suggest that Bakthin's model of "synchronous diachrony" is the most productive way to understand the ideas that Stirling conveyed in his architecture and teaching. The simultaneous focus on the architectural object and the city allowed him to animate the uninspiring lethargy of late-modernism with a sense of formal and conceptual ambiguity while also reinstating a cultural interest in architectural history.

Stirling's architectural practice was never disconnected from his teaching; his own projects are for the most part well known, but I propose that a brief discussion of some of the much less known projects of his students will help to conceptualise Stirling's architectural themes; they will furthermore help interpret his own projects in a new light. At Yale University, Stirling taught as a visitor from 1959 to 1964, and as the inaugural Charlotte Shepherd Davenport Visiting Professor of Architectural Design from 1965 to 1983—a professorship he shared in alternate semesters with Robert Venturi for five consecutive years. The teaching allowed Stirling to experiment with his ideas and develop his particular brand of a bifurcated, European-American aesthetic sensibility. There is no doubt that Socratic self-reflection was not the dominant mode of teaching in Stirling's studios, but that a very particular *modus operandi* was conveyed: this procedure was to deal with the analysis of precedents and context and it transmitted an ideology about how the architecture of the present defines itself as the tectonic bond between heterogeneous elements. In his studios Stirling was not interested in a zeitgeist-y synthetic form (or a formal veneer that smoothed over differences), but on the contrary, all projects should make architecture look very spatial and tectonic. Stirling believed in architecture as the witty art of joining and the combination of architectural ingredients taken from past and present moments in time.

Paul Rosenblatt took Stirling's studio at Yale in the fall of 1983, when Stirling assigned the Performing Arts Center at Cornell as the studio project. One of Rosenblatt's partial axonometric drawings is remarkable for the reason that, like Stirling's drawings for the Düsseldorf museum, it creates the aporetic fusion of both the temporalities of the architectural object and the city spaces in one and the same drawing. Indeed, Rosenblatt's representation is a "butterfly" or "open-book" axonometric: it allows for the viewer to look at the same space of his building twice: both up into the round lantern-like skylight, and also down, into the more meandering entrance hall with its connections to adjacent spaces. The drawing and the proposed architecture unite the features of both Choisy and Nolli—of the absolute time of the Platonic form of the round lantern, closed on itself, and looking up... with the episodic time of the labyrinthian entrance hall that is meant to be passed through, which is inserted in the network of public spaces in the urban context. What is most remarkable, however, is that Rosenblatt created a spatial "hinge" which graphically connects the two parts of the axon drawings. Not only does the drawing demonstrate a truth about Stirling's architecture, but it makes clear that the context of Yale was very important in generating this particular solution. Because Josef Albers, who taught at Yale from 1950 to 1958, provided the structural and aesthetic mechanism to make this double drawing work. Indeed, Albers created his study series *Structural*

James Stirling and Partner
Nordrhein-Westfalen Museum, Dusseldorf,
Germany: axonometric, 1975.
James Stirling/Michael Wilford fonds
Collection Centre Canadien d'Architecture/
Canadian Centre for Architecture, Montréal © CCA

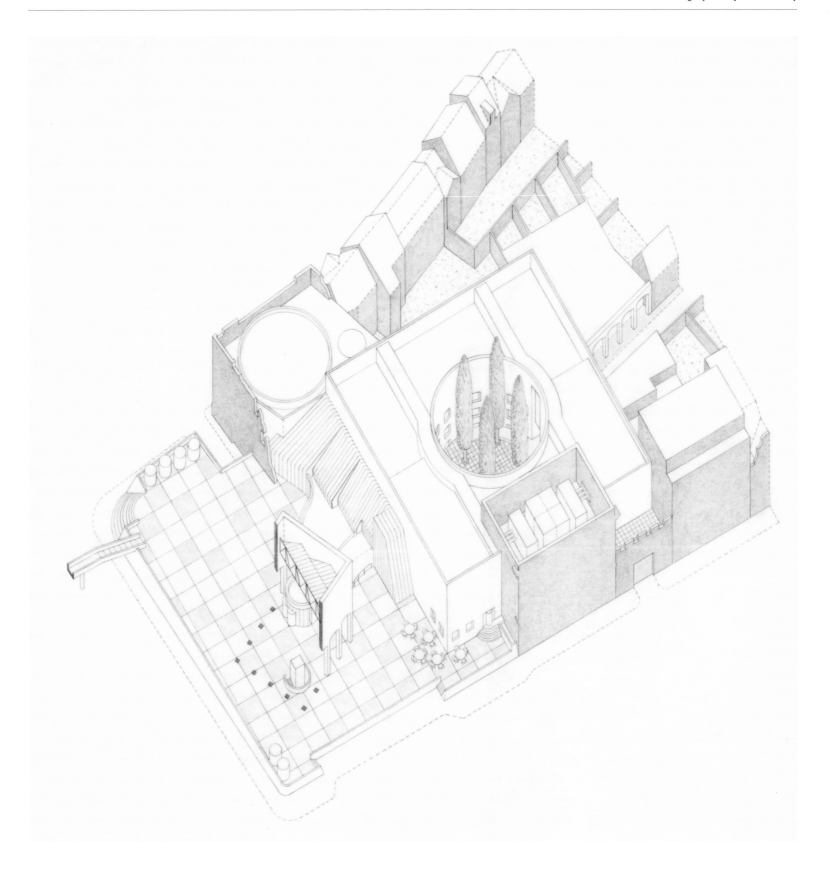

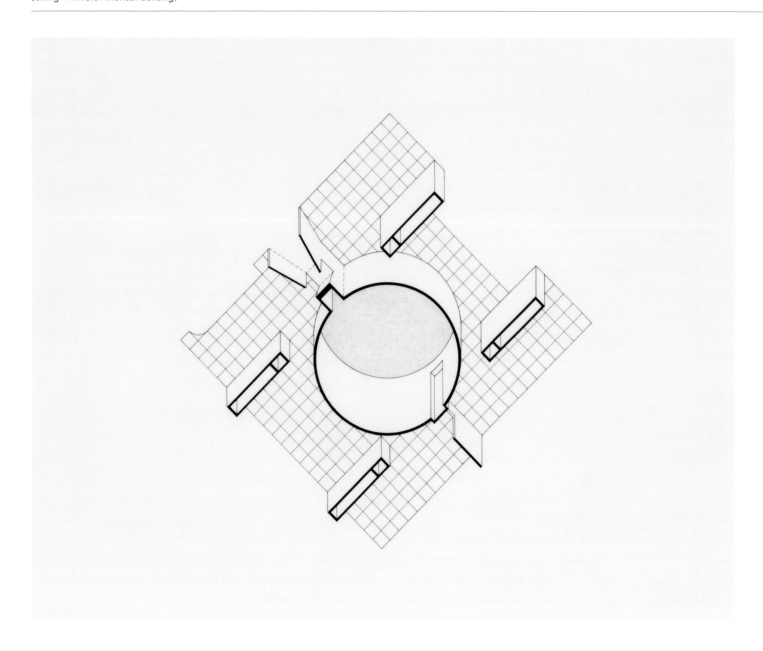

above

James Stirling and Partner
Nordrhein-Westfalen Museum, Dusseldorf,
Germany: worm's eye axonometric of
courtyard and gallery ceilings, 1972–1976.
James Stirling/Michael Wilford fonds
Collection Centre Canadien d'Architecture/
Canadian Centre for Architecture, Montréal © CCA

opposite

Paul Rosenblatt, Performing Arts Centre,
Cornell University: "butterfly" or "open-
book" partial axonometric drawing
James Stirling Studio, Yale University,
1983. Courtesy of Yale Manuscripts
and Archives, Yale University

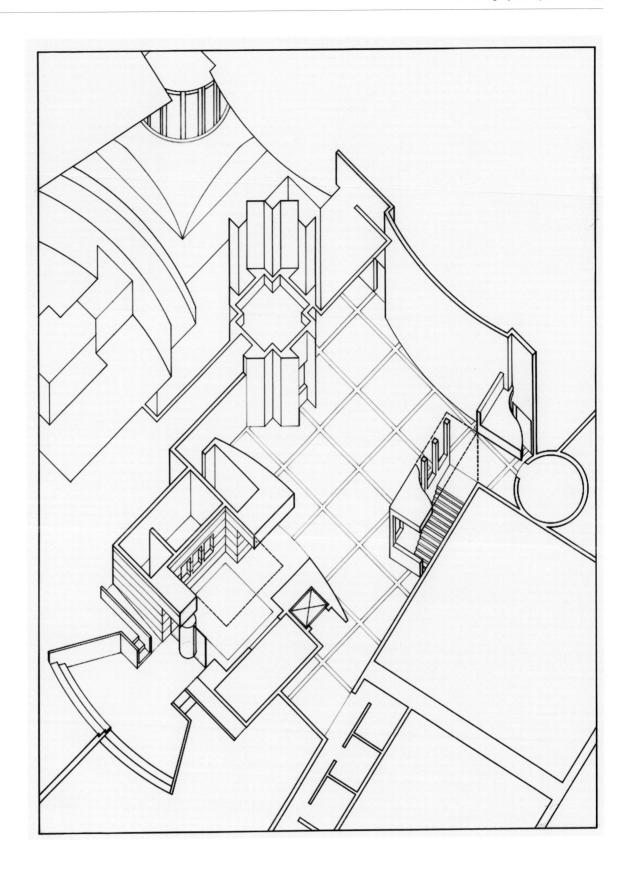

Constellations while at Yale. One can speculate that Stirling had himself been influenced by Albers' formal experimentations in the 1950s, given that the pinwheel dynamic and the alternating up and down movement in space had been part of Stirling's interest ever since his and James Gowan's Assembly Hall project in Camberwell, in London, 1958 to 1961. Rosenblatt was explicitly influenced by Albers and also by the American graphic designer and Cooper Union Professor Rudolph de Harak (who was at the time a Visiting Professor at Yale), and for whom Rosenblatt worked during some of his summers. Also, MC Escher's play with the graphic representation of spatiality should not go unmentioned. When two-dimensional drawings turn spatial and when spatial objects are transcribed into flat representations, certain "impossible" translations can happen: the translations between the world of three-dimensional things 'out there', and the world of ideas, conceptualised in the 2-D surface of a drawing. The potential for a creative misreading when the 2-D and the 3-D fuse is part of the intellectual potential of artistic activity... and had an influence on Stirling too: remember that in his essay "Real and English", Peter Eisenman had argued precisely that at Leicester, Stirling himself played with the intrinsic flatness of glass sheets when he paradoxically rendered them spatial, sculptural, and massive.

Stirling assigned the competition project of the Stuttgart Staatsgalerie in his Yale studio in 1978. For his student project, Richard Clarke created a hybrid drawing that combined the effect of the axonometric (built around an infinite vantage point) with the technique of perspective (built around specific viewpoints in real space). In conceptual analogy with Rosenblatt's later drawing, Clarke wanted to capture by his own account "both the analytical and the experiential aspects of the architecture as they coexist". The drawing thus gives the impression that it is some form of worm's eye view reminiscent of Choisy, yet in a strange spatial inversion, it looks down into the space—the project is built "into the earth", as Clarke insisted: every column is constructed around a different vanishing point sliding along the central axis, which, in fact, represents the movement axis of the museum visitor. In other words, the perspective of the drawing shifts with the anticipated movement of the visitor to the museum; thus, while the movement of a person unfolds in time as a sequence of diachronic events, Clarke's drawing absorbs that movement in the simultaneity of this idealised representation. Despite the overall symmetry of the space, the promenade it sets in motion is fundamentally asymmetrical and episodic. The point here is that this space, like so many instances of Stirling's own architecture, creates the incongruent simultaneity of heterogeneous elements and experiences. For Stirling, these types of conceptual-perceptual paradoxes were revitalising the vocabulary of modern architecture.

Had not Erwin Panofsky proposed, in his 1927 text "Perspective as Symbolic Form", that "the structure of an infinite, unchanging, and homogeneous space—in short, a purely mathematical space—is unlike the structure of psychophysiological space: "Perception does not know the concept of infinity?!"[4] Both Rosenblatt and Clarke's drawings challenge this notion and suggest, with Stirling, that architecture has the capacity to produce the kind of spatial paradox that enmeshes abstract ideas about space with a very real and physiological apprehension of space. This unlikely (and "impure") *mélange* of incongruous arguments makes it so difficult to theorise Stirling; this is the reason that in the later work, critical attention was always addressed at his use of historical quotation—an aspect which was considered a central phenomenon of his "postmodernism". But in fact, the real pivot of his postmodern mind lies precisely in the ability to carry out the alchemical fusion of abstract and physiological space concepts.

In the fall of 1979, Stirling assigned the extension of Harvard University's Fogg Museum (The Sackler Museum) in studio—this was one of the more contested projects he had realised because of its unusual facade with corpulent columns,

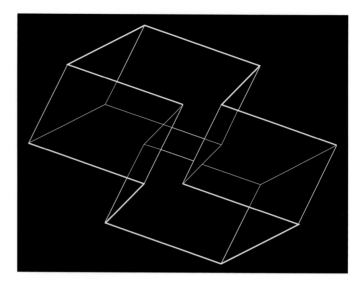

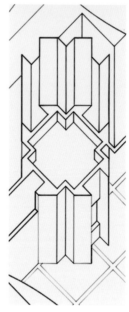

top

Josef Albers, *Structural Constellation*, 1954: incised vinyl. © 2014 Museo Thyssen-Bornemiza/Scale, Florence

bottom

Paul Rosenblatt, Performing Arts Centre, Cornell University: detail, "butterfly" or "open-book" partial axonometric drawing. James Stirling Studio, Yale University, 1983 Courtesy of Yale Manuscripts and Archives, Yale University

Richard Clarke, Stuttgart Staatsgalerie:
hybrid axonometric and perspective drawing.
James Stirling Studio, Yale University, 1978
Courtesy of Yale Manuscripts and Archives,
Yale University

truncated pyramid entry, rusticated frame, and use of colour as well as for its internal organisation with a monumental stair leading up through the middle of a quite narrow building. Alex Gorlin's studio project was characterised by a linear sequence of skylights in the form of three Platonic shapes (the circle, the square, and the diamond), strung together by the envelope of the building. The geometric volumes, which are visible from the street view extrude down through the building to organise the section and plan of the museum. One of the early sketches makes the provenance of the volumes clear: Gorlin puts them in front of a stage-set-like surface—very reminiscent of the parti of Le Corbusier's Salvation Army building in Paris. Anthony Vidler has emphasised the relevance of the Salvation Army parti to Stirling's buildings, claiming not least that the voided drum in the centre of the Staatsgalerie was ultimately taken from Le Corbusier. Just like in Le Corbusier, Gorlin's shapes appear as plastic volumes playing off a flat plane, and those spatial forms are meant to be passed through. The representation is an isometric and is disconnected from the particular contour of the urban site (and makes that geometric discrepancy quite evident. By using an isometric view, the sketch addresses the realm of ideality that is not yet adapted to meet the contingent geometries of the city; but then something happens in Gorlin's design which is not Corbusian at all, but very much in line with what Stirling would do: the simple volumes get wrapped in an envelope which aligns itself with the contour of the street; this facade does now not only mediate between the ideality of the Platonic volumes and the reality of the city, but its surface gets filled with the dense and multifarious texture of an architectural rhetoric—the rhetoric of urban

109

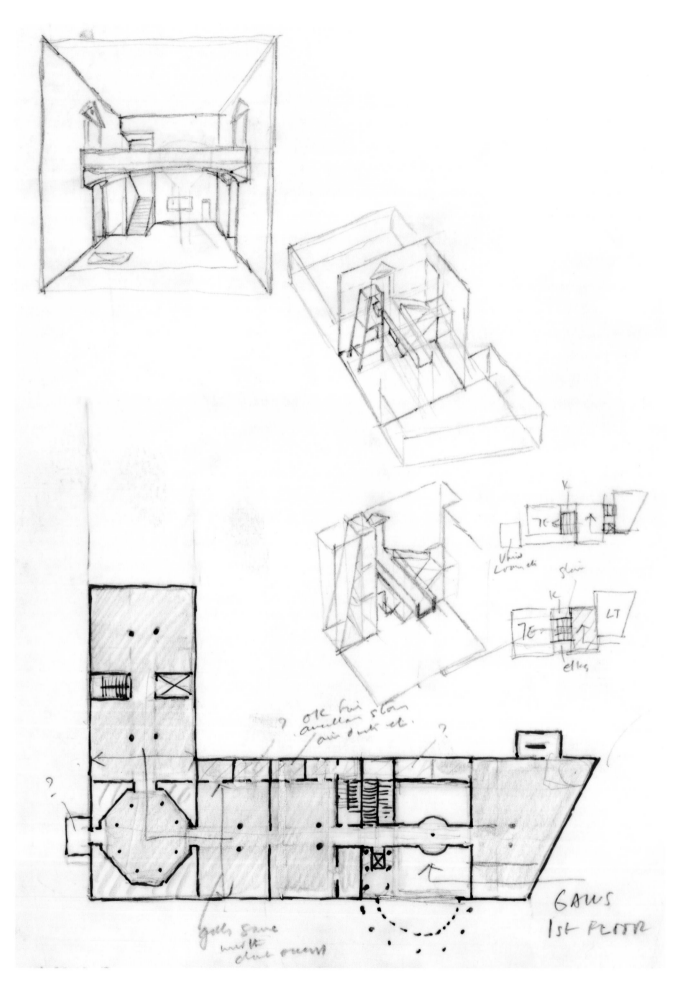

GAUS
1st FLOOR

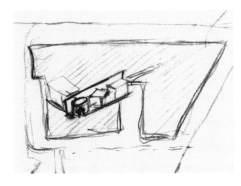

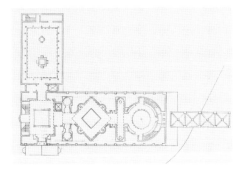

multiplicity (here extracted from Venetian-Byzantian architectural iconography: possibly the bridge between the Sackler and the Fogg evoked a connection to the Rialto in Venice, and hence some of the ogival and horseshoe arches of the Rialto's surrounding buildings are invoked). Where the site ends (because a street cuts it off), Gorlin establishes continuity by other means—by rounding off the building corner which can now act as a formal hinge to connect to the next urban artefact.

Stirling relied on such round corner hinges too, perhaps most graphically in his Meinekestrasse Hotel project in Berlin in 1976. Conceptually, this project depends on the pragmatic linkage of individual and recognisable architectural objects such as Tatlin's Comintern Monument, a pyramid, and other architectural objects that are normally free-standing. After lining up this catalogue of autonomous and independent objects extracted from different parts of history (with their internal object-temporalities), Stirling then introduces a continuous front which strings the history of architecture together as a street (one recognises the facades of Le Corbusier's villa Stein, Borromini's San Carlo, and other paradigmatic moments of architectural history... not least the Parthenon to turn the corner). The plurality of precedents adds up to a facade which is not as consistent, formally speaking, as the plans, but which proposes the idea of urban heterogeneity in a more anecdotal way... suggesting the adjacency of history with found objects of the historic town (or perhaps one should say *objets a réaction poétique* in reference to Le Corbusier's occasional play with the fragments of the historic city?) : architecture produces the simultaneity of diachronic ideas (i.e. independent architectural events that are conceived in subsequent moments of history), now chained together in the synchronous time of the urban street.

When the concept of infinity and the fact of spatial boundary are brought into dialogue with one another, "form" appears in a fragmented state: it claims its autonomy and, at the same time, indicates its finitude, its limit, its contingencies, as well as its willingness to act as a hinge in relation to "other" forms... based on "other" ideas. This double spatiality reflects the infinite dialectics of the philosophical tradition Romanticism had described as the source of heightened creativity: "While art is bounded on every side", German Romantic Friedrich Schlegel declared, "nature, on the contrary, is everywhere vast, illimitable, and inexhaustible." Only an ironic or oblique approach to this double spatiality can solve such an *aporia*. Conceptually, architecture's past always played a major role for Stirling as a resource for, and catalogue of, ideas which he recombined in ever fresh spatial assemblages. His earlier projects largely depend on abstract and unusual arrangements and combinations of typological fragments; with his later projects, and in fact in his buildings in the United States, he adds iconographic specificity to his combinatory vocabulary. To some, the increased iconographic recognisability undermines modern architecture's "advancement" towards abstract, elemental, and universal space. Yet despite his ability to expand the typological pluralism of architecture, Stirling also decidedly aimed to make architecture accessible outside the boundaries of the architectural cognoscenti. Thus, some of the metaphors and the humour he uses were addressed to the disciplinary elite in architecture, while sometimes his oblique approach expressed itself as a mere wink to the popular audience.

Solidified Space: The Use of the Void in Stirling and Wilford's American Work

Amanda Reeser Lawrence

So many accounts of James Stirling's architecture wrestle his varied oeuvre into a dialectical opposition as a means to account for the inherent complexity and the lack of an overarching style. Alan Colquhoun's incisive pairing of the tendency for "fragmentation/explosion" on the one hand and "unification/implosion" on the other is perhaps most emblematic.[1] Rafael Moneo identified a shift in Stirling's work from the section-centric projects of the 1960s (Leicester, Cambridge, Oxford) to the plan-centric projects of the later decades (Düsseldorf, Stuttgart, Wissenschaftszentrum).[2] And underlying nearly all Stirling commentary is the assumption of a modern/postmodern divide, with the "turn" from his earlier "heroic" work of the 1950s and 1960s to the—"neoclassical"—projects occurring sometime in the mid- to late-1970s. Even Stirling (who refused the term postmodernism outright, as well as in reference to his own work) resorted to binaries when describing his projects, noting the "oscillation" between the "abstract" and the "representational" as the underlying tension in his architecture.[3]

To these dialectical pairings of fragmented/unified, plan/section, and modern/postmodern we could add one more: British/not British. Nearly all of Stirling's early work was designed for or built in Britain (notably at the Universities of Oxford, Cambridge, Leicester and St Andrews) while an overwhelming majority of his later projects were international. After the technical and political failures of the Florey Building at Oxford—commissioned in 1965 though not completed until 1971—he was not given a single project in the UK until the Clore Gallery in 1980. At the same time, his international star power skyrocketed, particularly in Germany with the widely published competition entries for Düsseldorf and Cologne in 1975, and rising to a fever pitch with the media frenzy surrounding the design of the Staatsgalerie at Stuttgart, commissioned in 1977 and completed in 1984.

This architectural extradition from England in the 1970s was particularly poignant given that Stirling's Britishness was such a significant and driving force in his early work. For his thesis project at Liverpool in 1950 he had photographed the forthright, aggressive forms of the local docks.[4] During the 1950s he published articles comparing his own designs to British oast houses and Scottish Medieval fortifications.[5] He listed as among his favourite books in architecture school Saxl and Wittkower's monumental *British Art and the Mediterranean*, and

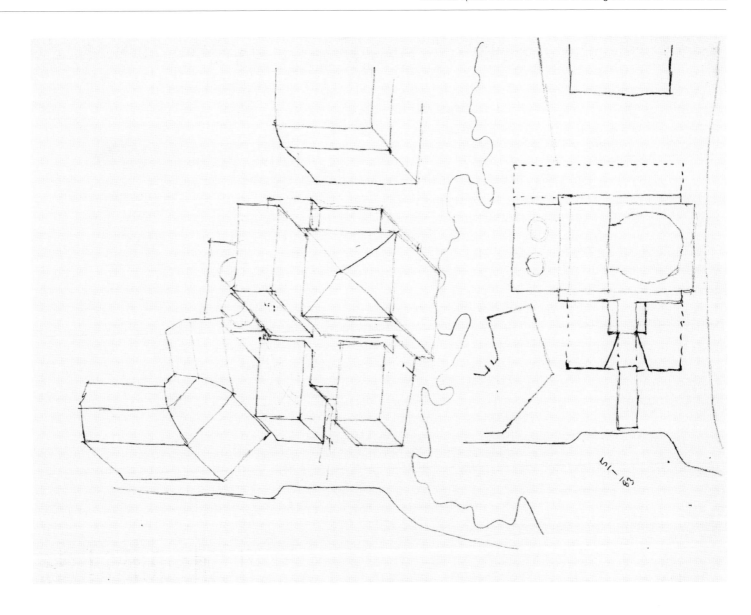

AE Richardson's *Monumental Classic Architecture in Britain and Ireland*, both of which chart how Britain imported and made its own various architectural styles from abroad.[6] He wrote with outrage that "since the crystallisation of the modern movement around 1920—Britain has not produced one single masterpiece and it must be practically the only European country which has not produced a 'great man'".[7] Moreover, he lamented Britain's seeming backwardness as compared to technology-driven America, which continued "inventing techniques and developing the appropriate expression of the modern attitude".[8]

Like Le Corbusier before him, Stirling's feelings toward America were a complicated mix of enthusiasm and antipathy. Stirling had spent a year in America while a student at Liverpool in 1949, largely in New York but also travelling to see projects by Frank Lloyd Wright, Mies van der Rohe, Louis Kahn, and others. Arguably, it was in America that he developed a more "modernised and globalised perspective", as Murray Fraser and Joe Kerr have argued was the impact of America more generally on Britain during the post-war period.[9] By the time he received his first American commission, 30 years later and in partnership with Michael Wilford, his status as an architectural expat was complete. Even the northern Englishman seemed to have forsaken his earlier British loyalties and adopted a more international identity. In 1986, when interviewed about the facade of the newly completed Sackler Building at Harvard Stirling replied, "Perhaps I was trying to make a face which was, shall I say, not British."[10]

Yet the shift to American soil was not, by most accounts, a success. Stirling and Wilford's four completed American Projects—the Architecture School at Rice, 1979–1981, the Arthur M Sackler Museum at Harvard, 1979–1984, the Cornell Center for the Performing Arts, 1983–1988 and the Science Library at University of California, Irvine, 1988–1994—are dismissed as the nadir of his postmodern period (after which our hero was allowed to rise again (in the Venice Biennale bookshop or Braun), if only briefly, before his untimely demise). In Stirling's obituary in the *New York Times* Paul Goldberger, described him as an "international" architect whose buildings "dazzle", but added the caveat: "His American buildings, at least those that got built, were generally not his best."[11]

Against this desire to separate the American work from Stirling's earlier "best" work, while also challenging and expanding the dialectical pairings of modern/postmodern, British/not British, or for that matter any attempt to divide Stirling's career into phases, I would propose that the American work—like all Stirling's work with his two different partners—is characterised not simply by a lack of stylistic unity—the eclecticism that Colquhoun rightly identified—but by its compositional technique. In the legacy of the "elementarist" work of Le Corbusier, Stirling's and Stirling and Wilford's design methodology focused on the accumulation of programmatic volumes—what Le Corbusier referred to as individual "organs" brought together to form a "synthetic solution". For Stirling, however, each element to be assembled wasn't simply a shape tied to programmematic function, but the result of a highly controlled and deliberate investigation of historical precedent. In other words, it wasn't simply the way he put the pieces together—or whether they were combined into a "unified" or "fragmented" composition—but the nature of the pieces themselves as generalised typological studies that distinguishes Stirling's work. With Gowan and later Wilford he probed deeply into a dizzying array of historical sources, searching for modern "principles", as a means to strip away their specificity and legibility and recombine them into novel compositions. Some of their sources are plucked directly from what was "discarded on the battlefield after the defeat of Modern Architecture", to recall Manfredo Tafuri's memorable phrasing.[12] Others are from lands and eras farther afield—from Oxbridge courtyards to Schinkel's museums to Scottish castles; and still more emerge from Stirling and Wilford's own collection of architectural solutions in flagrant acts of self-quotation. Regardless of the particular identity or origin of the source, the act of their combination and moreover the manipulation of volume and space—particularly the latter, as will be discussed—characterise Stirling and Wilford's architecture as it did Stirling's earlier work.

This compositional approach is immediately apparent at Cornell. The project is characterised by an assemblage of separate programmatic elements, each with its own volumetric identity and tied to a generalised historical type: the octagonal entrance pavilion, the shed-like volumes of the dance theatre and the main theatre, and above all the campanile that rises at its centre. The elements are arranged orthogonally on the site—unlike the splayed composition of the Wissenschaftszentrum—conceptually and programmatically tied together by the long open loggia (a revisioned stoa) at one edge, which overlooks the gorge below. Colquhoun argues that this project embodies the "fragmentation/ explosion" proclivity with a renewed vigour, converting "the early De Stijl-like work in to a new lyricism" with elements "collaged in a way that is apparently free but that in fact is tightly controlled".[13] Goldberger (here in a more generous mood) echoes Colquhoun, calling it an "idiosyncratic mix of inventively abstracted historical form and industrial elements, neatly composed so that they work both sculpturally and urbanistically".[14]

The architectural strategy of collage resonated both as a dominant design mode in architectural culture at the time, as well as more personally for Stirling, a former

above

James Stirling, Michael Wilford, and Associates
Wank Adams Slavin Associates
Center for Theatre Arts, Cornell University,
Ithaca, New York: forecourt and loggia, 1982–1989.
© Richard Bryant, photographer
James Stirling/Michael Wilford fonds
Collection Centre Canadien d'Architecture/
Canadian Centre for Architecture, Montréal

opposite

James Stirling, Michael Wilford, and
Associates Michael Wilford and Partners
IBI Group
Science Library, University of California at
Irvine, California: axonometric, 1988–1994.
James Stirling/Michael Wilford fonds
Collection Centre Canadien d'Architecture/
Canadian Centre for Architecture, Montréal © CCA

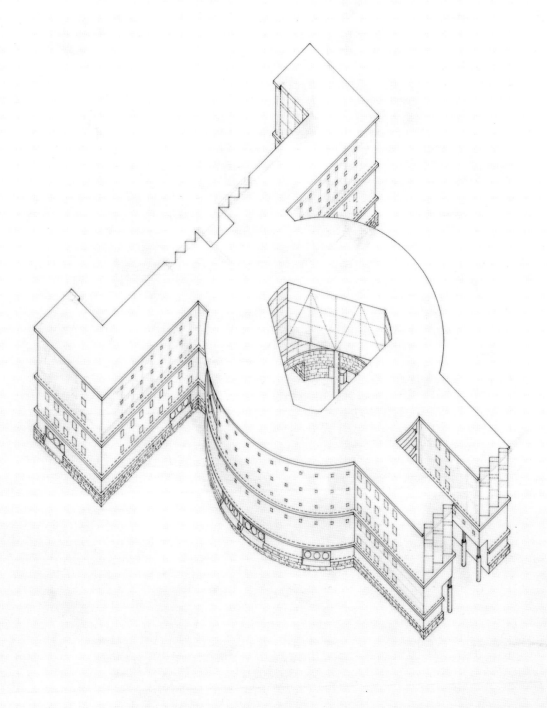

student and longtime friend of Colin Rowe. In his RIBA Gold Medal Acceptance speech of 1980 (awarded just after Stirling and Wilford received the Rice and Sackler commissions) Stirling made explicit his debt to Rowe, stating that his latest projects were "a collage of old and new elements, Egyptian cornices and Romanesque windows, but also Constructivist canopies, ramps and flowing forms—a union of elements from the past and present".[15] Certainly the popularity of collage at the time informed Cornell (where Rowe had been teaching the technique for years), but Stirling and Wilford had been working with this collage at least since the Düsseldorf and Cologne projects of 1975, in which the various programmemematic elements disaggregate across the site—largely, as Moneo noted, in a plan-based strategy—to become not one building but a collection of them.

But focusing solely on this notion of collage as a "pasted paper" technique— the "bricoleur" combining "conscripted" elements into a new composition, to use Rowe and Koetter's terminology from their 1975 article "Collage City"—misses an equally important but often forgotten aspect of the collage discourse, which had to do with a complex figural play of solid and void. In "Collage City" Rowe and Koetter juxtapose the voided interior gallery space of the Uffizi and Le Corbusier's Unité d'Habitation, describing the Uffizi as the negative volumetric equivalent or "jelly mould" for the Unité.[16] In addition to the compositional strategy of "collision", they stress a balance between the "continuous solid" of the traditional city and the "continuous void" of the modern one. In other words, void space is equal in importance to its "solid" counterpart. At its core "Collage City" is an investigation of figure/ground drawing techniques and a testament to the influence of gestalt-based theories; the key operation of the gestalt diagram is the reversal in our perception of the image vs the background, the activating of the ground as a figure. Of the rotunda at the Staatsgalerie, Stirling wrote: "It is no longer acceptable to do classicism straight and in this building the central pantheon, instead of being the culminating space is but a void—a room like a non space; instead of a dome open to the sky."[17] For Stirling and Wilford, as for Rowe and Koetter, negative space/ground was as important as positive/figure.

This "non space" had in fact been a crucial aspect of Stirling's design methodology since the 1950s, influenced by the Italian architect and editor Luigi Moretti. Moretti's 1952 article "The Structure and Sequence of Spaces" in his journal *Spazio* featured a series of plaster casts made from models of the interiors of historical buildings.[18] In a kind of proto-Rachel Whiteread exercise—though at a much smaller scale—void became solid. Stirling discussed Moretti's article a few years later:

> Luigi Moretti illustrated in *Spazio* the plaster castings taken from inside accurate models of certain historical buildings. By treating the external surface and the inner constructions of a building as a three-dimensional negative or mould, he was able to obtain solidified space. If space can be imagined as a solid mass determined in shape and size by the proportion of a room or the function of a corridor, then an architectural solution could be perceived by the consideration of alternative ways in which the various elements of the programme could be plastically assembled.[19]

This mastery of "solidified space", gleaned from Moretti and then continued through the influence of "Collage City", defined Stirling's work beginning in the late 1950s: the courtyard spaces at Churchill and Florey, subtracted from volumetric solids; the voided courtyards at Düsseldorf and Stuttgart, empty spaces that anchor the composition around them; and perhaps most powerfully the unbuilt scheme for Cologne in which the play of subtraction and addition define an archeology of volumetric solids and spaces, including the subtracted footprint of the cathedral itself, in miniature. As Stirling's reading of Moretti

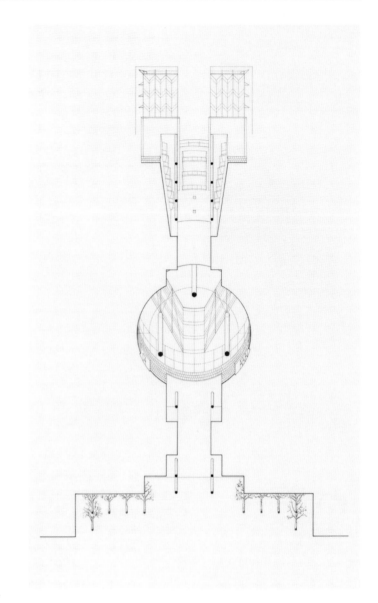

James Stirling, Michael Wilford, and Associates
Michael Wilford and Partners
IBI Group
Science Library, University of California
at Irvine, California: worm's eye
axonometric of public walkway.
James Stirling/Michael Wilford fonds
Collection Centre Canadien d'Architecture/
Canadian Centre for Architecture, Montréal © CCA

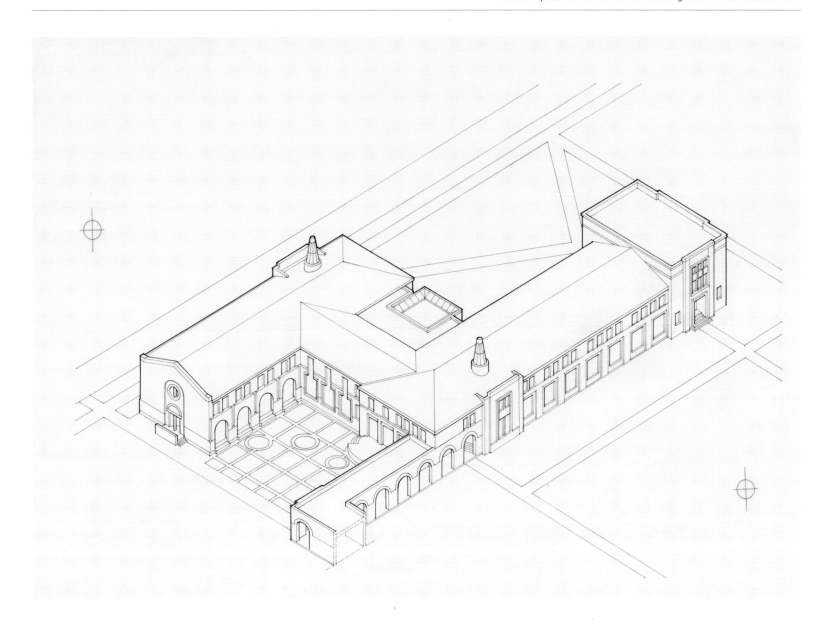

James Stirling, Michael Wilford, and
Associates Ambrose and McEnany Architects
School of Architecture Addition, Rice
University, Houston, Texas: plan and
axonometric from south west.
James Stirling/Michael Wilford fonds
Collection Centre Canadien d'Architecture/
Canadian Centre for Architecture, Montréal © CCA

reveals, solids were simply another version of the negative, space "reimagined" as a "solid mass", turned inside out. Through this lens the jutting lecture halls at Leicester can be understood as a kind of inside out "jelly mould" of their interior functions, as are the elements at Cornell.

Continuing this compositional trajectory, the void is the dominant design move in all four American examples. At Irvine it is perhaps most clearly articulated: the extended linear passage bisecting the building appears to rend it in two with an extended circular courtyard that morphs into a gateway at either end. This void both separates and unifies the two halves of the scheme and can be seen in the trajectory of the centralised "evacuations" at Stuttgart—the "non space" courtyard that Stirling describes—which was itself a revisioning of Düsseldorf. In fact the central rotunda at Irvine borrows directly from the self-same element at Düsseldorf: both are open, centralised, circular courtyards, with a pair of ramps leading up from the mid-point of the space. Unlike at Düsseldorf, however, the central space at Irvine is more ambiguous and complex: at the upper levels the circle morphs into a hexagon, while at the ground level it bleeds out through the two gateways at either end. The plan of Irvine is a kind of gestalt diagram; as with the famous face and vase combination, our mind shifts between seeing the two sides of the building as the figure, with the courtyard as ground, to instead seeing the void as the figure, with the adjacent buildings as ground. A

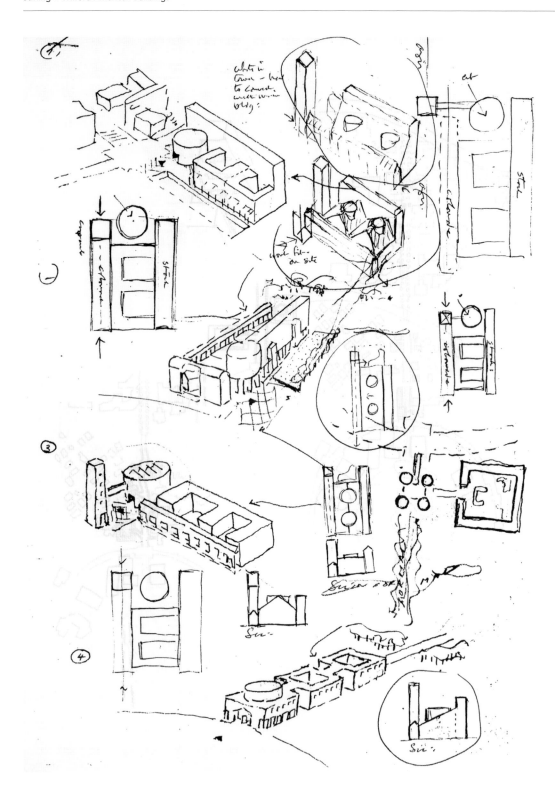

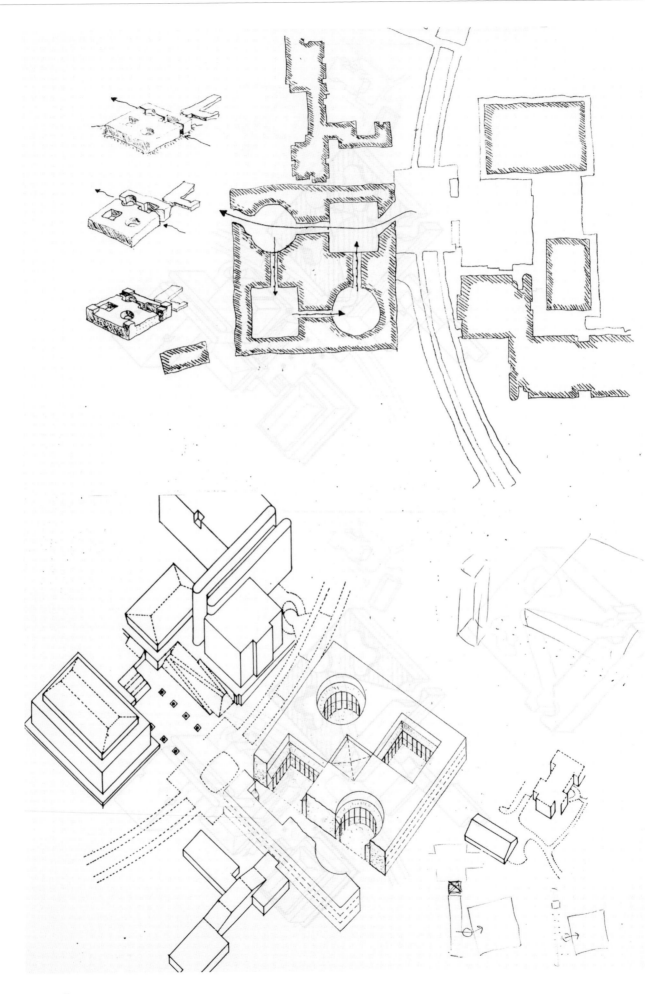

related ambiguity occurs with the building overall which we understand both as a singular figure, with a void extracted, and as a collection of three distinct volumetric elements—the library drum at the centre and the two symmetrical gateways on either side. The pieces are more tightly fused than at Cornell, and there are fewer of them, but a residual technique of assemblage remains. We can also place Irvine in the lineage of the courtyard interrogations begun at Churchill and continued at Florey in which the idea of an open space surrounded by a ring of cellular rooms—the Oxbridge courtyard typology—serves as an historical and cultural starting point from which revisions are made. At Irvine the adjacent Ring Mall—the mile-long circular pedestrian route and defining feature of the campus—provides an equally strong but distinct reference point which is filtered through the scheme and serves as another precedent that informs the circular layout of the design.

The Sackler is a less diagrammatic building than Irvine, and emerged within, or perhaps in spite of, complicated site constraints and client relationships. Nevertheless the use of the void and subtractive techniques inform the project as well. The idiosyncratic exterior form becomes more legible when we understand it as a solid urban block which was shaved off, twisted, and cut away to negotiate the numerous site restrictions—like an iceberg that had been chipped away.[20] The predominant void operation, however, is an interior one; the distinguishing programmematic space at the Sackler is the long, straight-run, interior stair running up the centre of the building. As at Irvine, this void space at Sackler effectively slices the project in two; rather than bisecting two equal parts, however, the Sackler stair runs between two different interior facades—on one side three levels of galleries, and on the other five-storeys of offices. This space is often described as an outside within the building, and indeed it gives one the feeling of being on an interiorised street, in contrast to the Irvine void in which the pair of exterior facades facing inward suggest an interior space. More importantly, this interior void at the Sackler retains a clarity of design intent in relation to Stirling's continuing use of the figural void. In a subtle way it challenges notions of inside and outside and becomes a counterpoint to the voided courtyard of the Fogg next door, to which a physical connection was unfortunately never realised.

Among the four projects, Rice is often dismissed as the most accommodating and contextual and would seem to be out of place in this investigation of Stirling's use of the void and of "solidified space". The simple design strategy of interlocking a new L-shaped building to an existing one, however, in fact generates two new courtyards on each side, both of which register the figure/ground ambiguity under discussion. The two courtyards are framed subtly, enclosed on only two of the four sides—one of the walls is from Stirling and Wilford's addition and the other from the existing building—a strategy similar to the one employed at the Clore Gallery at the same moment. This two-walled courtyard creates a perceptual question as to whether or not the space is actually enclosed or open. As at the Arts Centre at St Andrews, the addition at Rice clarifies the existing by adding an exterior void space that reorients the entire condition, setting the original building in "italics", as Rowe pithily described St Andrews.[21] This same strategy was employed at Derby, again through the use of an exterior void space, though at Derby the horseshoe-shaped space at the centre of the project reoriented an entire urban zone not simply a single building.

This use of the void is less pronounced at Cornell, and, as discussed previously, the assemblage of pieces as a classically collagist technique clearly predominates. With an expanded definition of collage as an investigation of both figure and void, however, the spaces between the various elements at Cornell emerge as critical aspects of the scheme. Moreover, if we understand each programmatic piece as an example of "solidified space", those same pieces—vertical campanile, octagonal pavilion, shed-like theatres—become legible as a space turned inside

James Stirling, Michael Wilford, and Associates
Staatsgalerie, Stuttgart, Germany: plan
between 1977 and 1984.
James Stirling/Michael Wilford fonds
Collection Centre Canadien d'Architecture/
Canadian Centre for Architecture, Montréal © CCA

out, as "three-dimensional negatives" of an interior condition. Similarly the glass window box askew in the front facade, seemingly unable to be contained within the overall volumetric perimeter of the shed building reinforces this sense of space as fluid and plastic; Stirling wrote that he considered glass "rather like polythene, to be pushed in and out enveloping the shape of the rooms".[22]

Although seemingly a motley crew of architectural forms and strategies, differing wildly in their material vocabulary and building functions, Stirling and Wilford's four completed American projects share an investigation of "solidified space". In this often maligned, and even more often ignored, work, we find the continuation of strategies that Stirling first discovered in the 1950s when working with Gowan. While the vocabulary may indeed be more contextual and even classical, the fundamental technique of investigating the relationship of building and ground, and moreover of developing a three-dimensional technique for working with volumetric elements not simply as positive forms but as residual moulds or negatives of interior space, persists. In a typical subversion, the emphasis shifts from the solid to the void—though one is never completely disentangled from the other. In this ambiguous and often subtle technique perhaps we find—at the very apex of postmodernism—an "appropriate expression of the modern attitude".

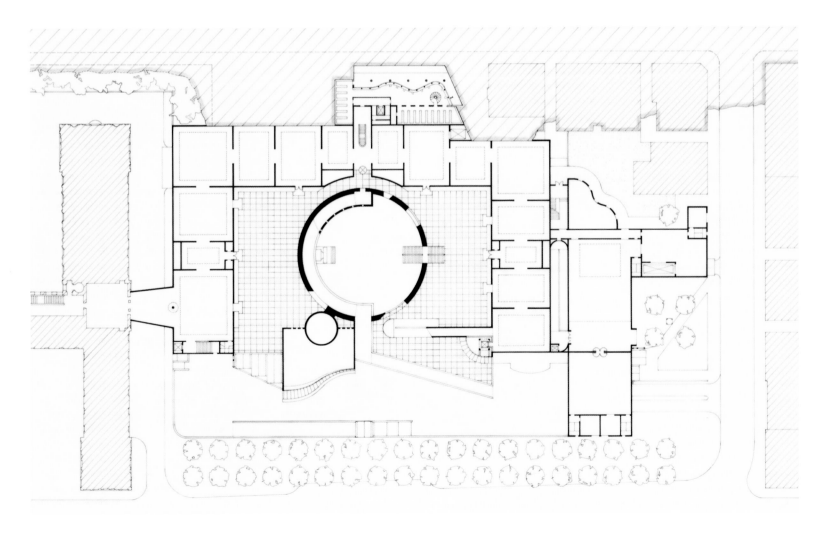

A Modern Mannerist

Robert Maxwell

America was important for James Stirling: not only did he believe himself to have been conceived there, but he worked there as an architectural student in 1948, and went back with increasing frequency throughout his career. Stirling and Michael Wilford built four times in America, and also completed several unbuilt projects for sites there. Many have queried how this American work fits in to his total output and in addressing this I shall focus mainly on a detailed examination of the two works that I've personally visited: the Sackler Museum, an extension to the Fogg Museum at Harvard University, and the Center for the Performing Arts at Cornell University.

The Sackler — originally intended as an extension but which became in effect a whole museum — was designed between 1979 and 1984 and dedicated on 18 October 1985 at the same time that The Clore Gallery extension to the Tate in London was being designed (1980–1986). This is the outstanding example of Stirling setting out to be a modern mannerist.

The arrangement of The Clore warrants consideration as it elucidates much about these other projects. In particular, the whole entrance sequence at The Clore gives the first time visitor a lived experience of mannerist space that can be unnerving. Passing the reception counter, stairs lead up to the galleries heading away from the upper entrance. Arriving at the top of the stairs, with no obvious way forward, the visitor must pause, look around, and turn to see the entrance arch into the galleries behind one. To reach this one traverses back along a narrow "gallery" that is on the side, and along the length of, the high entrance hall, before having to shift back onto the axis of the main stair in order to enter the galleries, through a high arched opening, which is boldly emphasised by a striped surround of bright colours. So in the contemporaneous Sackler Museum at Harvard we expect to find at least hints of a similar mannerist experience.

Stirling was aware of Mannerism as a way of "turning architecture upside down" as early as March 1956, when he published "Ronchamp: Le Corbusier's Chapel and the Crisis of Rationalism" in *The Architectural Review*. There he defines it as "a conscious imperfectionism". He was properly introduced to Mannerism by his tutor at Liverpool, Colin Rowe, who published "Mannerism and Modern Architecture" in *The Architectural Review* in 1950. So Stirling, who qualified in 1950, showed an interest in the subject from the beginning, which explains why

James Stirling, Michael Wilford and Associates
The Clore Gallery, Tate Britain, London: interior,
gallery entrance.
James Stirling/Michael Wilford fonds
Collection Centre Canadien d'Architecture/
Canadian Centre for Architecture, Montréal © CCA

Peter Eisenman was able to point to mannerist tendencies in the work which first brought Stirling to international attention: the Engineering Department building, at the University of Leicester designed from 1958 while he was in partnership with James Gowan.

But this interest, although always present in Stirling, does not really begin to manifest itself until it becomes allied with another tendency: the idea of the continuity of the city. Why this should be so is an interesting question that is seldom considered, although evidently always the case it is clear that Stirling had two vital concerns: firstly to be self-evidently a mannerist, and also to deal with architecture as part of the public realm, contributing to the space of the city. That there is a certain contradiction in these aims didn't trouble him.

This is probably due to a sort of rivalry that emerged between himself and Leon Krier, who joined his office in 1970. Krier was not himself a mannerist, but an architect who promoted architecture as a kind of fiction, that tells stories about how life might be—as can be seen in his own later work for Prince Charles at Poundbury, designed in the late 1980s: the fiction presented is of still living in the eighteenth century. But Krier also had a deep interest in urbanism, as seen in one of his early works with Stirling—the 1970 competition project for Derby Civic Centre, in which new offices are contained in a horse-shoe shaped building, smooth and modern, which adds decisively to the shape of the city by forming an important public place. This project established Stirling's stand as a protagonist for city space.

But for the Mannerist aspect, we have to look not just to the influence of Rowe, but to Stirling's wry sense of humour. The civic space in the Derby proposal has to be questioned as well as displayed. In the new space stand two jokes: a somewhat grandiose statue of the Winged Victory, which I take to be due to Krier, and a more puzzling idea: the old facade of an historic building, salvaged from the war damage on this site, now preserved, but inclined at an angle of 45 degrees, so as to form part of the acoustic backing for the proposed out-of-doors amphitheatre. This could only be due to Stirling. It is reverent towards the old facade, seeking to preserve it, and at the same time puts it in question—a typical mannerist duality. Mannerism arises from irony, and it involves not being too serious about oneself, or about life as a whole. This is an attitude that became deeply ingrained in everything Stirling did.

So what are the mannerist aspects of the work at Harvard and Cornell?

Discussing the Sackler with Michael Dennis Stirling stated: "Nowadays one can draw equally, without guilt, from the abstract style of modern architecture and the multiple layers of historical precedent", and in particular, referring to the Sackler Gallery, he says: "In some parts I hope there is the quality of ambiguity that you sometimes see in Soane...."[1] This answers to Summerson's comments on The Clore Gallery as "the kind of strange space that Soane would have enjoyed" and of course ambiguity is the essential quality of mannerism.[2] So we can deduce that mannerism was clearly part of Stirling's intention at that time.

Beyond that, there are decidedly mannerist qualities in the Sackler Museum's main staircase leading from the entrance hall up to the principal gallery level. It connects essential functions, but it is also, Stirling claims, an end in itself. The entrance hall runs across the full width of the building, creating an important cross-axis marked by pairs of monumental columns each side, but which lead on both sides to nothing more than subsidiary stairs down to the basement, while the main stair up to the galleries is beyond, through a narrow opening. In addition, the stair is not on the central axis of this imposing space, but shifted slightly to the left, so that the stair is effectively reduced to half its implied width—a cunning example of architectural know-how.

The possibility that the new building could be linked to the Fogg by a bridge provides a further—factual—ambiguity. It justifies the architect in

James Stirling, Michael Wilford, and Associates
Wank Adams Slavin and Associates
Center for Theatre Arts, Cornell University,
Ithaca, New York: interior of the foyer, 1989.
© Richard Bryant, photographer
James Stirling/Michael Wilford fonds
Collection Centre Canadien d'Architecture/
Canadian Centre for Architecture, Montréal

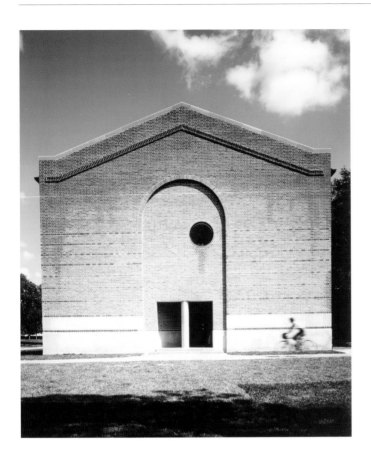

James Stirling, Michael Wilford, and Associates
Ambrose and McEnany Architects
School of Architecture Addition, Rice University,
Houston, Texas: exterior view, 1979–1981.
© Richard Bryant, photographer
James Stirling/Michael Wilford fonds
Collection Centre Canadien d'Architecture/
Canadian Centre for Architecture, Montréal

placing two supports for such a future bridge either side of his entrance porch, like sentries, and leaving an opening above, for the time being disguised as a window.

But none of these aspects explain the strange scale of the supports, which dwarf the entrance porch, and join with the outsize quoins in the wall beyond to make a hugely mannerist entity. This puts one in mind of the way the huge pilasters dwarf the windows in the rear of St Peters, Rome, by the arch mannerist Michaelangelo. There, it is the disparity between the delicacy of the windows and niches and the monstrous scale of the giant Corinthian order which seems to crush, if not extinguish, their perfection.

In the case of the Center for the Performing Arts, at Cornell, the trace of mannerism is altogether more subtle. It is a supremely lyrical building, much more integrated than the Sackler, and its mannerist aspect results from its over-all plan, rather than from key details of the architecture: it falls into Stirling's view of sources, described in his discussion with Michael Dennis above, as being both in the abstract style of modern design and drawing on "the multiple layers of historical precedent".

The location of the building itself establishes an ambiguity that is inherent in the whole project: the Performing Arts Center is formally part of the university campus, north of Cascadilla Gorge, but separated from the campus by the gorge and its raging torrent. And there are many other ambiguities in the design: Stirling's spreading loggia that faces the campus across the gorge expresses the connection to the campus as if a "front", but it accepts people only from each of its ends — the taxi drop-off or buses in College Avenue and those arriving from the car park building at the other end. All are brought to the centre of the loggia to enter the building on what is effectively its side so that when entering or leaving it, the university facing them as they turn to right or left is acknowledged. So the ambiguity of the site is intimately related to the functional planning.

The octagon placed on the main point of arrival on College Avenue has the air of a chapel or baptistery, but it merely shelters a bus stop, and gives access by stairs to a couple of offices above. It also masks the entrance to the building via the loggia and creates a sort of townscape, with the small piazza. There is an arbitrary fictional aspect to all this, which is what makes it mannerist. But it is redeemed by Stirling and Wilford's instinctive sense of form. The arbitrariness is of the same nature as that found in the Wizzenschaft Centrum in Berlin, 1979, where the required amount of office accommodation is provided in several buildings, none taller than the original building which is thus kept intact, but all following completely arbitrary plan shapes; or in the towers of his project for Canary Wharf, 1988, where the offices again are cylindrical towers of constant height, but these cylinders are cut into arbitrary segments of different shapes, as if they were made as toys for children.

The campanile which nails the main axis towards the university does not contain bells, but the lift. We are familiar with the phrase "lift tower", so there is nothing unfunctional about it being a tower. It is still cheeky to terminate the lifts so visibly, making it something of significance to the city. The large space facing the street contains the dance studio, its bulk did not have to be so reminiscent of a Florentine chapel, but this gives it a civic significance. The relation between form and function is thus rather loose, in a way that Alvar Aalto made important with his idea of "loose" function.

Stirling related that he overheard a family discussion in the cafe across the street, when the husband finally declared: "well, I guess it's some sort of Florentine rip-off". In shadowing an Italian chapel the building contains many aspects of what we used to call "historical allusions". This makes it a postmodern building, yet it is also clearly modern: the stone facing is hung, not a structural part of the wall and the steel structure of the loggia is nakedly exposed.

125

But this fictional aspect is not aimed at a picturesque illusion, as it is in Leon Krier's work. It is thoroughly tied into the analytical quality of modern design. In the "heroic" period of the 1930s we became familiar with the special shape that was awarded to auditoria, determined by the acoustic and visual properties that the space had to possess, as opposed to 'ordinary' rectangular rooms. This formal distinction declared the seriousness of "truth to function", and all modern architecture thereafter had to show this same analytical quality.

The loggia's last bays at either end turn at right angles as if to continue around the sides of a courtyard. This happens also in the Latino Library design, and in the project for an Opera House at Compton Verney, where it takes in an entire bay of the imaginary courtyard. This device, which Stirling and Wilford used in several designs, conveys a feeling of modernity and at the same time of incompleteness, even of disintegration. It may be taken as an indication of mannerism, similar to the "fallen" keystones of Giulio Romano at Palazzo Tè, Mantua.

Mannerism here is tied up with a certain fictional aspect of the building as part of an Italian town. The only point where it shows as a visual quality is in the main foyer, in what you see immediately on entering: the two square windows three floors up, right and left, take on the aspect of eyes: the building acquires a physiognomic character at the very point where it welcomes you.

Something of the same merging of historicist and functional aspects occurs also in the extension to the School of Architecture at Rice University, where round-headed arches are combined with stone coursing (without any key-stones) in a thoroughly mannerist way. It is perhaps most evident in the very prominent symmetrical gable end with its central door contained in a shallow round-headed arch, above which is a circular window but which is not symmetrically placed but is off to one side, where it marks the position of the corridor within. This is functionally correct, but visually disturbing.

In the un-built design for the Disney Philharmonic Hall at Los Angeles, 1988, there are evident mannerist elements in the way that enormous escalators stride through the main foyer, and also in the way the auditorium opens up into this space, without any sound barrier. Events in the auditorium thus become watchable for anyone using the building, against normal expectations.

In the Biological Sciences Library for the University of California at Irvine, 1988, the building is complete and self-sustaining. Ambiguity enters through strict functionality, but is prompted by the placement on the site. The main entrance is from the circular courtyard at the heart of the building, which at this point bridges the pedestrian route through the campus. The floor of this courtyard, built as truly horizontal, is broken into by a sloping ramp, as dictated by natural levels of the site. This works in a mannerist way to admit aspects of the site to the main space of the building as a conflict—a conflict that thus remains unresolved.

In this library project, there is no central reading room, as there is at the History Faculty in Cambridge, 1964: reading here is dispersed in a variety of situations. The glazing to the triangular upper courtyard is translucent, in order to reduce the exposure of the books to light, while the glazing bars remain constant; but it sometimes becomes serrated, the reason for which is not apparent from the outside. There is an extreme contrast between the generous areas of glazing, controlled by electrically operated sun blinds, and the dotted pattern of very small windows facing outwards, emphasising the inward social contact. As at Rice, this building conveys a mannerist merging of historicist and functional aspects.

James Stirling, Michael Wilford, and Associates
Los Angeles Philharmonic Hall: perspective view of the
performance space in the concourse, 1984–1989.
James Stirling/Michael Wilford fonds
Collection Centre Canadien d'Architecture/
Canadian Centre for Architecture, Montréal © CCA

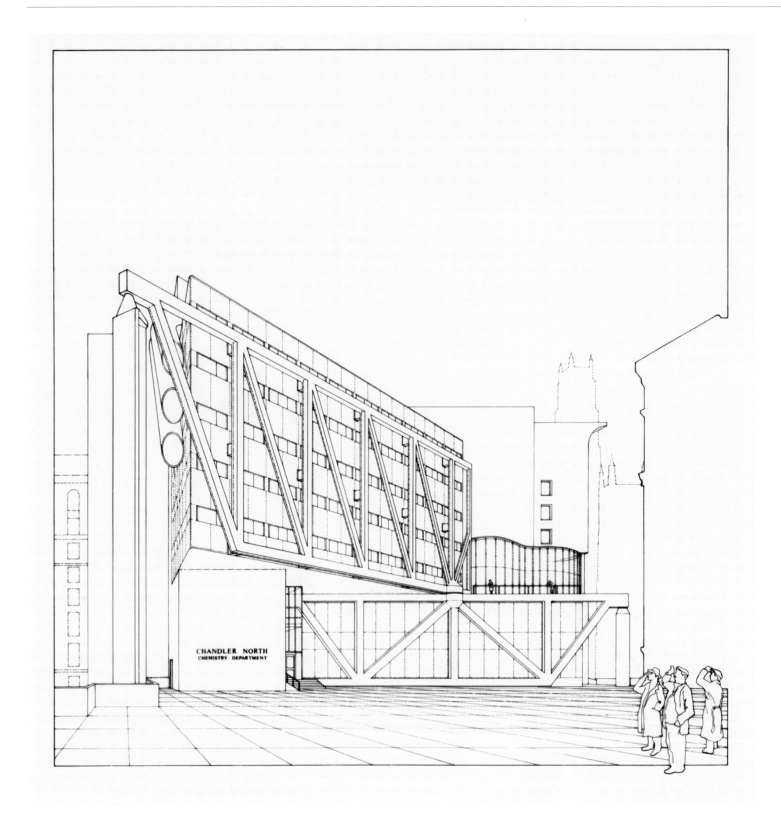

James Stirling, Michael Wilford, and Associates
Wank Adams Slavin Associates
Chandler North building, Department of Chemistry,
Columbia University, New York, New York: aerial
axonometric from 120th Street.
James Stirling/Michael Wilford fonds
Collection Centre Canadien d'Architecture/
Canadian Centre for Architecture, Montréal © CCA

Among the other un-built projects, mannerism is evident in the design for 11 town houses for East 67th Street, of 1978. The narrow projecting bays appear to support a projecting cornice, but only the actual projections, not in general. This produces an arbitrary effect on the whole block: a small touch that has an enormous effect.

In the case of the Chemistry Building for Columbia University, there is an extreme contrast between the courtyard side and the street side. The latter follows the street pattern, with a multitude of small windows, broken at one point by a recessed balcony marking the presence of a meeting room for receptions. The building is unexpectedly crowned by a massive coved cornice of the same form as that built in Stuttgart in 1977. Facing the courtyard we see a huge steel lattice of industrial scale, reaching to a single visible support, which bridges a large gymnasium that already existed on the site. The overhang of this outsize structure is used to protect the main entrance. This solution of a difficult problem is superb, and necessitates the acceptance of visual effects in one building that are heterogeneous and disconcerting.

It seems then that while Stirling and Wilford's American buildings display mannerist tendencies, they are no different in following the same approach that they employed in all of their buildings. They remain always concerned about their functionality, but without making a fetish of it. By employing a sort of loose fit functionalism, as advocated by Alvar Aalto, they gave themselves the space to introduce arbitrary effects where they were wanted. These effects were not modified in pursuit of what might be assumed to have been more down-to-earth American clients. Jim Stirling, with Michael Wilford remained true to themselves, and true to the principles that Stirling, from the earliest days, and later with Wilford, were engaged in discovering how to be at once a good architect and modern mannerist.

An English Eclectic Abroad

Nicholas Ray

James Stirling's projects in America, carried out with Michael Wilford, are by all accounts distinguishable from his work up to the trilogy of red buildings that were designed up to 1966—unquestionably "later" works, or part of a second phase. There have been numerous accounts of Stirling's apparent "turn", firstly to the overtly "pop" architecture of Olivetti at Haslemere, 1969, and then to the apparent postmodernism of the later work, beginning with the three German projects, 1975–1979, but already anticipated in the project for the St Andrews Arts Centre, 1970, and the Derby Competition, 1970. Superficially, he appears to have abandoned modernist principles and embraced the postmodernism that was emerging at the time; reviewing the Performing Arts Center at Cornell, Roger Kimball described his "transformation from eccentric modernist to confirmed postmodernist".[1] But of course it was not as simple as that.

Most thoughtful critics have stressed the continuity of Stirling's position: he was always an eclectic, from his student days onwards, encouraged no doubt by the scepticism of his teacher at Liverpool, Colin Rowe, whose whole career can be seen as a meditation on what was lost and what could be recovered from earlier traditions after the revolution of Modernism. Robert Maxwell has claimed that he was a mannerist, and it is this which provides the consistency of his work, going on to argue that great works of Modernism, such as Joyce's *Ulysses* and TS Eliot's *The Waste Land* were always full of allusions, and suggesting that there is a latent aspect of Mannerism in all great art.[2] Stirling's own diaries and notes from his student days onwards reveal his self-conscious preparation as a "third-generation" modernist: the heroic simplifications of the first generation simply cannot be sustained in a period that is aware of its own history, but the weak accommodations of the second generation are insufficient. There is a palpable anxiety here about where to move, which is reflected in Stirling's published response to the later work of Le Corbusier. He would prefer the ethics of early Modernism to be sustainable, but he has to acknowledge that it is not. Ham Common can be seen as an answer to the too-overtly rustic Jaoul Houses that Stirling reviewed for *The Architectural Review* in 1955—the precision of the brickwork deliberately eschewing the romantic textures of the Paris buildings.[3] But the unbuilt houses for Basil Mavrolean, as published in the 1984 'Black Notebook', reveal the extent to which Stirling was prepared from the earliest days to consider proscribed stylistic motifs, such as round-headed openings, when occasion demanded it.[4]

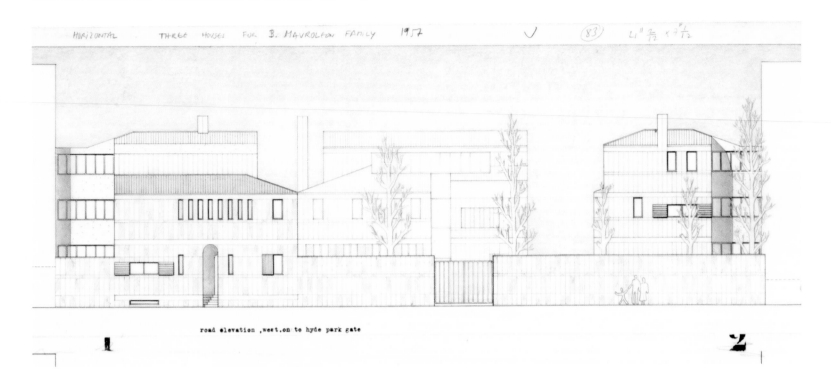

road elevation ,west.on to hyde park gate

James Frazer Stirling

Three Houses for B Mavrolean Family, London

(competition entry): West elevation from road, 1957.

James Stirling/Michael Wilford fonds

Collection Centre Canadien d'Architecture/

Canadian Centre for Architecture, Montréal © CCA

By common consent Stirling and Gowan's Leicester Engineering Faculty, 1959 to 1963, represents the moment when the formal vocabulary that the practice had been developing, in the competition for Churchill College and the unrealised project for Selwyn College, finds its fulfilment. Multiple influences have been detected: Hannes Meyer (League of Nations competition), Wright (Johnson Wax), Kahn (Richards Research), and even the early ideas of Archigram, amongst others.[5] The shift, therefore, in the 1970 project for Derby, to a figure-ground composition that emphasises the space of the city rather than a treatment of buildings as objects, whilst undoubtedly a response to Rowe and Koetter's *Collage City* and the presence of the young Léon Krier in Stirling's office, had been prepared for: Stirling was always an architect with exceptionally sensitive antennae adept at absorbing multiple influences to serve his compositional ends. But what sort of eclectic or mannerist does this make Stirling, and can this shift, when considering buildings as part of the city, be seen through another lens?

I examine below the way in which Stirling and Wilford's work in America can be seen not only as a reflection of its time, but as an example of a deeply embedded tradition in British architecture.[6] I will suggest that the cultural context of the American commissions made demands which Stirling's aesthetic position was particularly well-suited to provide an appropriate response. Finally, I will propose that the success of the best examples can largely be explained by the similarities of the problems to those for which a British eclectic position is best equipped to solve. The argument is not that Stirling was influenced by his British predecessors—he was more overtly interested in Schinkel, or Le Corbusier, or a host of others—but that he shared elements of their sensibility.

In nineteenth century British architectural history, as elsewhere, two traditions can be identified, a romantic Gothic strand, and an apparently opposed classicism. But they always inter-twined. The Gothic George Gilbert Scott was forced by Palmerston to build the Foreign Office in classic dress, while the classical Cockerell built Tudor Gothic churches. More significant for my purpose is the trajectory of two of the assistants of GE Street—Philip Webb and Richard Norman Shaw. Nikolaus Pevsner saw Philip Webb's development of an architectural language for the Red House—an eclectic and pragmatic use of vernacular, Gothic and classical elements, unprecedented in a house for a wealthy young client—as one of the origins of Modernism.[7] But Webb could equally be viewed as an exemplar of a British eclectic tradition that in some way seems to anticipate the procedures of postmodernism. Philip Webb's last major house design, Standen, would serve as an example. The drawings of the house survive, as do Philip Webb's hand-written diary and a transcription of the specification, in the care of the National Trust.

After a brief investigation of a larger and more elaborate plan a simple strategy was evolved for the house, one that was to recur again and again in the plans for smaller houses by members of what was loosely describes as the English Free School: principal rooms facing south, a central entrance and staircase on the north side and an extended kitchen wing. A courtyard is formed for the entrance, enclosed on one side by the retaining walls of a bank of trees and on the other sides by existing buildings that Webb was careful to retain. This accounts for the picturesque angle at which the kitchen wing abuts the main house but Webb cannot have been unaware of the device of adding a wing at an apparently odd angle, as George Devey did at Coombe Warren and Norman Shaw had at Grim's Dyke and Pierrepont. Lethaby's reverent, sentimental, but moving biography of Webb appears to be correct in its assessment of his priorities—a concern for the site, the conscious avoidance of stylistic posturing by a builderly concentration on the materials to be used—whilst at the same time a willingness to employ whatever motifs he required, from history or from the immediate context, to fashion his composition.[8] The elevations indicate both the strengths and weaknesses of Webb's approach. Where, as in the entrance to the kitchen court, he is dealing with common vernacular elements, pier, gate hinge and step—dealing in fact with the everyday apparatus that had been the common currency of the country house and its outbuildings for the previous century—his particularity and sensitivity to detail raise what he creates to the plane of unaffected art. But when we look at the main south facade, sporting his favourite boarded gables, we are bound to question the curious meanings and associations that Webb's composition must convey. The facade on the ground floor is punctuated and centred by a projecting porch-like structure with a deep coved cornice that turns out to be a bay off the living room. There is no evidence that at any stage in the design this was thought of as a porch, since access to the garden was always intended to be through the conservatory. This element seems to take on more meaning than is intended: too straight-laced to be read as witty and paradoxical, as Lutyens' effects were later to be interpreted, it merely appears heavy-handed.

So Webb is one kind of British eclectic: inventive but awkward. And we may observe that such an architectural character has well-known antecedents. As long ago as 1936, in an essay entitled "The Mind of Wren", Sir John Summerson argued that Wren was an intellectual who lacked an intuitive visual imagination, "a fancy controlled empirically not intuitively", and whose intellectual framework was close to that of Locke, the quintessential English Empiricist.[9] He uses the example of St Paul's Cathedral, but the same working through of formal problems in a dogged and somewhat pedestrian way can be seen in Emmanuel College Chapel in Cambridge and even in the later and more successful Trinity College Library. This is also the mind of Webb, but it is not the mind of Shaw, nor, in the next generation, of Lutyens—British eclectics of a different flavour.

The work of Webb's fellow-assistant at Street's office, Norman Shaw, was never awkward in this way. Distinguishing himself from his earnest contemporary, Shaw described Webb as "a very able man indeed, but with a strong liking for the ugly".[10] In 1940 Reginald Blomfield's short biography portrayed Shaw as "a cool clear headed Scot, of first rate ability, with immense powers of concentration".[11] He was "always moving on" stylistically, was "blessed with a most fertile imagination and a brilliant intuitive "compositional eye". But Blomfield also tried

top
Standen House by Philip Webb
East Grinstead, West Sussex, England,
1892–1894.

bottom
1 Palace Green by Philip Webb,
Kensington Palace Gardens, London
1868–1870.

to show that Shaw had been "subconsciously searching all his life" for... "the grand scale... scholarly restraint (and) quiet dignity of the eighteenth century", and illustrates Chester's, 1889–1891, which he considers his greatest house. The young Nikolaus Pevsner, reviewing Blomfield's book, characteristically attempted to see Shaw, especially in his earlier domestic work, as a precursor of Modernism.[12] But in his 1976 monograph Andrew Saint took a more balanced view.[13] Shaw borrowed throughout his career, and the precedents he called upon depended on the task at hand. Saint noted that as late as 1894, at "The Hallams", Shaw was still employing half-timbering and tile hanging in a large country house much as he had in the virtuoso composition of Leys Wood in 1870. It is obvious that some principle of "decorum" is at work here, in the choice of style, and the attempt to see a logical stylistic progression is unproductive. Voysey had one explanation for the general shift in taste: "a severe climate favoured the Gothic, while a mild and sunny one induced the Classic. It is easy then to see how the commercial prosperity and peace... down to the commencement of the Great War, led the public to express itself in a Classical rather than a Gothic manner. This tendency was accelerated by the greatly increased facilities for foreign travel."[14] "The Gothic spire, pinnacle and pointed arch" (he pointed out), "like the spearhead, lightning and angularity, are all associated with ideas of conflict, aspiration and movement. While the dome, the round arch and the sphere, globe or ball are associated with luxury, ease, repose and amusement." But in the case of Shaw, a shift towards Classicism seems much more likely to be a function of coming to terms with creating a street architecture, or an architecture that can take its place in the city, by endowing it with some of the resonance and dignity that classicism can confer. Shaw told Lethaby in 1902:

> I was trained on the older Gothic lines, I am personally devoted to it, admire it in the abstract, and think it superb; but it is totally unsuited to modern requirements. When it came to building, especially in places like the City we found it would not answer.[15]

This is a shift that is not just convenient—it is necessary, and the much-discussed "shift" in Stirling's style can be seen as a similar response to the conditions of working within the city. As Michael Wilford explained to Geoffrey Baker in 1998:

> You and others have alluded to a significant shift in '75 for the museums projects in Germany. Jim and I have always explained that for the first time, apart from St Andrews and Derby, we were working in historic city centres. A lot of the earlier university work was on fringe site around cities. Leicester was on the edge of the campus. Cambridge is way out of the established university pattern, Oxford the same, the St Andrews Hall of Residence is on the periphery. All those projects were on edges, the three German museum projects were right in the middle.[16]

In other words: "when it came to building, especially in places like the City we found it would not answer". It is tempting, if Stirling can be seen as a version of Shaw to interpret Gowan as a version of Webb—"a very able man indeed, but with a strong liking for the ugly".[17]

The parallels between Shaw and Lutyens have often been pointed out, and one can argue that Lutyens travelled the same road between 1896, with the early Godalming houses (such as Munstead Wood), and 1906 (Heathcote), as Shaw had between 1871 (Leys Wood) and 1890 (Chesters). Both men were prolific compared to Webb, and certainly Lutyens admired the work of Norman Shaw, writing, in his often-quoted letter to Hubert Baker of 1906, at the time he was working on Heathcote, that "Shaw has the gift".[18] This is the letter in which he confesses to Baker that he is adopting the High Game of Classicism. Yet he also admired Philip Webb and yearned perhaps to give his houses something of Webb's direct unaffectedness that his Shavian facility did not permit.[19]

One of Lutyens' problems was how to endow his houses for the nouveau-riche with a suitable dignity, on a relatively low budget. One method was to enlarge the composition, by the incorporation of out-buildings and loggias into an extended elevation. Another favourite device was the use of a spurious archaeology, so that Tigbourne Court looks as if a Tuscan Loggia has been inserted by others into a seventeenth century vernacular house, and at Little Thakeham, by Lutyens' own description "the best of the bunch", not only has a service wing been apparently attached at a later date at the rear, but a conversion in the central hall seems to have taken place, where the Jacobean interior has been invaded by a Gibbs screen of stonework which is itself fragmented and incomplete. Thus, where a formal heavy-handedness, or earnest awkwardness, seems to lend authenticity to the work of an architect like Philip Webb, the employment of wit rescues the eclectic architect of a different cast, who is cursed with compositional virtuosity. Reviewing the Butler memorial volumes on Edwin Lutyens in *The Architectural Review* of April 1951, in an article entitled "Building with Wit", Nikolaus Pevsner was confused. Lutyens' work was paradoxical: he introduced "motifs which seem to have nothing to do with each other", and his work seems to degenerate into fantasy: "The Drum Inn at Cockington is the cottage straight out of the pantomime, Castle Drogo is a fairy castle, the Viceroy's house a fairy palace, and New Delhi as planned by Lutyens a fairy city". Most distressingly, here was an architect of "prodigious gifts" who, because he was a revivalist, "contributed nothing whatsoever to the main stream of development in twentieth-century architecture".[20]

In these terms, Stirling is unambiguously a Shavian, an inheritor of a British tradition that goes through Lutyens, where facility is tempered by wit. Stirling's most admired project in the second stage of his career, the Stuttgart Staatsgalerie, is a brilliant blend of pragmatism, in the use of the garage to establish a podium for the building, sensitivity to the urban context, in the way in which the building meshes with its immediate context, and virtuoso episodes of formal invention and quotation. Its composition is strong enough to be able to absorb even the literalness of half-buried Tuscan Doric columns—elements that were immediately to seem somewhat dated and could have been embarrassing in the work of a less skilled operator. When Stirling is invited to build in America, he brings to the task a particularly British temperament, and set of skills, which distinguishes his work from that of other architects, whether from within the United States, or from South America or from elsewhere in Europe. The cultural context is also very different to that in the United Kingdom in the 1950s, when Pevsner was so disconcerted by Lutyens.

The projects for universities in the United Kingdom to which Michael Wilford referred (Leicester, Cambridge, Oxford, St Andrews) had each suffered from inadequate budgets and poor standards of construction, and, while serving to establish Stirling's international reputation, were generally not admired by their users, so that Stirling found no further patronage from British universities in his career.[21] In the United States, however, ever since Gropius' involvement with Harvard Yard and Aalto's dormitory for MIT, there had been consistent patronage of modern architects, and mostly they had delivered recognisably "modern" solutions.[22] Venturi's commission for the Faculty Club at Penn was not until 1974, and from then on, on university campuses as much as for other purposes, a "postmodern" manner might be expected. The purpose of inviting Stirling to compete, or be considered for, commissions in American campuses was to patronise an internationally renowned architect of acknowledged formal virtuosity, who could be expected to respond to the particular briefs by producing

top

Sir Edwin Lutyens, Little Thatcham, West Sussex, England, 1903: the south exterior, 1909. © Country Life

bottom

Sir Edwin Lutyens, Little Thatcham, West Sussex, England, 1903: the hall, 1909. © Country Life

a memorable building—selectors at both Harvard and Cornell refer to his ability to satisfy practical requirements. The sensibility Stirling brought to bear was most obvious in his appreciation of context. At Irvine, he responded to the powerful radial arrangement of the existing campus, though the library building is somewhat over-scaled and diagrammatic in comparison to his best work. At Cornell, the problem is the reverse: in constructing a picturesque miniature city of separate elements, he runs the risk of the pantomime that Pevsner complained about in Lutyens' work. The Fogg extension, which delivers a brilliant resolution of its brief by Stirling's manipulation of its section, has too effortful an external expression because it tries to refer to a complex context. Paradoxically, it is at Rice, where the constraints were most stringent and seemingly the opportunities most limited, that his "prodigious gifts" are most apparent, in a modest work of considerable subtlety. The planning of the extension makes sense of the pre-existing building, concentrating movement in a way that ensures a strong social atmosphere, and creates spaces that are adaptable and reinterpretable, all within a skin that is deferential to Cass Gilbert's architectural language without being directly imitative. It is apparently effortless. Because of its subtlety, some critics have yearned for an earlier version of Stirling, but this is a misunderstanding: given the context (not exactly urban, but part of a coherently considered ensemble), a stringent modernist expression "would not answer".[23] Intriguingly, the effect is achieved by means of a version of the "spurious archaeology" such as Lutyens might have employed: within an extension that appears at first glance to be simply part of the original building, a conversion seems to have taken place, whereby a colourful abstracted "modern" space has invaded the fabric. Clues as to the internal disruption are legible externally, in the asymmetrically placed bulls-eye window for example. This is building with wit, an eclecticism that has little to do with postmodern posturing, but plays the necessary game with consummate skill.

If they are by no means his masterpieces, the four built American projects represent the breadth and consistency of Stirling's interest, and something of his "English Eclectic" sensibility and manner: the bold response to the pre-existing 'urban' conditions in the Irvine library, the free quotation from numerous precedents at Cornell and Harvard, and the use of a narrative whereby different architectural languages can be subtly integrated into a satisfactory whole at Rice. In each, in different ways, this apparently iconoclastic international architect reveals a particular sensitivity to context—the contribution of the Englishman abroad.

Stirling Under Review

Marco Iuliano

The Italian journal *Casabella*, in the issue of September 2006, published posthumously a conference paper by Manfredo Tafuri on James Stirling. The original speech had been delivered by Tafuri many years before in Bologna, in October 1990, at the opening of an exhibition of Stirling's work. Only later was a recording found and a transcription made. The paper, bright, evocative and not generally known in the Anglophone countries, starts with the analysis of a curious object that Stirling displayed at Whitechapel, in 1956, at the famous exhibition This is Tomorrow, organised by Theo Crosby: this object, a rather informal *papier -mâché*, full of ravines, was irreverently entitled by Stirling *Primitive Habitat*. Tafuri's message was clear. It is impossible to separate the future and the past in Stirling's architecture, and this will be the leitmotif of this essay.[1]

It is reasonable to suppose that Stirling borrowed the notion, of the continuity between past and future, as well as many others, from Le Corbusier via Colin Rowe, when he was his student at the Liverpool School of Architecture from 1947–50. A potential precedent to the *Primitive Habitat*, indeed, could have been an exhibition of sculptures, tapestries and paintings, entitled 'Primitive Art', hosted in 1935 at Le Corbusier's studio in Paris, as precisely recorded in volume three of the *Œuvre Complète*. Although Rowe writes—in his lively introduction to Stirling's *Buildings and Projects* of 1984—that in the 1950s the first three volumes of the *Complete Works* were not on the shelves of the Architecture School's Library at Liverpool, we know that Stirling was in possession of the published works of the Swiss-born master. Indeed, in the late 1940s, when still a student, he purchased from Charles Wilson, a bookseller in Liverpool, volumes one to four of the *Œuvre Complète*. Stirling himself states his particular devotion for Le Corbusier ten years later [2]:

> In the process of knowing more, we pored through the pages of Corb's *Œuvre Complète*, our designs were eclectic, a necessary stage to the formation of a personal style. The books of Corbusier were thus utilised as catalogues, as had been previously the books of Alberti and Palladio in the Renaissance. Thus one's first acquaintance with Corbu's buildings, and also the work of Gropius and Mies and the other masters was through the medium of the printed page. The formative process was an

costruire in altezza
alejandro aravena
antonio monestiroli
mecanoo
vittorio gregotti

747 CASABELLA

tafuri su stirling
jean baudrillard
francesco dal co
tadao ando
peter zumthor
alberti a firenze

above

Cover of *Casabella* 747, September 2006. Courtesy of *Casabella*

opposite

Casabella 747, September 2006, with images of the Primitive Habitat, James Stirling and Manfredo Tafuri. Courtesy of *Casabella*

... e ...
Manfredo Tafuri

Fra le prime opere di James Stirling, oltre alle
architetture ben note, vi è uno strano oggetto,
vale a dire un *papier mâché*, che viene esposto,
a firma di Stirling (insieme a Michael Pine
e Richard Matthews), ad una mostra del 1956
a Londra. La mostra si chiamava: *This Is Tomorrow*.
Ma, sardonicamente, questo strano oggetto,
vale a dire un *papier mâché* piuttosto informale,
pieno di anfratti, viene chiamato dagli autori,
quindi anche da Stirling, un *Abitato primitivo*.
Dobbiamo ricordarci dell'atmosfera in cui
è immerso Stirling nei primi anni Cinquanta
e del momento di questa mostra. È il momento
in cui Stirling, insieme a Peter e Alison Smithson,
ad Alan Colquhoun, a Theo Crosby, a Cedric Price,
a Richard Hamilton, aveva dato vita ad un Institute
for Contemporary Art e si riuniva con costoro
in quello che veniva chiamato *Independent Group*,
vale a dire una delle espressioni di quella
che poi venne chiamata la generazione arrabbiata
inglese di quegli anni. A queste riunioni,
che si tenevano, prima, in un pub di Soho a Londra,
e che poi si trasferivano nell'abitazione di Rainer
Banham, molto spesso partecipavano sia Edoardo
Paolozzi che Joseph Rykwert. È un momento
di spregiudicato, direi addirittura scanzonato,
riesame di tutto ciò che era non solamente
la tradizione dell'architettura moderna fino
a quel momento, ma della realtà. Scanzonato,
dicevo. In fondo, se si pensa di nuovo a questo
strano oggetto, una sorta di enorme alveare
bucato, che viene presentato da Stirling e dai suoi
amici alla mostra *This Is Tomorrow*, quello che
è divertente è che il primitivo, l'abitato primitivo,
cioè l'ancestrale e il futuro, il *tomorrow*
della mostra, sono da loro congiunti insieme.
Quando io guardo architetture di Stirling, anche
molto recenti (penso ai suoi boccaporti in colori
molto violenti: blu violentissimo, verde
violentissimo, giallo violentissimo -anche nella
Neue Staadstgalerie di Stoccarda), non riesco
a staccare la considerazione storica che ho di lui
da queste origini; e, in fondo, ritrovo anche
nelle sue architetture recenti un tipo

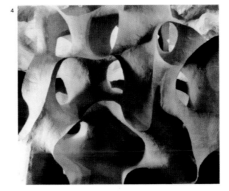

1 Achille Castiglioni e James Stirling,
Bologna 1 ottobre 1990
Achille Castiglioni and James Stirling,
Bologna 1 October 1990
2 James Stirling con le calze viola
mentre ironizza sulle pareti sospese
approntate da Achille Castiglioni
per la mostra *I Musei di James Stirling,
Michael Wilford and Associates*, Bologna,
1 ottobre 1990
James Stirling with violet socks as he jokes
about the suspended panels prepared by
Achille Castiglioni for the exhibition *I Musei
di James Stirling, Michael Wilford and
Associates*, Bologna, 1 October 1990
3 Achille Castiglioni, 1990
allestimento della mostra *I Musei di
James Stirling, Michael Wilford and
Associates*, Bologna
exhibition design for *I Musei di James
Stirling, Michael Wilford and Associates*,
Bologna
4 Richard Matthews, Michael Pine,
James Stirling, 1956
The "bubble" sculpture, mostra *This Is
Tomorrow*, Londra
The "bubble" sculpture, exhibition *This Is
Tomorrow*, London
5 6 Manfredo Tafuri e James Stirling,
Bologna, 2 ottobre 1990
Manfredo Tafuri and James Stirling,
Bologna, 2 October 1990

intellectual one (…). With the exception of buildings by Lubektin, there were few others in this country, which could be visited, and therefore assimilated emotionally.

If we look carefully at Corbu's books, alongside the visual analogies between architecture and painting, there is a clear relationship between the natural shape and the project, which Stirling seems not only to have introjected but extended to a detailed observation of the past, starting at Liverpool. A sort of sequential continuum between things far from each other in time and space, encapsulated in a vision of architecture that we could say is harmonic.[3]

Rowe encouraged his students to analyse buildings of all periods, as part of their learning to see. As another primary source states—this time Robert Maxwell—"with Rowe, Stirling learned how to look".[4] When, in 1961–1962, Rowe was with David Roberts in charge of second year students as studio master at the Cambridge School of Architecture, the two things that he told his pupils to look at were the Italian city and the work of Le Corbusier.[5] Again, we see him advocating the best of the past—according to his own lights—and the better possible future.

left

James Stirling's signed copy of the
Œuvre Complète, vol. 2, 1946 edition.
Private collection

right

Cover of *The Architectural Review*, April
2011. Courtesy of *The Architectural Review*

opposite

Some of James Stirling's visual analogies
inspired from Liverpool to his later
projects, as published by Brian Hatton in
The Architectural Review, April 2011.
Courtesy of *The Architectural Review*

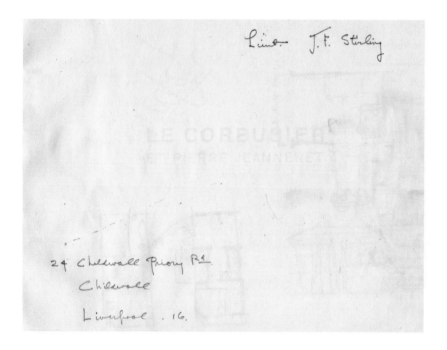

Why should we read Stirling's late projects in the light of this premise which I have described at some length? Because, with Michael Wilford, even if the four American buildings—at Harvard, Rice, Cornell and Irvine—did not enjoy the same public acclaim, and although they are very different in terms of architectural quality, they can each be read in connection with the past, and with his entire production.

Nothing could explain this concept better than the textual/visual material of a lecture presented by Stirling at the Iranian Congress of Architects in 1974, and published in *The Architectural Review* a year later under the indicative title "Stirling connexions":

I consider 99 per cent of modern architecture to be boring, banal and usually disruptive when placed in older cities (…). The collection (in a building) of forms and shapes which the everyday public can associate with and be familiar with—and identify with—seems to me essential. These forms may derive from staircases, windows, corridors, rooms, entrances, etc. and the

1 & 2 Liverpool's Custom House with the roof blown off is very similar to Stirling's Neue Staatsgalerie

3 & 4 Ships in Liverpool docks. Stirling surely recalls seeing ships dry docked in his design for the Florey Building

5 & 6 Stirling's 1969 axonometric of the Olivetti Training School resembles landing stages, as featured on the Meccano magazine cover, February 1937

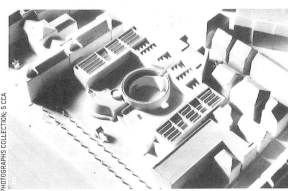

5

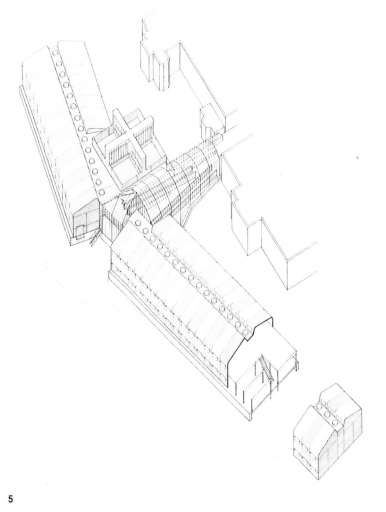

6

Stirling connexions

At the end of September 1974 the second Iran International Congress of Architecture was held at Persepolis at the behest of the Iranian Government. Architects invited included Fuller, Sert, Soleri, Soltan, Tange, Maki, Bakema, van Eyck, Doshi, Hollein, Candela, Safdie, Erickson, Candilis, Zevi, Quaroni, Fathy, Stirling. The over-riding theme of the five-day congress was 'The role of architecture and urban planning in industrialising countries'. As is usual with such large architectural gatherings, most of the talk was sociological, but on later days, in addition to slide shows, there was some discussion on architecture, much of it related to the question: to what extent should/can modern architecture be influenced/affected by the buildings of the past? James Stirling's statement made at the congress (below) is related to that question.

I consider 99 per cent of modern architecture to be boring, banal and barren and usually disruptive and unharmonious when placed in older cities.

In England the government—either local authorities or central government—are politically concerned to build the greatest number for the common good, be it schools, houses, factories, etc. Private enterprise developers are concerned with building the greatest quantity of square footage (ie offices) at the least cost to maximise profits. Both see shoebox-style modern architecture with its stripped-down puritan aesthetic and repetitive expression as very suitable for building to the lowest costs. Government and developers are eliminating the perhaps more costly element of 'art' in architecture; and many would agree that this is right and proper in a social democratic society. In this situation an architect who is concerned to produce architecture has to revert to lowdown cunning to make his buildings of any consequence.

*Stirling & Gowan

1, Maison Cook, Paris, 1926

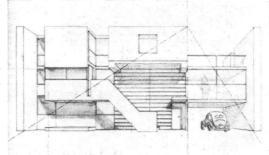
1a, core and crosswall house, 1951

2a, cylinder section (20th century)

2b, Sheffield University, 1953

3a, Cotswold barn (18th century)

3b, Woolton house, 1954

4a, Queen's Docks, Liverpool, 1860

4b, Preston housing, 1957*

5a, Blenheim Palace, 1705

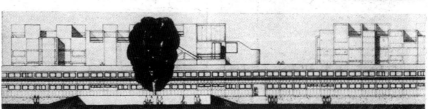
5b, Churchill College, 1958*

273

total building could be thought of as an assemblage of everyday elements recognizable to a normal man and not only an architect. For instance, in a building we did at Oxford University some years ago, it was intended that you could recognise the historical elements of courtyard, entrance gates towers, cloisters: also a central object replacing the traditional fountain or statue of the college founder. In this way we hoped that students and public would not be disassociated with their cultural past (…). Hopefully there might be some humour in modern architecture, and in this context there is a rich vein in serious puritanical modern that can be satirised and commented upon. I realise that an interaction between the design for a new building with associations of the past is a dangerous tightrope to walk, with compromise and sentimentality on either side. The illustrations that accompany this statement indicate, in pairs, a relationship between the past and one of our projects. Not that the first illustration of each pair has in any way influenced the design of the building which follows. Nevertheless there is, I hope, a connexion, be it in material constructional method, or association.[6]

As the layout of The Architectural Review pages clearly illustrates, Stirling was inviting the reader to reflect on the continuity of the historical, spatial and physical relationships beyond any epoch, style or formal result. This logical process was powerfully and provocatively illustrated by a simple mise en page, juxtaposing 18 images of the past with 18 of his recent projects. The only exception to this rationale was his 1969 Olivetti Training School building, intended as a "connexion" with a design object: the 1973 Olivetti Divisumma, a calculator machine. These relationships should not be considered "literal connexions" — as, of course, is the comparison between Christchurch at Spitalfields and the Leicester building — but they certainly suggest a modus operandi which could easily, by and large, be applied to Stirling's imaginative approach to architecture.

It is well known that the fortune of the reputation of a work of architecture depends upon its positive reception in the media. Stirling was particularly attentive to this aspect of self-publicity — another lesson learned from Le Corbusier.[7] As Mark Girouard recalls in his rich and documented biography on Big Jim, for instance, Léon Krier was literally conquered by the Leicester Engineering building published in Casabella of June 1967, a special edition of Jim's architecture. After this illumination — "it seemed like something fantastic", he says — Krier went to work with him, because "I was looking for a second Le Corbusier".[8]

Stirling's cited approach towards the presentation of his projects to the public was understood by John Summerson in his article "Vitruvius Ludens", of 1983. He went further in analysing the architect's stylistic position:

There are photographs galore, published designs for unbuilt projects, many thousands of descriptive words and, more significantly, the architect's own idiosyncratic drawings, exhibited and published. On this evidence assessments of a sort can, I hope, be made and an answer attempted to the question: what is it Stirling has brought to architecture and released, to loud and prolonged applause, into what seems to have been an aching void? 'Imagery' is a word more often used in the discussion of works of literature than those of architecture but it is a word we can hardly do without in discussing Stirling's work from 1970 onwards. I see Stirling as the architect who, more than any other in this country, or perhaps anywhere, has identified himself with this transfiguration, turned the old seriousness back to front and re-engaged it as play. He is essentially a great player — even something of a gambler — an architect cast more distinctly than most in the role of homo ludens.[9]

above

Casabella 315, June 1967.

Courtesy of Casabella

opposite

The Architectural Review, May 1975.

Courtesy of Architectural Review

But the "gambler" was not always so lucky. The fortuna critica of the four American buildings was controversial and largely negative. The extension of the Fogg Museum at Harvard is the best known between these four efforts and it was widely published in the United Kingdom before, during and after its completion by *The Architectural Review*: in March 1983, April 1984 and July 1986 with articles respectively written by John Coolidge, Gary Wolf and Michael Dennis. The last of these three pieces in the British journal, entitled "Sackler Sequence" is an extremely well organised interview with Stirling, who explains, with clarity, the design intentions. Furthermore, the building at Harvard had more than ten pages of description devoted to it in *Architectural Record* (March 1986): the project was not a masterpiece for its stylistic language, but a *coup de théâtre* which took particular care in the composition of its internal spaces. Again, Rowe gave perhaps the most balanced judgement in the review of the building appearing in the cited issue of *Architectural Record* by noting, for example, that "the exterior is certainly not an invitation to applause". "Who, but Stirling?" was the title of the article—a clear enough indication of his view of the design.

The extension at Rice encountered harsher criticism from the very beginning, starting with Philip Johnson's sarcastic statement: "I went to Rice to see the building, but I couldn't find it." Johnson's view was, this time, partially echoed by Rowe, but the real blow for the American projects was epitomised in Michael Sorkin's trenchant judgements, particularly on the extension at Rice, which appeared in *The Architectural Review* of April 1984:

> It is a work caught in the bind of emulating mediocrity and the result is what one might expect from such an enterprise. Rice shows a compendium of failed details, unconvincing rhythms, and kitsch wit. Still, taken as a whole, it's a wimpy and undistinguished work... I want the old Jim back.[10]

As often happens in architecture, these assessments from influential critics significantly inhibited the reception of the building by a wider public and by the scholarly community. It was not sufficient that a detailed and informed review of the Rice project, written by Peter Papademetriou, had been published two years before in *The Architectural Review*, February 1982, with a captivating set of photographs shot by Paul Hester. In a correspondence I had with Hester in September 2012, he remembers his interesting involvement in the photographic project: he toured the building with Papademetriou and Michael Wilford to learn their specific concerns about the photographic representation of the architecture. These photographs were originally conceived by Hester for another article by Papademetriou, which appeared in the American magazine *Progressive Architecture* in December 1981 and were later borrowed by the British journal.

We will return to the analysis of Rice as a case study later; instead, it is interesting to see the "publishing luck" of the other two buildings, Irvine and Cornell. We can quickly comment on the Science Library at Irvine, University of California, which was completed, posthumously, in 1994: at that time it received only a brief note in *Progressive Architecture* for its "curious shape", October 1994. *The Architectural Review* avoided in-depth analysis of this built project as did *Architectural Record*; the only journal which considered it at some length, was *Lotus* (no. 89, 1996), with an issue largely dedicated to the whole new University campus of Irvine, written by Alessandro Rocca. Stirling and Wilford's architecture, completed two years earlier had ten pages devoted to its description. A technical text accompanies the colourful images of the campus shot by Richard Bryant. Although it provides a translation from Italian to English in between the pages, *Lotus* probably could not assure the same degree of public impact as journals with a widespread global coverage.

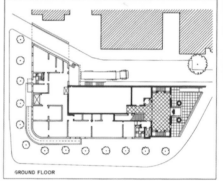

Once through the Sackler's "neo-Mycenaean" glass entry vestibule, museum visitors, students, and staff enter a monumental, if austere, hall (facing page). The slate floor was salvaged from the building razed to make way for this one, and the rusticated stucco walls reiterate the overscaled quoining surrounding the entrance. The great room's 34-foot height is emphasized by two pairs of spindly piers that take their place to either side (facing page and plan below). As the eye follows the piers upward, the source of the anteroom's natural light is revealed in the ceiling-level strip windows with brise-soleil troughs. Encased within the piers are lights that help guide students down the two flights of stairs leading to a 281-seat lecture hall below (photo below). The subterranean room, with its gently vaulted pink ceiling and row of robust structural columns (flattened to face the aisle) contains a large niche cut away from the ceiling—a "psychological window," according to Stirling—intended to frame large horizontal works of art that have, as yet, not been installed. Back upstairs in the anteroom, a luminous tubular information desk acts as a "lantern" to direct visitors to a pair of galleries—one small for exhibitions used in classroom study, the other large for temporary exhibitions.

GROUND FLOOR

above

Architectural Record, March 1986.
Courtesy of *The Architectural Record*

opposite

The Architectural Review, February 1982.
Courtesy of *The Architectural Review*

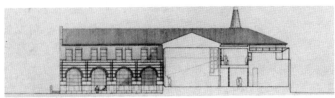

section A-A through gallery, bridge and Jury Room; new south elevation beyond

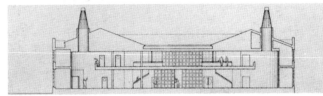

section B-B through bridge showing two-storey voids and conical skylight lanterns over entrances; sliding panels in centre are earlier design

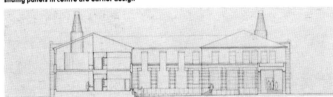

section C-C through new wing showing preferred parti of studios, off-centre corridor and offices facing court; elevation of existing building shown with intended 'bottle windows' on two-storey gallery facade

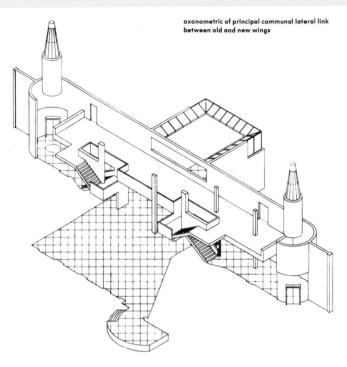

axonometric of principal communal lateral link between old and new wings

Stirling at Rice

ARCHITECTS: JAMES STIRLING-MICHAEL WILFORD ASSOCIATES

SCHOOL OF ARCHITECTURE, RICE UNIVERSITY, HOUSTON, TEXAS

James Stirling's recent building for the School of Architecture at Rice University is a response to the particular setting and history of the university. In order to understand the work, both in relation to Rice and to Stirling's past designs, the AR asked Peter C. Papademetriou, associate professor at Rice's architecture school, to assess Stirling's achievement (p55).

Facing page: 1, new east elevation, with existing wing of Anderson Hall on left. New porch entry replicates the themes of the existing wing, whereas the Aalto-like Jury Room with clerestory glazing is stated as a collage element.
2, the new wing blends unobtrusively into the campus, subtly reflecting the forms of neighbouring buildings.

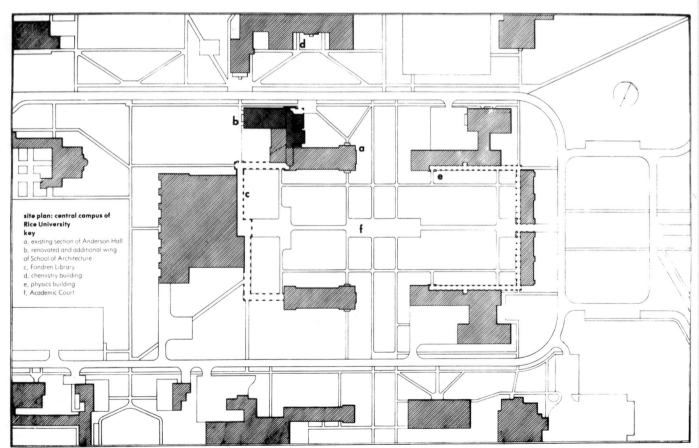

site plan: central campus of Rice University
key
a, existing section of Anderson Hall
b, renovated and additional wing of School of Architecture
c, Fondren Library
d, chemistry building
e, physics building
f, Academic Court

The Cornell ensemble had a different published destiny, and could be paradigmatic in understanding the different cultural approaches shown by American and English journals. The project deserved attention and appeared almost simultaneously in the US and in the UK, in *Architectural Record* and *The Architectural Review*, respectively in October and November 1989: both the journals dedicated their covers to the new building.[11] Written by Deborah Dietsch, the article in the US journal opens with a symptomatic "American Universities have a curious affinity for the work of British architect James Stirling". Despite the numerous pages given over to the Performing Arts Center, the review was a generic description of the campus with a minor criticism of the interiors that, in the author's view, were "the parts of the building most lacking Stirling's strong hand". The rest of the short essay was illustrated by two-dimensional drawings, some long captions and, also on this occasion, by Richard Bryant's photographs.

On the other hand Robert 'Bob' Maxwell wrote the analysis of Cornell for *The Architectural Review*, in an article also illustrated by Bryant's images (some of the photographs are the same in the two issues). A close friend of Stirling, and his contemporary as a student at Liverpool in the 1940s, Maxwell has an enviable knowledge of the architect's personal history, which was demonstrated, in a masterly manner, in his commentary on the project. There is no space in the present essay to recall Maxwell's article in detail: but, even today, it is worth retrieving that issue of *The Architectural Review* to read carefully the dense pages of his article, which gives a clear understanding of Stirling's references, his way of manipulating spaces and, therefore, beyond any formal assessment, his compositional method. Perhaps, the only thing we might add today, is when Maxwell rightly compares Cornell to an "Italianate hill village" it could be considered a tribute by Stirling to his old mentor, Rowe, who was Professor at Cornell at the time. Rowe presented the Italian city as an example to his pupils, and his talented and receptive student now gave back to him this formal surrogate of an Italian village.

Returning to the analysis of Rice—especially to highlight how sometimes primary sources can be often undervalued—we should note that before any articles had been published, during the ceremony for his 1980 Gold Medal of the Royal Institute of British Architects, Stirling, who was aware of forthcoming critical judgements, had the opportunity to speak about this work. He clearly sets out what he calls his 'oscillating' approach to architecture in a passage that is worth repeating here:

The last project is for extending the School of Architecture at Rice. The original campus by Cram, Goodhue & Ferguson is from the 1920s in a sort of Venetian, Florentine, Art Deco and we were asked to work within a limited range of bricks, pantiles, and pitched roofs which is reasonable for this eccentric but elegant campus where there are many arcades, marble balconies and fancy spires. The School of Architecture is an L-shaped building and we are extending it with another L-shaped piece. The interlock is joined by a surgical splint—a galleria of circulation core binding the pieces together and connecting the old entrance with a new entrance at opposite ends of the splint. These entrance areas are lit through glass spires on the roof. The galleria overlooks a new exhibition space on one side and a jury room on the other. The existing building is connected with a colonnade to an adjoining building and the L-shaped extension creates a three-sided courtyard—a new sheltered garden in an otherwise very open campus. It may be difficult to distinguish the facades of the new building from the existing ones and for those who think this design is uncharacteristically quiet or conventional, I would point to the Mavrolean Houses, a project from the 1950s, to indicate that reserve and

above and opposite

Cover and page from *The Architectural Review*,
November 1989. Courtesy of *The Architectural Review*

PERFORMING ARTS CENTRE, CORNELL UNIVERSITY

PHOTOGRAPHS
RICHARD BRYANT

10

7, east elevation. According to its prominence external walls are surfaced in marble, stucco with marble string courses, or all stucco.
8, close up of east elevation with Vermont marble cladding in two degrees of finish. Below semi-circular stucco panel is window to dance studio and below that the pergola that edges the piazza. Purple and white wisteria will one day climb over the pergola.
9, piazza, edged by pergola, closed by octagon and with view of university through end of loggia.
10, east end of loggia with entrance to enclosed and ramped part to left of stairs.
11, loggia seen from where gorge edge footpath skirts octagon.

11

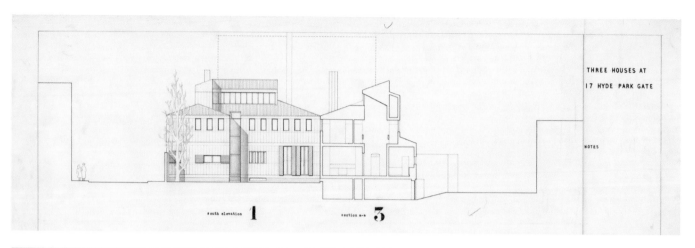

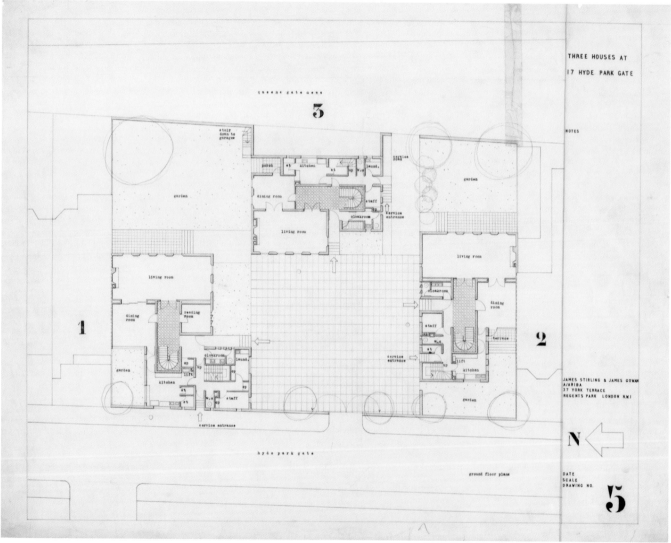

top

Stirling and Gowan

Three Houses for B Mavrolean Family,

London (competition entry): sectional

elevation from road, 1957.

James Stirling/Michael Wilford fonds

Collection Centre Canadien d'Architecture/

Canadian Centre for Architecture, Montréal © CCA

bottom

Stirling and Gowan

Three Houses for B Mavrolean Family,

London (competition entry): floor plan, 1957.

James Stirling/Michael Wilford fonds

Collection Centre Canadien d'Architecture/

Canadian Centre for Architecture, Montréal © CCA

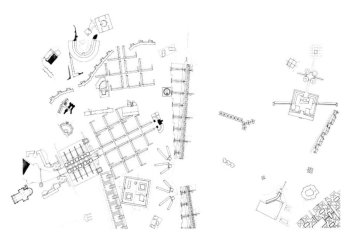

top to bottom

Sheet of Giovani Battista Nolli's map of Rome, 1748; Sheet
of Stirling's earlier projects, Cambridge, Leicester, Oxford, St
Andrews, etc. at same scale; Composite sheet with Stirling's
buildings overlaid on Nolli's map.

James Stirling and Partners proposal, Roma Interrotta
exhibition, 1978, Mercati di Traiano, Rome, Italy. The
exhibition travelled to the Architectural Association, London,
the Cooper Hewitt Museum, New York and other venues.
James Stirling/Michael Wilford fonds
Collection Centre Canadien d'Architecture/
Canadian Centre for Architecture, Montréal © CCA

restraint—like the formalism of other projects—is not a change in our
work. Both extremes have always existed in our vocabulary; so if we have
a future, I see us going forward oscillating, as I did as a student, between
the formal and the informal, between the restrained and the exuberant.[12]

It is important to read the clear and concise description of the project at Rice
in conjunction with the relevant drawings from Stirling's office housed at the
Canadian Centre for Architecture (CCA). The project, indeed, is still paradigmatic
today as an example of a sensitive approach to architecture and its relation to
the *genius loci*—an exemplary insertion of the new in the old that Stirling and
Wilford achieved without mimesis. It is difficult to separate the contribution of
Michael Wilford in the work of the atelier, and for the present we will consider on
this occasion the Rice project as a single product of two minds.[13]

My focus is particularly on some sheets housed at the CCA, which are
exemplary in the delicate approach to the gestation of the plan and of the facades
that they illustrate. These study-drawings show how much respect Stirling and
Wilford have for the history of the site. There is a sketch study for the insertion
of the new volume into the existing building so that it reads not as a contrast
but as continuity. It shows consideration of 11 different solutions, and is a clear
indication of the reasoning that led to the exclusion of most of them. The old
L-shaped building was integrated in every possible way: amongst others, there
are solutions with an isolated cube on the right, probably connected with a ramp;
a flipped L; a scheme that creates a rectangular enclosed court; and many others,
that loosely recall to mind—but in plan only—the famous summary of four villa
types sketched by Le Corbusier in plan and axonometric view, published in the
Complete Works.[14] The final solution chosen was the second in the left row (note
that the plan in the drawing of Stirling and Wilford is upside-down compared with
the usual plan widely published).

Another important aspect of these drawings and sketches is that, they
reveal the studies that were undertaken of the facades of the buildings already
present on the campus. Many of the suggestions for the new project are clearly
a transformation or elaboration of historical elements seen in a new light: this is
evident for the "rockets", the skylights that must be seen as a reinterpretation
of the pinnacles of the earlier architecture on the campus, as Hester also clearly
documents in his images. Furthermore, the way that the facade elevation of the
new addition is conceived, simplifies the main lines that exist in the adjacent
buildings, with the triangular conclusion of the roof taken as a model for the
short-side elevation of Stirling and Wilford's extension.

A feature to consider in strict relation to history is that Stirling and Wilford
imagined a new pattern in bricks and stone for the facades, that it is not mimetic
but, again, a reinterpretation of the logic of the early twentieth century buildings.
As one of the CCA sketches indicates, the design of the new facades was
considered carefully. The final result gives an apparently homogeneous effect,
though the well-educated eye can distinguish the old bricks and stones from the
new. We can associate this type of approach with that of the most sophisticated
practitioners in building restoration, where the architect plans an intervention
that reintegrates lost parts of the building in a subtle manner, visible only to the
attentive eye through its distinction of materials. In greater detail, we can see, for
example, how Stirling and Wilford envisioned at Rice the three facades in their
new intimate courtyard: on one side there is the previously existing principle of
arcades; in the centre, part of the old building, respected, and a new invention
where Stirling and Wilford conceive the ground-level rectangular windows and
the smaller openings in the upper part as a sort of mediation between old
and new; and, finally, on the third side, arched windows are introduced with a
patterned treatment (stone and brick) that relates well with the existing open

arcades on the opposite side, but with a deep vertical void between every arch to highlight the new intervention. It is worth noting that, on the other side of the new building, the architects invert the use of brick and stone on the facade, proof of the different approach to the inner and outer condition that we might encounter in any sensitive design with or without reference to historical precedent.

The last point to mention is the surgical splint, the galleria—as Stirling calls it. Papademetriou was able to find the historical precedent in a German building by Hans Saedler realised in the 1920s which, compared with part the of the new plan of the Rice extension, represents another potential "stereoscopic pair" of Stirling's 1975 article.[15] In terms of plan there is certainly a strong relationship between Rice and the Saedler's project, even if in the American circumstance the meaning is completely distinctive: the gallery is the functional connection within the building, the only immediate evidence of modernity in the entire project, in terms of its architectural language. The skylights, which are uncompromisingly different, lie at the extreme ends of a path that links different levels and gives a privileged view over the jury room that is positioned in the middle of the gallery. This jury room, placed on the opposite side of the external courtyard already described, is illuminated by a continuous strip of glass at the edge of the roof; on the exterior, this volume is a pure cube encased in stone and, with the gallery, is the element presented in the axonometric view that fulfilled the role of the icon, the imagery, for the entire project.

To conclude, in the light of the reception of his architecture as seen in the medium of the printed page, we could speak of an "almost Stirling". I have tried here, especially through the use of Rice as a paradigm, to highlight that, despite either positive or negative reviews, the real architectural object needs focused investigations and attention to first hand sources, if it cannot be visited and, to use Stirling's words, "therefore assimilated emotionally". The Rice case shows how architectural history is clearly considered and deeply reinterpreted, in a very refined manner, in the making of the project.

But there is another meaning that we could give to the "almost Stirling" concept, strictly related to his own personal history. Indeed, in 1993, one year after Stirling's untimely death, Colin Rowe closed his article for the Spanish journal *Arquitectura Viva*, "Las cenizas del genio/The genius's ashes" with these words:

> And, in other ways, what else can I say but almost? He began his career as almost a student of mine—almost but not quite; and I myself will almost close my own career as a student of his—again not quite. And, meanwhile, there remains that brilliance, that truculent, that ongoing argument, lots of things looked at together and a ceaseless hospitality such as, otherwise, I have never experienced and can no longer hope to enjoy.[16]

This very poignant passage is a symptom of how deep the relationship between the two men must have been. I would simply conclude by adding that, when we look at Stirling's built works, we need to think immediately of the legacy of his most influential mentor at the Liverpool School of Architecture.

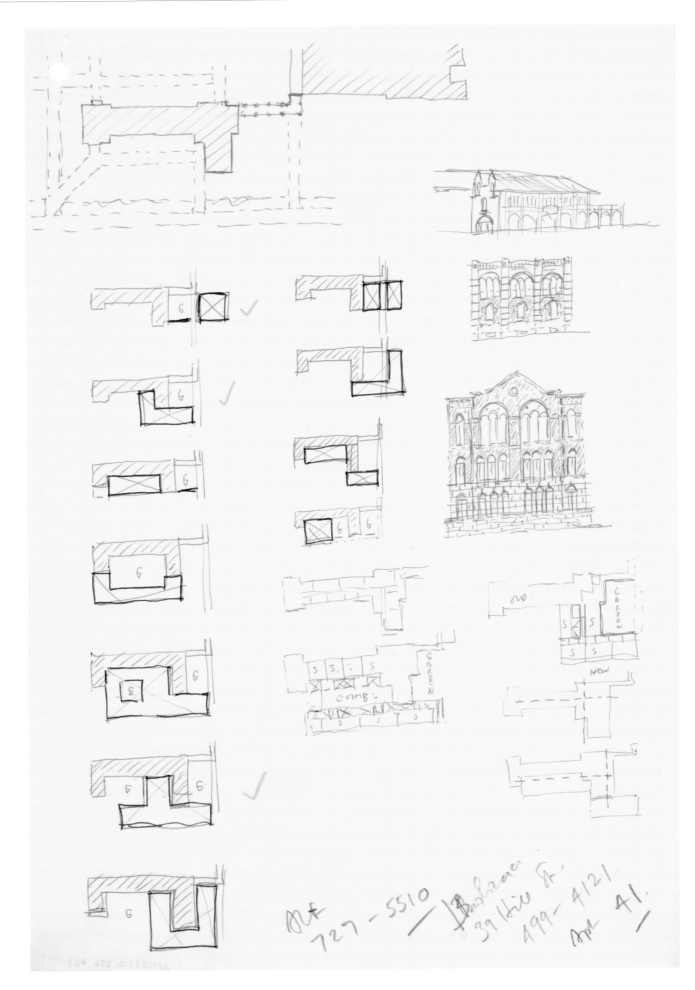

Modernity and Postmodernity in the Work of James Stirling and Michael Wilford

Kenneth Frampton

If one compares the creative trajectory of Stirling's career to the radical, revolutionary white architecture of the European avant-garde between the two world wars, one realises that the British Brutalist movement, under the rubric of which James Stirling came into prominence in the early 1950s, was already a postmodern syndrome, even though its ethical attitude towards the expression of raw material, social as well as technical, saved it from the Swedish petit-bourgeois contemporary style which the Brutalists despised. At the same time, Stirling, like Alison and Peter Smithson, was quite disenchanted with the implicitly socialist agenda of the pre-war Modern Movement. We need to bear this in mind when it comes to evaluating his eventual turn towards some sort of historicised stylistic postmodernism in the 1970s.

Fair-faced, load-bearing brick construction first appears in Stirling's work as an expressive element in an unrealised project for a house in north London of 1953. This may have been a response to a somewhat similar house in brick that Alison and Peter Smithson had designed for a site in Soho, London in the previous year. This was the stereotomic syntax that Stirling, in collaboration with his first partner James Gowan, would emphasise throughout the next decade of their practice. A particular feeling for landscape also first appears in his architecture around this time, most certainly in the Woolton House project of 1954; a chunky, loadbearing brick house with intersecting monopitched roofs. The alternating slopes of these roofs seem to inflect the form of the house towards the incline on which it sits.

A similar load-bearing brick cross-wall technique is adopted in Stirling's Team X Village Project of 1955, which had a linear castellated character despite the fact that there was no specific site. The resulting syncopated assembly of load-bearing brick walls and monopitched roofs echoed the form of a traditional village street, comparable to that of West Wycombe, which Stirling cited after Thomas Sharp who had featured this village in his seminal study *The English Village* of 1945. Stirling and Gowan would achieve something similar in their two-storey, flat-roofed Ham Common Flats, designed in calculated, load-bearing brickwork and built near Richmond in 1958. This work was clearly influenced by Le Corbusier's Maison Jaoul of 1956, as is suggested by the exposed concrete floor slabs and rainwater gargoyles draining the inset first floor balconies. These

Brutalist concrete details had the effect of emphasising the precise coursework of the flanking brick walls. Similar brick walls, without exposed concrete flooring, make up the castellated form of Stirling and Gowan's Preston housing of 1957–1959, with which they intended to induce the spontaneous social life of the adjoining by-law terrace houses. This social agenda was virtually identical to that aspired to by the Smithsons in the design of their Golden Lane housing in 1952. In Preston this sentiment was related to Stirling and Gowan's particular sympathy for the working class ethos of the moment as evident from their descriptive text: "In this project we tried to retain the spirit of the alley, yards and street terraces that the new development was replacing and from which its occupants were being moved...." When this housing was first published in Stirling's collected works, it was accompanied by the image of a northern industrial town, as this was habitually depicted at the time by the painter LS Lowry, accompanied by a citation from Somerset Maughan's characterisation of Charlie Chaplin's nostalgia for the slums of his childhood.

The Stirling and Gowan 1958 competition design for Churchill College, Cambridge was conceived as a heterotopia in as much as the entire project was surrounded by two-storey residential accommodations plus a continuous arcade on its inner face and a berm reinforcing its outer perimeter. This hermetic boundary enclosed a large courtyard in the middle, of which there were a pair of five-storey dormitory blocks plus a free-standing, three-storey library and an adjoining dining complex, both covered by monopitched roofs. At the time, the staccato castellated profile of this composition was affectionally characterised by Colin Rowe as the Blenheim of the Welfare State. A similar monopitched roof-work set over a monumental, bermed earthwork would be realised in the same year as a free-standing, school assembly hall for the London borough of Camberwell. The square plan of this building was covered by three monopitched roofs pin-wheeling about a central column, surrounded on all four sides by berms covered with turf and lit by clerestory curtain walls, the gable ends of which were of precision brickwork. As with Churchill College, this building was a sharp response to the rather non-descript flat landscape in which it was situated.

The four-storey, faceted plan form adopted by Stirling and Gowan for their Selwyn College dormitories projected for Cambridge in 1959 was also conceived as resting on top of a bermed earthwork, thereby reinforcing the boundary of the existing college garden. These dormitories, had they been realised, would have demonstrated for the first time the crystalline, red brick and curtain wall palette of the so-called "red trilogy". What is unique about this work is that it is Stirling's first treatment of a curtain wall as a faceted and stepped skin which, in this instance, is in strong contrast to an undulating rear of the complex, faced in brick and punctuated by Kahnian stair/elevator towers, also clad in brick. These last, assuming the form of a hammer-head in plan, will become transformed into the freestanding, red tile faced access towers which will become a signature elements in the next four projects; i.e. the Leicester Engineering Building, 1959, the History Faculty Building, Cambridge, 1964, the head offices projected for the Dorman and Long Steel Company, 1965, and the Florey Building for Queen's College, Oxford of 1966; the last three being credited to Stirling alone.

The Selwyn College design is remarkable for its audacious projection of a continuous curtain wall as a cascade of glass, stepping out at each floor toward the top, with two overlapping large glass sheets covering a single floor. This double shift in section and plan produced a faceted and stepped glass profile which was the counterform of a rear wall in brick. This wall was stepped back so as to provide for a shallow clerestory light at each floor; a detail which will be repeated, almost exactly, in the Florey Building. Inspired in some measure by Mies' glass skyscrapers of the early 1920s, the faceted glass front of Selwyn was conceived as breaking up the overall form of the building through tessellated reflections, of which they wrote: "The glass screen was really an enormous window faceting in and out, approximately indicating on the exterior the scale of the students' rooms and sets; and college members walking in the grounds would have seen reflected in the glass a shattered Cubist image of the trees in the garden."

In 1959, at the Leicester Engineering Building, the main vertical feature which dominated the composition was a six-storey curtain-walled office tower, raised into the air on top of an exposed reinforced concrete frame. The other crystalline component was the faceted engineering workshops, bounded on all four sides by a floor-height, windowless, red brick wall. The triangulated, 45 degree greenhouse roof of this space was in effect handled as a space-frame, covering the entirety of its orthogonal plan at grade. A narrower crystalline roof of exactly the same format covered the upper level workshops on the third floor. An alternation between the 45 degree geometry of these "space-frame" roofs and the orthogonality of the plan itself permeates the entire composition with the exception of the cantilevered lecture halls on the first and second floors. As a consequence of this interplay between the two geometries, 45 degree clipped corners are employed throughout, particularly at the corners of the office tower and at the corners of the four-storey diagrid floors which make up the brick-faced laboratory block "bustle" to the rear of the tower. Hence the curtain wall of the tower itself stands in strong contrast to the elevator/stair shaft, finished in red tiles, which rises for the full height of the building. Here the syntax of the "red trilogy" is fully articulated, including the cantilevered concrete lecture halls, also clad in red tiles. These striking forms seem to have taken their cue, as others have remarked, from Konstainin Melnikov's Rusakov Worker's Club in Moscow of 1929. Neither Leicester nor its freestanding successor, the Cambridge History Faculty Building which followed in 1964 may be considered works which are particularly sensitive to the contexts in which they are situated. In fact, one could say that each embodies an artificial site within its own constitution, that is to say, an earthwork base which, in each instance, is comprised of podia and ramps.

If the Leicester Engineering building was informed in various ways by both Constructivism and by the British nineteenth century engineering tradition, Cambridge History Faculty was largely determined by the panoptic plan of its top-lit library, ingeniously roofed in greenhouse glazing. This dominant crystalline motif will reappear again in the 12-storey megastructural slab which Stirling designed for the headquarters of the British steel company of Dorman Long. It is ironic and somewhat perverse that this tour de force in patent glazing and exposed steel framework should become an occasion for Stirling to make an argument against any kind of structural verisimilitude. In a 1966 address he stated:

> They asked for the building to be of steel construction and to be an exposition of their standard products. Not only had the building to be made of steel, it had to be seen to be made of steel.... An interesting situation arose when a particular design of the external grid of column and beams was being considered by the structural engineers. It transpired that there was a choice of about six alternatives for this structural mesh... it could be all diagonally braced, or it could have horizontal stiffener beams at every floor level, etc.. The choice of a particular structural appearance was therefore arbitrary.... To resolve this problem we made an architectural decision and kept the horizontal wind stiffener beams adjacent to each floor on the upper part of the building but on the splayed front we omitted them at every other level, replacing them with diagonal structure to maintain the strength of the structural mesh. The scale of structural grid therefore relates to the building section and graphically indicates the smaller accommodation at the top and the larger accommodation below.

While Dorman Long was hardly more than an esquisse, the dormitory facility for Queen's College, Oxford, designed at the same time, would become the last building of the "red trilogy". It was, in effect, a similar condensation of the brick and glass syntax which had been first envisaged for Selwyn. Arranged around a five-sided podium/courtyard facing north over the River Cherwell and inflected towards the tower of Magdalen College, this work, the so-called Florey Building completed in 1971, may be seen as a coiled up version of the Selwyn plan with virtually an identical contrast between a continuous curtain-walled front and a largely opaque rear facade faced in red tile. As in Leicester and Cambridge, this material is also applied to the paved surface of the court and the ramp rising up from the river walk to access a paved ambulatory that bounds the court on all sides. The most singular departure from Selwyn is surely in the dormitory section which steps back as it rises, thereby affording each room a view over the court which opens to the river and the riverside walk. Topographic by definition, this is also a structural tour de force in that the reinforced concrete frame which supports the set-back profile of the dormitory is inclined at the same angle throughout, so that its canted reinforced concrete struts span over both the ambulatory and the overhang of the set-back block. One of the most consistent aspects of the structure is the fact that each facet of the cranked plan, with the exception of its widest face, is supported by pairs of struts equidistantly spaced. The widest facet is carried by three sets of struts, the same distance apart, with Stirling's characteristic stair and elevator shaft being set on either side of the central strut, along with a glazed passerelle affording access from the elevator tower to each floor. As in the rest of the "trilogy", twin-towers are once again deployed in this instance as a kind of signature. As in Selwyn, with comparable ingenuity, lavatories, showers and kitchenettes are built into the sloping rear of the dormitory section. However, unlike Selwyn, a central social focus of the entire complex is the breakfast room, which, clerestory lit and partially sunken into the earthwork, rises above the ambulatory to provide a belvedere terrace on its roof overlooking the river.

While totally eschewing the syntax of the "red trilogy", the 250-student residence, designed in 1964 for St Andrews University in Scotland and built entirely of prefabricated and in situ concrete, must still be seen as the typological and topographic apotheosis of the practice up to the arrival of Leon Krier in the office in 1969. It is significant that these twin, four-to-seven-storey, dormitory blocks, splayed in plan with windows angled so as to gain optimum views over the sea, should be clad throughout in floor-height, precast concrete modules, lifted into position against a reinforced concrete superstructure by mobile cranes. Possibly inspired by Alvar Aalto's 1957 competition entry for the town hall of Marl in Germany, Stirling arrived, in this instance, at a compelling topographic solution which he will not be able to broach again until the Braun AG campus projected in 1986 for Melsungen in Germany. From a structural standpoint, the extraordinary breakthrough at St Andrews was the use of large ribbed prefabricated concrete panels, cast from welded steel moulds. With the perfection of this ingenious technique, Stirling came up with a precast *produktform* which was not only economical but also much more capable of withstanding the rigors of the northern climate. It could also be read tectonically as a metaphor for rusticated stonework. In Stirling's typical understated manner, his description touches only the pragmatic advantages of the system while totally overlooking its cultural connotations.

Labour and material were unavailable in this part of Scotland, and the repetitive elements of the building were therefore prefabricated in Edinburgh and transported to the site. The assemblage method is visually stressed by the contra-diagonal ribbing on the surface of precast concrete units which articulates each unit in the wall. This diagonal ribbing produces controlled patterns of weather-staining and three-inch margins give better edges for handling as well as visually outlining the unit.[1]

In a well-known axonometric, Stirling depicts this precast cladding being hauled into position by a mobile crane. One sees this in retrospect as the swansong of Brutalism in that the axonometric depicts exactly the same crane system as the Smithsons had envisaged for their hypothetical reconstruction of bombed out Coventry in the early 1950s.

In retrospect, one has the sense that Brutalism was out flanked by the arrival of high-tech building systems which, having been first imagined by Archigram after Buckminster Fuller in the early 1960s, were then being realised a decade later in the first works by Team 4 and Renzo Piano. As a consequence of this development, Stirling seems to have adopted one rationalised building methods after another, ranging from his habitual penchant for patent glazing to his brief use of prefabricated concrete panels and his subsequent move towards self-finishing, clip-on GRP moulded panels as these appear first in the Runcorn New Town Housing of 1967 and then in the Olivetti Training School, realised in Haslemere in 1969. Soon after, Stirling, will indulge in a mélange of such techniques with postmodern forms. This odd mixture will first come together in such heterogeneous projects as Derby Town Hall of 1969 and the Olivetti Headquarters for the new town of Milton Keynes of 1971—now with Michael Wilford.

Soon after, with Leon Krier becoming an increasingly influential figure in the office, Stirling seems to have found himself gravitating towards an eclectic historicism of a neoclassical character. This incipient postmodern style, coinciding, as it happens, with the decline of the British welfare state, led to a climate in which Stirling's regionally inflected modernity could no longer be convincingly sustained. With this he began to embrace a neoclassical postmodernity that attained its initial apotheosis in his megastructural proposal for Siemens of 1969. In this instance, we encounter a monumental matrix conceived in part as a mega-machine and in part as a double loaded classical allée complete with cypresses, the perspective rendering of which was populated with otherworldly Wagnerschule figures delineated by Krier. Looking back at his Siemens project, it is hard to imagine a more synchronous introduction to the flowering of his late career in both Germany and the United States.

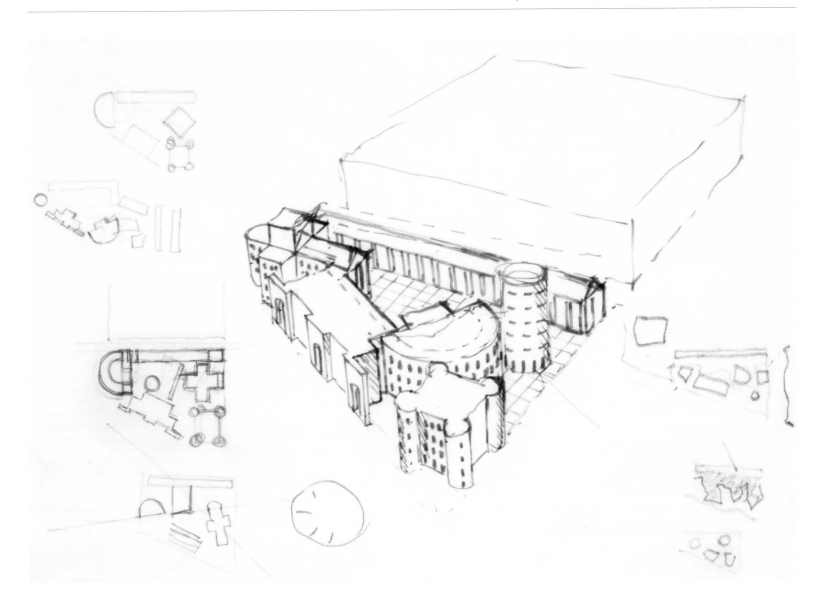

Anticipating by a decade Paolo Portoghesi's 1980 Venice Biennale slogan "The End of Prohibition and the Presence of the Past", Stirling, working in full partnership with Michael Wilford after 1971, projected one archly neoclassical, postmodern set piece after another: from the memorably iconographic entry for the Dusseldorf Nordheim Westfalen Museum Competition of 1975 to his more authoritative, civic proposal for the Wallraf Richartz Museum, Cologne, submitted in the same year. The consistent dressed stone revetment employed in these two projects was already a manifestation of an appropriately restrained neoclassical language, which was only incidentally inflected by free-form entry foyers clad in patent glazing. This was a subtly different variation on the 'new monumentality'; at once neoclassical, yet simultaneously Sittesque, and in each instance carefully integrated into the surrounding urban context. This accomplished civic manner will see its fulfillment in the 1983 completion of Stirling and Wilford's masterly Stuttgart State Gallery. The completion of the Staatsgalerie constitutes a rather decisive break in the nature of Stirling's production: in the first place, because of the exuberance of his plastic inventiveness from this point onwards and, in the second, for the overwhelming output of the Stirling and Wilford office in what was to be the last decade of Striling's life, leading to his untimely death in 1992. This exuberantly ludic but somewhat sardonic creativity amounted to a total of 40 projects, large and small, in the space of ten years, only nine of which will be brought to completion during this period; five in Europe and four in the US.

With Krier's departure from the office in the mid-70s, the elegiac neoclassical strain begins to fade from the practice and is soon replaced by a discernible turn towards the language of Louis Kahn, and via Kahn back to Emil Kaufmann's *Three Revolutionary Architects*, published in 1952, which had been the fundamental source of Kahn's own balancing act between tetrahedral structure and Neoplatonic form as we find this first in Kahn's Yale Art Gallery of the same year. Kahn's "servant vs. served" syndrome had already been an influence on Stirling, as is evident from his rather casual borrowing of brick-faced access towers in his early Brutalist work. However, what also obtains after Stuttgart is a certain penchant for grotesquely mannered primitive form, the proto-modern origin of which would seem to lie in CN Ledoux's Saline de Chaux of 1779 and in the barrières that Ledoux erected around the perimeter of Paris since 1785. In the last analysis, however, the catalyst that seems to have set off the exceptional fertility of Stirling's postmodern imagination from this moment onwards was the exaggerated iconographic manner of Michael Graves from the late 1970s onwards, as we find this in Graves' project for the Fargo Moorhead Cultural Center and in the Plocek House projected for Warren, New Jersey in 1977. It is not that Stirling and Wilford literally follow Graves' entry into the grand mannerist game of oscillating between Piranesi and Ledoux, but that Graves' flamboyant scenography enabled Stirling to dispense totally with any vestige of the original Brutalist ethic.

Thereafter, in one project after another, often enriched by an alternating colour banded treatment, as in the surface of Stuttgart, a schematic, somewhat cacophonic Piranesian freedom became the main compositional stratagem driving each project forward, although in the Wissenschaftzentrum, Berlin (1979–1987) the project seems to take its essential parti from Louis Kahn's 1965–1968 proposal for the Dominican Convent in Media, Pennsylvania. With the Sackler Museum, Harvard University, put in place at virtually the same time, the iconography of Fargo Moorhead is soberly transformed in brick and stone into the totemic front of the new museum building.

Of all the practice's American work, the Sackler establishes most decisively the shift from Brutalism to postmodernism. I have in mind the three-dimensional emblematic frontispiece where the representational essence of the institution is concentrated. The rather incommodious four-storey, straight flight of stairs which follows hardly seems to be an adequate response to such a bold overture, even though a similar Aztec doorway reappears at the end of this seemingly endless climb to the top of the building. Moreover, despite the generous classical enfilade of the galleries themselves, it is hard to accept the Dadaist logic used to justify the random distribution of windows on the Quincy Street elevation, the irregular placement of which depends on the somewhat arbitrary rule of placing the windows in the centre of each room. The net effect in terms of relative decorative status is to render the street front facade of the building as if it were a non-descript back. As for the initial, monumental emblematic front, this surely would have been totally compromised by the projected covered box bridge to the original Sackler Museum.

The other theme cropping up in the work during this period is the idea of returning to some kind of Edenic timber-framed structure; that is to say, having recourse to a faux naïf primordial shed. This is surely the unifying motif of the street facade to the Cornell Center for the Performing Arts, completed on the Ithaca campus, New York in 1988 and this trope surfaces again in a number of other projects; above all in the precocious design for a Municipal Library in Latina of 1986 and in the load-bearing stone loggia with an exposed timber roof which was envisaged as flanking one side of St Paul's Cathedral in Paternoster Square, London. The somewhat perverse motif appears at the Clore Gallery, London in 1980 and also at the Abando Transport Interchange projected for Bilbao in 1985, where a shallow four-storey arcade bounding a square could have provided neither shade nor shelter.

With the development of the site known as No 1 Poultry, projected as a *bâtiment d'angle* in 1986 and realised in London shortly after his death, we encounter a particularly ingenious synthesis of diverse postmodern tropes including a cylindrical atrium excised out of the depth of the triangular city block. From 1983 on, a central cylinder, rendered either as a void or as a solid, will serve as the essential nexus for one civic set piece after another including the Staatsgalerie. It is there in the music school and theatre academy projected for the adjacent site in Stuttgart, 1987, and it is there again in the Science Library projected for the centre of the UCI campus at Irvine in 1988. In the late 80s, it often circumscribes a tectonically symbolic equilateral triangle; the two together constructing and deconstructing themselves in a whole sequence of dynamic compositions, one more ingenious and irreverent than the next as though the master architect was now quite certain that, given the total decadence of the society of spectacle, there was little risk that anyone would actually commission him to realise any of these extravaganzas. The one article of faith that he and Michael Wilford sustain in all of this is their commitment to the reconstruction of the European city, a postmodern critical stance stemming in part from Leon Krier and in part from Colin Rowe's remedial thesis known as *Collage City*, published as a book of this title in 1984. This is surely the essential parti pris of No 1 Poultry, as opposed to Mies van der Rohe's 1969 *tabula rasa* project for the adjacent Mansion House site. It is just this spirit that accounts for the eloquent, somewhat Sitteque play with archetypal elements, i.e. amphitheatre, loggia, *impluvium*, as these appear in their project for the Kaiserplatz in Aachen in 1987.

Stirling and Wilford will finally break with this mannered repertoire at the end of Stirling's life in two exceptional works, which were profoundly affected in each instance by the unique qualities of the context in which they are situated. These

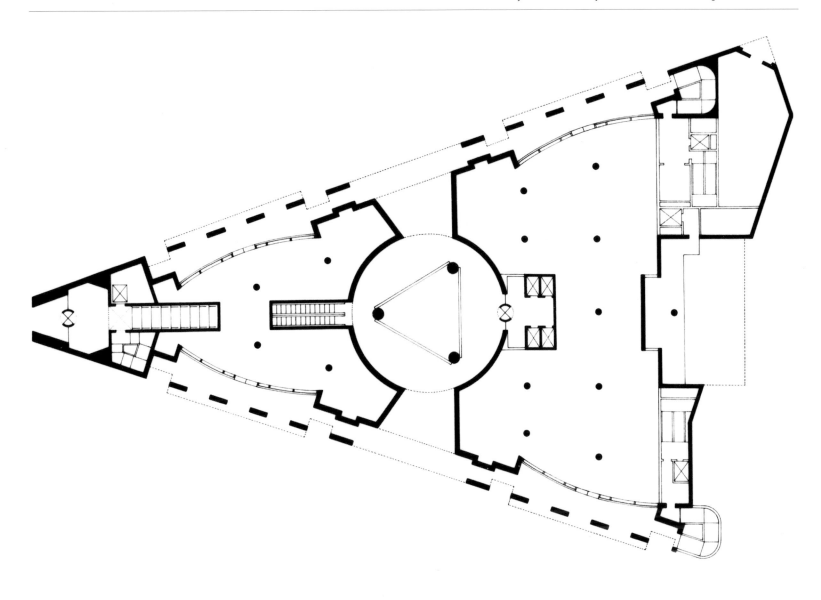

opposite

James Stirling, Wilford
& Associates No 1 Poultry,
London. © Tom Cronin

above

James Stirling, Michael Wilford, and Associates
Michael Wilford and Partners
N°1 Poultry, London, England:
floor plan, 1986–1988.
James Stirling/Michael Wilford fonds
Collection Centre Canadien d'Architecture/
Canadian Centre for Architecture, Montréal © CCA

breaks enabled him to return to the topographic as the primary inspiration of his work from the beginning. These works are the Braun AG campus, designed in association with Walter Nägeli and Renzo Vallabuona and completed outside of Melsungen in 1992, and the Biennale bookshop, completed in the tree covered *giardini pubblici* of the Biennale in Venice, realised in the same year. In both works it is the genus loci that has determined the main thrust of the project; in Melsungen the entire work is essentially conceived as a large-scale, spread-eagled juxtaposition of engineering forms set into a bucolic landscape, whereas in Venice the overall motif of the form oscillates between the thatched corn casons of the Venetian marshes and the vaporetti plying the canals of the city. Stirling's description of this work reads like a last will and testament as he attempts to account for the compact form of this boat-like form of the building, nestled into its site as though it were just another national pavilion:

> Perhaps the fault of modern architecture has been its doctrinaire seriousness, but given a waterside site and a nautical atmosphere, things seem to loosen up; mysteriously, it would seem that the closer modern architecture gets to water and boats, the more amusing it becomes. For it to survive, it will need to reinvigourate itself and become more credible and acceptable. If the Bookshop stimulates the senses and pleases the intelligence, then it maybe fulfilled some of that purpose.[2]

Here surely one encounters a profound auto-critique at the end of the day, inspired by his own achievement of a taut, copper roofed structure with standing seams, covering a shape halfway between an agricultural barn, sustained by elegant timber trusswork, and an upturned barge. Stirling's text reads not only as a critique of the tradition of the initial Modern Movement, but also, by implication, of Brutalism and, above all, of the excesses of a spectacular postmodernism in which he had fully participated. It is an appeal for an architecture that is at once ludic, modest and accessible; the precedent that is to be found in the work of Alvar Aalto who Stirling always admired. To leaven all this, however, there is that touch of wit by which the British have always been able to overcome the embarrassment of art. It is ironic, to say the least, that the last building of his life should be realised on the very same site where the momentary exuberance of postmodernism had its beginnings.

Notes

Introduction

1 Calvino, Italo, *Why Read the Classics*, London: Penguin, 1991, p. 9.

2 Butler, Christopher, *Early Modernism: Literature, Music and Painting in Europe 1900–1916*, Oxford: Oxford University Press, 1994, p. 16.

3 Berman, Alan, ed., *Jim Stirling and the Red Trilogy. Three Radical Buildings*, London: Frances Lincoln, 2010.

4 John Toumey in *Jim Stirling and the Red Trilogy*, p. 104.

5 Sorkin, Michael, "Big Man on campus", *Architectural Review* no.1046, April 1984, p. 28.

6 Vidler, Anthony, *James Stirling Frazer Notes from the Archive*, CCA, New Haven: Yale Center for British Art and Yale University Press, 2010.

7 Lawrence, Amanda Reeser, *James Stirling Revisionary Modernist*, New Haven: Yale University Press, 2012.

8 Long, MJ, *Jim Stirling and the Red Trilogy*, p. 112.

9 Prasad, Sunand, in Berman, *Jim Stirling and the Red Trilogy*, p. 91 This is an exceptionally lucid and concise. exposition of Stirling's skill.

10 St John Wilson, Colin, *Architectural Reflections*, Oxford: Butterworth Heinemann, 1992, p. 3.

11 St John Wilson, *Architectural Reflections*, p. 4.

12 Banham, Reyner, "The Style for the Job", *New Statesman* no. 67, 14 February 1964.

13 Woodman, Ellis, *Modernity and Reinvention The Architecture of James Gowan*, London: Black Dog Publishing, 2008, p. 201.

14 Summerson, John, "Vitruvious Ludens", *The Architectural Review* 173, March 1983, p. 19.

15 Ray, Nicholas, unpublished lecture "Contemporary Approaches to Architectural Theory".

School of Architecture, Rice University

1 Acceptance speech, Royal Gold Medal in Architecture, 1980, entitled "Architectural Aims and Influences" [cited in "Stirling Gold", *Architectural Design*, 1980, vol. 50, no. 7–8; *RIBA Journal*, September 1980; Maxwell, Robert; *James Stirling Writings on Architecture*, Milan: Skira, 1998].

2 "Acceptance Address for the Pritzker Prize" [cited in Maxwell, *James Stirling Writings on Architecture*].

3 Pevsner's categorisation of James Stirling as "rude", and his Cambridge History Faculty Library as "actively ugly" is noted in Susie Harries' *Nikolaus Pevsner: The Life*, Chatto & Windus, 2011.

4 "In 1980... [firm name change to] James Stirling Michael Wilford & Associates—better expressed the close collaboration..."; Maxwell, Robert, *James Stirling Michael Wilford*, Boston: Birkhäuser Verlag, 1998, p. 12.
"No less than five commissions came to Stirling and Wilford in 1979... awaited with eagerness, and on the whole greeted with disappointment... partly, perhaps, in the nature of what Stirling and Wilford were doing"., Girouard, Mark; *Big Jim*: The Life and Work of James Stirling, London: Chatto & Windus, 1998, p. 212.
"Most observers... expect something other than what he has produced in Houston.... Now, this is not a normal debut at all—one of the most eminent architects in the world, trying his hand for the first time in the United States, doing nothing but imitating the older building next door? What could be going on here?", Goldberger, Paul; *GA Document* 5; Fall 1982.
"But something has happened! The master has been somehow seduced: the new projects carry the uniform taint of complacency and the current (American) thing. It's all so well-mannered and genial it doesn't even seem to be there. The standard anecdote among architects making their first pilgrimages to Rice is the one about not being able to find the building.", Sorkin, Michael, "Big Man on Campus", *The Architectural Review*, 1984.

5 "Data", *Progressive Architecture*, December 1981.

6 "Architecture was one of the first disciplines offered at Rice, and its first chairman was William Ward Watkin, representative for Cram, Goodhue & Ferguson who stayed on in Houston.", Papademetriou, Peter, "Texas Contextualism", *Progressive Architecture*, October 1980.

7 Robert Venturi and Denise Scott-Brown had conducted a Third Year Rice Studio in 1969, (Venturi participated in a 1967 Rice design charette, Scott-Brown had known the then Rice Dean while both were students at the University of Pennsylvania) but ultimately were seen as a tough ideological call; Mitchell/Giurgola were regarded as the "safety factor"; Maki was a Visitor but ultimately the job would be logistically difficult for its size; Michael Wilford had been teaching at Rice as Visiting Critic and was well-liked by students.

8 The earliest publication of the scheme was headlined "Rice University School of Architecture renovation and expansion project, 1979; architects: James Stirling and Michael Wilford in collaboration [emphasis added] with Ambrose and McEnany", "Stirling Gold", *Architectural Design*, 7/8, 1980.

9 Diagonally opposite from Anderson Hall, Sewall Hall by Houston architects Lloyd, Morgan & Jones, 1971, simply duplicated the facade of the 1914 Physics Building, adjacent to Anderson Hall.

10 Cram, Ralph Adams, "Have I a Philosophy of Design?", *Pencil Points* 13, November 1932 [cited in Fox, Stephen; *The General Plan of the William M Rice Institute and Its Architectural Development*, 1981, *Architecture at Rice Monograph* 29]. Cram was best known as leading proponent of disciplined Gothic Revival architecture in general and Collegiate Gothic in particular.

11 In 2000, Venturi, Scott-Brown & Associates was hired to renovate Fondren Library, but the design was politely rejected six months later: "It was also felt that the traditional guidelines and expectations for Rice architecture might not be compatible with the Venturi proposal", *News from Fondren*, vol. 10, no. 1, fall 2000. Michael Wilford was then retained, presented a provocative design strategy in 2001 that "matches the material, look and scale of the academic quad while, as it moves west, transitioning into the future." "Board approves new $130 million library", *The Rice Thresher*, 23 March 2001. Regretfully, not built.

12 Acceptance Speech, RIBA.

13 Stirling, James, "The Functional Tradition and Expression", *Perspecta* 6, 1960.

14 Stirling, James, "Regionalism and Modern Architecture", *Architects' Year Book 8*, 1957, which cites Richards, JM, "The Functional Tradition", *The Architectural Review*, July 1957, discussed, with JS photos, in Vidler, Anthony, "III. The Crisis of Rationalism", *James Frazer Stirling Notes From the Archive*, 2010; both cited by Lawrence, Amanda Reeser; *James Stirling Revisionary Modernist*, 2012, p. 67.

15 Acceptance Speech, RIBA.

16 The Campus Business Manager, as he micro-managed the project's budget, was referred to as "Dr No" by the author, as one of JSMW's young Rice Faculty advocates.

17 "The building upon which Stirling performed his act was a half-hearted version of historicism —a characteristic of American collegiate architecture in the years immediately after World War Two... ", Gebhard, David, "Critique", *Progressive Architecture*, December 1981.

18 Stirling had, in spite of the vicissitudes of the 1950s, a firm grounding in Modernism, as noted, "Jim told him [Alberto Sartoris] how much his book *Encyclopedie de l'Architecture Nouvelle* [sic: *Elementi dell'architettura funzionale*] had meant to him,... so Jim produced the book, to show how he had valued it so much that he had it bound in white fur fabric...", Girouard; *Big Jim: The Life and Work of James Stirling*, London: Chatto & Windus, 1998, p. 268.

19 Such as Wolfsburg's Library, Mount Angel, or Rovaniemi, Stirling had received the 1978 Alvar Aalto Medal.

20 Ham Common, 1955, where three living units are rhetorically connected by an articulated "bridge", little more than a stair landing and the multi-level interior vertical lobby of common spaces at Leicester, 1959, Olivetti/ Haslemere, 1969, or Olivetti/Milton Keynes, 1971, for example.

21 Another Modernist quotation: Pierre Chareau's Maison de Verre: refer to the cross-hatch areas on both floor plans, Sartoris included the Chareau design in *Elementi dell'architettura funzionale*.

22 Actually "Burnt Caramel" (Benjamin-Moore paint 2167-10) and "Pink Pansy" (Benjamin-Moore paint 2083-50); described in detail Girouard; *Big Jim*, pp. 212, 213; the entire interiors are now totally white.

23 A carry-over from other projects: State Gallery & Chamber Theatre, Stuttgart, 1977–1983, terrace level entry canopy; Arthur M Sackler Museum, Harvard, 1979–1984, rear loading dock service bay canopy; Wissenschaftszentrum (WZB), Berlin, 1979–1987, courtyard entry canopy.

24 "It is said that when Philip. Johnson was visiting Rice and looked for it, he could not find it, because it was so like everything else.", Girouard, *Big Jim*, p. 213.

25 Stirling was in Section 8, This is Tomorrow, 1956, Whitechapel Gallery; as a loose member of The Independent Group, which he characterised as "... a bit casual and tongue-in-cheek about the project...", "Retrospective Statements", T*he Independent Group: Post-war Britain and the Aesthetics of Plenty*, 1990; Robbins, David, ed., also: "The 'As Found' and the 'Found'", Smithson, Alison and Peter; notwithstanding Stirling's antipathy to Alison, Girouard, *Big Jim*, pp. 69, 70. "Stirling and Wilford had not, in fact, been involved with fully air-conditioned buildings before."; Papademetriou, Peter C, "Stirling in Another Context", *Progressive Architecture*, December 1981.

26 A direct 'crib' from Robert Venturi's Guild House, 1961; both architects were Fellows at Yale University in the late 1960s.

27 "... a circular lunette set just below the springing [of the tall recessed arch], not bang on centre, as might be expected, but off to one side.", Maxwell, *James Stirling Michael Wilford*, p. 82, Maxwell's observation is unfortunately confused by reproduction of an axonometric view illustrating the initial version with centered window.

28 The issues emerged early on, as both the Associate Architects and Contractor, as well as the Campus Business Manager, predetermined choices; additionally, "Stirling and Wilford had not, in fact, been involved with fully air-conditioned buildings before.", "Stirling in Another Context", Papademetriou, Peter C, *Progressive Architecture*, December 1981.

29 Crinson, Mark, *James Stirling Early Unpublished Writings on Architecture*, 2010, Routledge and Girouard, "Chapter Eleven-After Stuttgart", p. 211. Interestingly, Anderson Hall/Rice is not included in any of the six editions of Charles Jencks' *The Language of Post-Modern Architecture*, although Stuttgart is featured, and Cesar Pelli's Herring Hall/Rice University (Jesse Jones School of business and Public Administration/1982–1984) is illustrated in the 1991 edition.

30 "At least externally his easy-going contextualism at Rice seems more American in its historical overtones than his current projects now being designed for Harvard and Columbia.", Gebhard, "Critique".

31 The author recalls, "When I interviewed JS, I eventually came 'round to ask him to comment on a photostat drawing; it was the Söder isometric, a dead ringer for the 'spine' Axon. I said, 'Oh, would you care to comment on this?'; Michael blanched slightly, and Jim simply said, 'Hruumph!',... to which I responded, 'Thank you very much'."

32 Hitchcock, Henry-Russell, "American Architecture in the Early Sixties", *Zodiac 10*, 1962.

33 Collins, Peter, *Changing Ideals in Modern Architecture*, 1967, McGill University Press.

34 From a talk at Rice School of Architecture, 1979; cited in Maxwell; *James Stirling Writings on Architecture*, pp. 158, 159.

Arthur M Sackler Museum, Harvard University

1 Brush, Kathryn, *Vastly More Than Brick & Mortar: Reinventing the Fogg Art Museum in the1920s*, Cambridge, Massachusetts: Harvard University Art Museums, 2003.

2 *The Arthur M. Sackler Museum, Harvard University*, Cambridge, Massachusetts: Harvard University Art Museums, 1985. Introduction by Seymour Slive; essays by John Coolidge and John M. Rosenfield; discussion between James Stirling and Michael Dennis. Quotes from Seymour Slive,John Coolidge, John M. Rosenfield and James Stirling, pp. 6, 29-32, 37, 41.

3 The author interviewed Seymour Slive on May 22, 2012; John Rosenfield on May 25, 2012; and Donald Tellalian and Frederick (Tad) Stahl on June 26, 2012.

4 Girouard, Mark, *Big Jim: The Life and Work of James Stirling*, London: Chatto & Windus, 1998, p. 213.

5 Huxtable, Ada Louise, "A Style Crystallised", *New York Times*, 31 May 1981. (Republished in James Stirling, Architectural Design Profile, 1982.)

6 Rowe, Colin, "Introduction" in Arnell, Peter and Ted Bickford, *James Stirling: Buildings and Projects*, New York: Rizolli, 1984, pp. 22, 23. Kenneth Frampton postcard, p. 295.

7 Coolidge, John, *Patrons and Architects: Designing Art Museums in the Twentieth Century*, Fort Worth, Texas: Amon Carter Museum, 1989, pp. 110-122.

8 Rowe, Colin, "Who, But Stirling?" *Architectural Record*, March 1986. (Republished in *Architecture + Urbanism 86:11*, and in *As I Was Saying*, Cambridge, Massachusetts: MIT Press, 1996, Vol. 2.

Center for the Performing Arts, Cornell University

1 Girouard, Mark, *Big Jim: The life and work of James Stirling*, London: Chatto & Windus, 1998, p. 226

2 *James Stirling Michael Wilford & Associates*, London: Academy Editions, 1990, p. 10.

3 *James Stirling*, London: RIBA Publications Ltd, 1974, p. 16

4 Girouard, *Big Jim: The life and work of James Stirling*, p. 228.

5 *James Stirling Michael Wilford & Associates*, p. 10.

6 *James Stirling Michael Wilford & Associates*, p. 10.

American Dreams?

1 Arnell, Peter and Ted Bickford, ed., *James Stirling, Buildings and Projects*, New York: Rizzoli, 1984, p. 162.

2 Arnell and Bickford, *James Stirling, Buildings and Projects*, p. 162.

3 Girouard, Mark, *Big Jim: The Life and Work of James Stirling*, London: Chatto & Windus, 1998, p. 43.

4 Girouard, *Big Jim*, p. 42

5 Girouard, *Big Jim*, p. 44.

6 Girouard, *Big Jim*, p. 45.

7 Crinson, Mark, *James Stirling*, Routledge, 2010, p. 19.

8 *British Architecture Today Six Protagonists, James Stirling, Michael Wilford Associates*. Milan: Electa, 1991, p. 156.

9 Girouard, *Big Jim*, p. 46.

10 Girouard, *Big Jim*, p. 56.

11 Alloway, Lawrence, *This is Tomorrow*, Introduction 1, 1956, (no page number).

12 McCallum, Ian, *Architecture USA*, London: The Architectural Press, 1959, p. 9.

13 Crinson, *James Stirling*, p. 37.

14 Girouard, *Big Jim*, p. 120.

15 Stirling, James, "The Functional Tradition and Expression", *Perspecta 6*, New Haven: Yale University Press, 1960, pp. 102, 104.

16 Girouard, *Big Jim*, p. 127

17 Arnell and Bickford, *James Stirling, Buildings and Projects*, p. 269.

18 Louis L Kahn Collection, University of Pennsylvania and the Pennsylvania Historical and Museum Commission, Office drawings folder 865.003.

19 McCarter, Robert, *Louis Kahn*, London: Phaidon, 2005, p. 7.

Jim Stirling: Synchrony and Diachrony

1 Etlin, Richard A, "Le Corbusier, Choisy, and French Hellenism: The Search for a New Architecture", *The Art Bulletin*, June 1987, vol. LXIX, no. 2.

2 Reported by Robert Kahn, who studied with Stirling at Yale in 1979 and was as one of his teaching assistants in 1983.

3 Bakhtin's notion of "synchronous diachrony" was a critique of the modern linguistic Ferdinand de Saussure's strict separation of synchrony/diachrony (cf. language/parole).

4 Panofsky, Erwin, *Perspective as Symbolic Form*, New York: Zone Books; Cambridge: MIT Press, 1991, p. 3.

Solidified Space: The Use of the Void in Stirling and Wilford's American Work

1 Colquhoun, Alan, "Architecture as a Continuous Text", *ANY*, no. 2, September 1993, p. 18.

2 Moneo, Rafael, *Theoretical Anxiety and Design Strategies in the Work of Eight Contemporary Architects*, Cambridge: MIT Press, 2004.

3 Stirling, James, "Design Philosophy and Recent Work" in *Architectural Design Special Issue*, London: Academy Editions, 1990, p. 8.

4 Lawrence, Amanda Reeser, *James Stirling Revisionary Modernist*, New Haven: Yale University Press, 2013, p. 11.

5 Stirling, James, "Regionalism and Modern Architecture", *Architects Year Book 8*, 1957, pp. 62–68.

6 Girouard, Mark, *Big Jim: The Life and of James Stirling*, London: Chatto and Windus, 1998, p. 36. Notably he did not include Wittkower's much better known book *Architectural Principles in the Age of Humanism*.

7 Girouard, *Big Jim*, pp. 79–80.

8 Stirling, "Regionalism and Modern Architecture", p. 68.

9 Fraser, Murray and Joe Kerr, *Architecture and the "Special Relationship": The American Influence on Post-War British Architecture*, London: Routledge, 2007, p. 10.

10 Stirling, James and Michael Dennis, "Notes from an Informal Discussion" in *The Arthur M. Sackler Museum*, Harvard University, The President and Fellows of Harvard College, 1985, p. 37.

11 Goldberger, Paul, "James Stirling Made an Art Form of Bold Gestures", *The New York Times*, July 19, 1992.

12 Tafuri, Manfredo, "L'Architecture dans le Boudoir: The Language of Criticism and the Criticism of Language", *Oppositions 3*, October 1974, p. 292.

13 Colquhoun, "Architecture as a Continuous Text", p. 19.

14 Goldberger, "James Stirling Made an Art Form of Bold Gestures".

15 Stirling, James, "Acceptance of the Royal Gold Medal in Architecture 1980", *Architectural Design 7–8*, 1980, p. 6.

16 Colin Rowe and Fred Koetter, "Collage City", *The Architectural Review* 158, August 1975, p. 68.

17 Stirling, James, *James Stirling: Writings on Architecture*, Robert Maxwell ed., Milan: Skira, 1998, p. 156.

18 Moretti, Luigi, "The Structures and Sequences of Spaces", Thomas Stevens trans., *Oppositions 3*, October 1974, pp. 109–139; Moretti, Luigi, "Strutture e sequenze di spazi", *Spazio 7*, 1952–53.

19 Stirling, James, "The Functional Tradition and Expression", *Perspecta* 6, 1960, pp. 91–92.

20 Stirling similarly described Leicester as an "iceberg," diminishing in size as it rose. Stirling, James, *An Architect's Approach to Architecture*, 72, May 1965, p. 233.

21 Rowe, Colin, "James Stirling: A Highly Personal and Very Disjointed Memoir", in *James Stirling: Buildings and Projects*, Peter Arnell and Ted Bickford eds., New York: Rizzoli, 1984, p. 21.

22 Stirling, *Architects Approach to Architecture*, p. 233.

A Modern Mannerist

1 Maxwell, Robert, ed., *James Stirling: Writings on Architecture*, Milan: Skira, 1998, p. 49.

2 Maxwell, *The Architectural Review*, April 2011, p. 75.

An English Eclectic Abroad

1 Kimball, Roger, "A Stirling performance at Cornell" in *The New Criterion*, June 1989.

2 Maxwell, Robert, "Situating Stirling", *The Architectural Review*, March 2011.

3 "From Garches to Jaoul: Le Corbusier as Domestic Architect in 1927 and 1953", *The Architectural Review*, September 1955.

4 Stirling referred to these houses in his address given on the occasion of his 1980 Royal Gold Medal, subsequently published in Maxwell, Robert, ed., *James Stirling: Writings on Architecture*, Milan: Skira, 1998, pp. 148–149.

5 Rafael Moneo, for example, whose admiration for Stirling is principally on account of his ability to absorb lessons from such diverse sources and maintain a compositional unity, lists these influences; Archigram's projects were not published until Leicester was on site, but Moneo's point was presumably that Leicester illustrates the spirit of that movement, "where the exaggerated presence of mechanical installations in itself became an image". Moneo, Rafael, *Theoretical Anxieties and Design Strategies in the work of eight contemporary architects*, Barcelona: ACTAR, 2004.

6 Born in Scotland, though there is nothing Scottish in his architecture, Stirling was brought up in Liverpool. Pedantically, Stirling is more correctly 'British' than 'English'. The question of national identification remains fraught in the (as yet remaining) "United Kingdom".

7 Pevsner, Nikolaus, *Pioneers of Modern Design*, London: Faber, 1936.

8 Lethaby, W R, *Philip Webb and his work*, London: Raven Oak Press Ltd, 1979. Chapter Five is entitled "Some architects of the nineteenth century and two ways of building"; Lethaby contrasts the inheritors of a moral Gothic tradition, such as Webb and Butterfield, who believed that "living architecture must have more in it than imitated style", with those, such as Shaw, who were prepared to accommodate themselves more readily to classical tastes.

9 Summerson, John, "The Mind of Wren" in *Heavenly Mansions*, London: Cresset Press, 1949.

10 Lethaby, *Philip Webb and his work*, p. 75.

11 Blomfield, Reginald, *Richard Norman Shaw R. A.: Architect 1831–1912*, London: B T Batsford, 1940.

12 *The Architectural Review*, June 1941, pp. 41–6.

13 Saint, Andrew, *Richard Norman Shaw*, New Haven and London: Yale University Press, 1976.

14 I noted this remark by Voysey some years ago, but have failed to locate its source subsequently.

15 Lethaby, *Philip Webb and his work*, p. 76.

16 Baker, Geoffrey H, *The Architecture of James Stirling and His Partners James Gowan and Michael Wilford*, Farnham: Ashgate, 2011, pp. 180, 394–5.

17 The particular strength of the Stirling and Gowan practice could then be seen as a product of the unique combination of the two strands of architecture deriving ultimately from the office of Street.

18 Quoted in Summerson, J, *The Classical Language of Architecture*, Cambridge MA: MIT Press, 1966

19 See Lutyens' review, "The work of the late Philip Webb", *Country Life* vol. 37, 1915, p. 619.

20 Pevsner, Nikolaus, "Building with Wit", *The Architectural Review*, April 1951.

21 See Berman, Alan ed., *Jim Stirling and the Red Trilogy: Three Radical Buildings*, London: Francis Lincoln, 2010. See also my essay "The Cambridge History Faculty, a case study in ethical dilemmas in the 20th century", in *Architecture and its Ethical Dilemmas*, Nicholas Ray ed., London: Taylor and Francis, 2005.

22 For trenchant criticism of a number of modernist university buildings by the pupils of Gropius, including I M Pei's 1973 Herbert F. Johnson Museum of Art at Cornell, see Herdeg, Klaus, *The Decorated Diagram*, Cambridge MA: MIT Press, 1985.

23 Sorkin, Michael, "The Big Man on Campus" in *Exquisite Corpse — writing on buildings*, London & New York: Verso, 1991.

Stirling Under Review

1 Tafuri, Manfredo, "...e...", *Casabella*, 747, September 2006, pp. 69–77 (English translation of the text at pp. 92–93). Crinson, Mark, "The Uses of Nostalgia. Stirling and Gowan's Preston Housing", *Journal of the Society of Architectural Historians*, vol. 65, n. 2, June 2006, pp. 216–237, addresses Stirling's reinterpretation of the past. Most importantly, in the same paper, he states that "Any attempt to write in depth about Stirling's work immediately reveals the scarcity of scholarly writing about him—astonishing given his prominence" (p. 234). This gap has been partially filled with some publications over the past years, but we are still in the process of a critical re-evaluation of Stirling's work. See, in this perspective Crinson, Mark, *James Stirling: early unpublished writings on architecture*, London: Routledge, 2010, pp. 74–75, 108–139, which presents previously unavailable writings by him, in particular the transcription of the Black notebook, written between late 1953 and March 1956 (pp. 17–68); Vidler, Antony, *James Frazer Stirling: notes from the Archive*, New Haven and London: Yale University Press, 2010; Crinson, Mark, *Stirling and Gowan: architecture from austerity to affluence*, New Haven and London: Yale University Press, 2012; and Reeser Lawrence, Amanda, *James Stirling Revisionary Modernist*, New Haven and London: Yale University Press, 2013.

2 Stirling's four volumes of the *Œuvre Complète* are now in a private collection. The inscriptions in the books are as follows: vol. 1: "J.F. Stirling" (no date or address); vol. 2: "Lieut. J.F. Stirling" and the address "24 Childwall Priory Road, Childwall, Liverpool 16" (no date); vol. 3: "J.F. Stirling" (no date or address); vol. 4: "J.F. Stirling" (no date or address). Volumes 1, 2 and 4 are 1946 editions, volume 3 is 1947 edition. The address in Childwall Priory Road, Liverpool, was Stirling's parents' house; the bookseller's name is enclosed in the books. I have to thank Neil Jackson for the precious information. For Stirling's citation on architectural books see Girouard, Mark, *Big Jim: The life and work of James Stirling*, London: Chatto & Windus, 1998, pp. 36, 303.

3 Recently discovered visual documentation reveals that Le Corbusier was already extremely interested not only in paradigmatic architectures from the past, but also in the natural realm, during the interwar period: see Benton, Tim, "Le Corbusier's secret photographs", in *Le Corbusier and the Power of Photography*, Nathalie Herschdorfer and Lada Umstätter eds., London: Thames & Hudson, 2012, pp. 32–53, especially pp. 46–49. This concept will be exemplified by Le Corbusier commenting his sketch of a bone; Le Corbusier, *My Work*, London: Architectural Press, 1960, p. 209: "Everywhere objects like these are spread before us. If you have a pencil in your hand, look at them and you will understand; you will then have storehouse of inspiration to draw upon, the lesson taught by natural phenomena. The chance occurrence, too: the broken shell, the shoulder of beef sliced by the butcher's saw, have riches to offer which the mind cannot conceive."

4 Maxwell, Robert, "Situating Stirling", *The Architectural Review*, April 2011, pp. 72–75. On the importance of Stirling's visual materials see the insightful essay by Brian Hatton on the same issue of *The Architectural Review*, pp. 76–79. Hatton evokes Stirling's Liverpool (recorded in photographs) as source of inspiration for his future architectural practice. We could add Stirling's own words in the early 1950s: "Dimension alone is meaningless in architecture. Only visual or comprehensible proportion is valid"; see Crinson, Mark, *James Stirling: early unpublished writings on architecture*, p. 18. See also Stirling, James, "The functional tradition and expression", *Perspecta* vol. 6, 1960, pp. 88–97.

5 Personal memory of Nick Bullock: I would like to thank him and Nicholas Ray for the extremely fruitful exchange of ideas on this text. Rowe's remains one of the very best assessments of Stirling's architecture and its importance, as states Antony Vidler, *James Frazer Stirling: notes from the Archive*, p. 24.

6 Stirling, James, "Connexions", *The Architectural Review*, May 1975, pp. 273–276; reprinted in Maxwell, Robert, ed., *Stirling: Writings on Architecture*, Milan: Skira, 1998.

7 Like Le Corbusier, Stirling was extremely attentive to direct the photographers in shooting images of his work. See Iuliano, Marco, and Penz, François, "The Cambridge Experiment", *Arts*, 3, 2014, pp. 307–334 (open access issue on architectural photography). It is also interesting to note here that Stirling himself spoke, on a later occasion, about his disappointment, "a sad shock" at seeing the Pavillon Suisse, which he had previously known from the *Complete Works*. It was simply a different object, out of context and far from the glossy images he remembered. See Mark Crinson, *James Stirling: early unpublished writings on architecture*, p. 41.

8 Girouard, Mark, *Big Jim*, p. 187; Luigi Biscogli, "L'Opera di James Stirling", *Casabella* 315, June 1967, pp. 30–55 (pp. 48–49 for Leicester).

9 Summerson, John, "Vitruvious Ludens", *The Architectural Review*, March 1983, pp. 19–21. In this issue three projects are discussed: Fogg, Columbia and the Museum at Stuttgart, pp. 22–41.

10 Johnson is cited in Arnell, Peter and Ted Bickford eds., *James Stirling, Buildings and Projects*, New York: Rizzoli International, 1984, p. 285; Rowe, Colin, "Las cenizas del genio", *Arquitectura Viva* (Special Issue: James Stirling), 42, July–August 1993, pp. 3–6: "At Rice, in that quasi-Byzantine milieu, the extensions to the architecture building are so unassertive that it becomes difficult to discover them"; see also Marzo, Mauro ed., *L'Architettura come testo e la figura di Colin Rowe*, Venice: Marsilio, 2010, and Sorkin, Michael, "The Big Man on Campus", *The Architectural Review*, April 1984, pp. 25–28.

11 Dietsch, Deborah K, "A Stirling performance", *Architectural Record*, October 1989, p. 98–107 and Maxwell, Robert, "Compact at Ithaca", *The Architectural Review*, November 1989, pp. 38–47.

12 James Stirling, address given at the ceremony for the presentation of the 1980 Royal Gold Medal, now in Robert Maxwell ed., *Stirling: Writings on Architecture*, pp. 148–149.

13 James Stirling, Michael Wilford and Associates, School of Architecture Addition, Rice University, Houston, Texas: plan and elevation sketches, 1979–1981, AP140.S2.SS1.D56.P2.1; elevation studies, 1979–1981, AP140.S2.SS1.D56.P8.4. In an interview held in 1998 with Michael Wilford, Geoffrey Baker asked him in which projects he had a major involvement: "I worked on Leicester, Cambridge and Dorman Long. I worked on Runcorn Housing, then the museums. I worked on Rice. I led the Olivetti Milton Keynes, Columbia, Cornell and Irvine projects". Baker, Geoffrey H, *The architecture of James Stirling and his partner James Gowan and Michael Wilford: a study of architectural creativity in the twentieth century*, Farnham: Ashgate, p. 382. For the Rice project see Mark Girouard, *Big Jim*, pp. 212–213: "Jim, as always, made the input, but the project was run by Wilford and he was much involved in the design".

14 Le Corbusier and Pierre Jeanneret, *Œuvre Complète 1910–1929*, Willy Boesiger and Oscar Stonorov eds., Zurich: Girsberger, 1937, p. 189.

15 Papademetriou, Peter, "Stirling in another context", *Progressive Architecture*, December 1981, pp. 53–61 and "Stirling at Rice", *The Architectural Review*, February 1982, pp. 51–57; see also *Architectural Design*, 7–8, 1980.

16 Rowe, Colin, "Las cenizas del genio", p. 6. In the same article, Rowe expresses a clear satisfaction speaking about "Jim as architectural conoisseur. He knew where all the bits and pieces of St. Paul's came from: for the west front a combination of east facade and the Louvre and Sant'Agnese in Piazza Navona; Pietro da Cortona's semi-circular of Santa Maria della Pace for the transept; and, for less eminent areas the facade from Palazzo Thiene Vicenza and a casual quote, a false perspective window from Palazzo Barberini", p. 5.

Modernity and post-modernity in the work of James Stirling and Michael Wilford

1 Jacobus, John, *James Stirling: buildings & projects, 1950–1974*, London: Thames & Hudson, 1975, p. 104.

2 Wilford, Michael and Thomas Muirhead, *James Stirling, Michael Wilford, and Associates: buildings & projects, 1975–1992*. London: Thames & Hudson, 1994, p. 251.

Bibliography

Books

Arnell, Peter and Ted Bickford, ed., *James Stirling, Buildings and Projects*, New York: Rizzoli, 1984.

Baker, Geoffrey H, *The Architecture of James Stirling and His Partners James Gowan and Michael Wilford*, Farnham, UK and Burlington, VT: Ashgate, 2011.

Berman, Alan, ed., *Jim Stirling and the Red Trilogy. Three Radical Buildings*, London: Frances Lincoln, 2010.

Brush, Kathryn, *Vastly More Than Brick & Mortar: Reinventing the Fogg Art Museum in the 1920s*, New Haven, CT: Yale University Press, 2003.

Collins, Peter, *Changing Ideals in Modern Architecture*, Montreal, Quebec: McGill University Press, 1967.

Chatel, Kersten Geers, Amanda Lawrence, Patrick Lynch, *The Architecture of James Stirling, 1964–1992*, OASE 79, Rotterdam: NAI Publishers, 2009.

Crinson, Mark, ed., *James Stirling Early Unpublished Writings on Architecture*, London: Routledge, 2010.

Crinson, Mark, and Claire Zimmerman, ed., *Neo-avant-garde and Post Modernism: Post War Architecture in Britain beyond*, New Haven, CT and London: Yale Center for British Art, 2010.

Crinson, Mark, *Stirling and Gowan: Architecture from Austerity to Affluence*, New Haven, CT and London: Yale University Press, 2012.

Crosby, Theo, ed., text by Lawrence Alloway, Reyner Banham, David Lewis, *This is tomorrow*, London: Whitechapel Art Gallery, 1956.

Fox, Stephen, *Architecture at Rice Monograph 29: The General Plan of the William M. Rice Institute and Its Architectural Development*, Houston, TX: Rice University Press, 1980.

Girouard, Mark, *Big Jim: The life and work of James Stirling*, London: Chatto & Windus, 1998.

Gordon, Leonie, ed., *The Arthur M Sackler Museum, Harvard University: design by James Stirling, Michael Wilford Associates*, Cambridge, MA: Harvard University Art Museum, 1985.

Harvard University, *The Sackler Museum, Cambridge*, Cambridge, MA: Harvard University Arts Museums, 1985.

Irace, Fulvio and Colin Almery, *British architecture today: six protagonists: Norman Foster, Nicholas Grimshaw, Michael Hopkins, John Outram, Richard Rogers, James Stirling & Michael Wilford*, Milan: Electa in collaboration with the British Council, 1991.

Jencks, Charles, *Modern Movements in Architecture*, New York: Penguin, 1973.

Jencks, Charles, *The Language of Post-Modern Architecture*, New York: Rizzoli, 1977.

Maxwell, Robert, essays by Michael Wilford and Thomas Muirhead, *James Stirling Michael Wilford and Associates: Buildings & Projects 1975–1992*, London: Thames and Hudson, 1994.

Maxwell, Robert, *James Stirling: Writings on Architecture*, Milan: Skira, 1998.

Maxwell, Robert, *James Stirling, Michael Wilford*, Basel: Birkhauser, 1998.

McCallum, Ian, *Architecture USA*, London: The Architectural Press, 1959.

Moneo, Rafael, *Theoretical Anxiety and Design Strategies in the Work of Eight Contemporary Architects*, Cambridge, MA: MIT Press, 2004.

Papadakis, Andreas C, ed., *James Stirling Michael Wilford & Associates*, London: Academy Editions, 1990.

Ray, Nicholas, ed., *Architecture and Its Ethical Dilemmas*, Abingdon, UK and New York: Routledge, 2005.

Lawrence, Amanda Reeser, *James Stirling Revisionary Modernist*, New Haven, CT: Yale University Press, 2012.

RIBA, introduction by Reyner Banham, *James Stirling: RIBA Drawings Collection*, London: RIBA Publications, 1974.

Jacobus, John, *James Stirling: Buildings and Projects 1950–1974*, Oxford: Oxford University Press, 1975.

Stern, Robert AM, with W Gastil, *Modern Classicism*, New York: Rizzoli, 1988.

Vidler, Anthony, *James Frazer Stirling: Notes from the Archive*, New Haven, CT: Yale University Press, 2010.

Wilford, Michael, and partners, *Wilford Stirling Wilford*, London: Michael Wilford & Partners, 1996.

Articles

Abrams, Janet, "Indecision mists Fogg Museum's extension plan", *Building Design*, No. 583, 26 February 1982, p. 28.

Abrams, Janet, "Getty Museum planned for LA", *Architects' Journal*, Vol. 179, No. 3, 18 January 1984, p. 31.

Biscogli, Luigi, "The work of James Stirling", *Casabella*, No. 315, 1967, pp. 30–55.

Buchanan, Peter, "Stirling triumphs again: Genesis of the designs for Fogg museum extension on show", *The Architectural Review*, Vol. 169, No. 1011, May 1981, pp. 258–259.

Cannon-Brookes, Peter, and Michael Williams, "The Arthur M Sackler Museum", *International journal of museum management and curatorship*, Vol. 5, No. 4, December 1986, pp. 319–336.

Cohn, David, "Four recent American museums", El *Croquis*, Vol. 6, No. 3, August/October 1987, pp. 116–139.

Dal Co, Francesco, "Special issue: James Stirling", *The Architectural Review*, Vol. 191, No. 1150, December 1992, pp. 4–13, 17–78.

Dennis, Michael, and James Stirling, "Sackler sequence", *The Architectural Review*, Vol. 180, No. 1073, July 1986, pp. 26–33.

Dietsch, Deborah, "A Stirling Performance: Cornell University Center for the Performing Arts, Ithaca, New York", *Architectural Record*, October 1989, pp. 98–107.

Dober, Richard P, "April was a Stirling month. James Stirling has nearly completed his designs for the Fogg Museum", *Building*, Vol. 240, No. 7189, 8 May 1981, pp. 14–15.

Doubilet, Susan, "Stirling and Wilford in progress", *Progressive Architecture*, Vol. 65, No. 10, October 1984, pp. 86–87.

Du Toit, Roger, "Competitions. The Toronto Ballet Opera House", *Canadian Architect*, Vol. 33, No. 8, August 1988, pp. 16–35.

Fisher, Thomas, "Stirling performs at Cornell", *Progressive Architecture*, Vol. 70, No. 6, June 1989, pp. 21, 26, 28.

Gandee, Charles K, "Best laid plans: Arthur M Sackler Museum, Harvard University, Cambridge, Massachusetts", *Architectural Record*, Vol. 174, No. 3, March 1986, pp. 112–123.

Goldberger, Paul, and Peter Papademetriou, "School of Architecture, Rice University, Houston, Texas, 1981", *GA Document*, No. 5, 1982, pp. 50–71.

Goldberger, Paul, "Architecture View: James Stirling made an art form of bold gestures", *The New York Times*, 19 July 1992

Grey, Christopher S, "Apartments in New York: investigation of an urban type", *International Architect*, Vol. 1, No. 5, 1981, pp. 27–36.

Hitchcock, Henry-Russell, "American Architecture in the Early Sixties", *Zodiac*, No. 10, 1962, pp. 5–17.

Jacobus, John, "Stirling at Harvard: the Sackler wing", *Progressive Architecture*, Vol. 66, No. 10, October 1985, pp. 27–28.

Kimball, Roger "A Stirling performance at Cornell", *The New Criterion*, Vol. 7, June 1989, pp. 56–60.

Maxwell, Robert, Brian Hatton and others: "Situating Stirling: new perspectives on his legacy", *The Architectural Review*, Vol. 229, No. 1370, April 2011, pp. 72–81.

Maxwell, Robert, "Compact at Ithaca", *The Architectural Review*, November 1989, p. 37–37

Miller, Michael W, "Addition to Fogg Museum, Harvard, USA", *Architectural Design* (news supplement), No. 6, 1981, p. IV.

Morris, Neil, "Stirling, Wilford in top three for Getty Arts Center", *Building Design*, No. 688, 4 May 1984, p. 3.

Muirhead, Thomas, Colin Rowe and Robert Kahn "Special issue: James Stirling Michael Wilford & Associates: Stirling since Stuttgart", *A&U*, No. 11, November 1986, pp. 21–156.

Papademetriou, Peter, critique by David Gebhard, "Stirling in Another Context. Remodelling and Extension of Rice's Architecture School", *Progressive Architecture*, Vol. 62, No. 12, December 1981, pp. 53–61.

Papademetriou, Peter, "Stirling at Rice", *The Architectural Review*, Vol. 171, No. 1020, February 1982, pp. 50–57.

Pawley, Martin, "Not the Last Word", *Architecture New York*, Vol. 1, No. 2, September/ October 1993, p. 62.

Rocca, Alessandro, "Irvine Campus, California. Irvine, plan and architecture of the campus", *Lotus*, No. 89, May 1996, pp. 6–49.

Rowe, Colin, "Who, but Stirling?", *Architectural Record*, Vol. 174, No. 3, March 1986, pp. 112–123 .

Scolari, Massimo, "The Extension of the Fogg Museum, Harvard", *Casabella*, Vol. 46, No. 480, May 1982, pp. 2–13.

Sorkin, Michael, "Anderson Hall Expansion: School of Architecture, Rice University", *Arts and Architecture*, Vol. 1, No. 2, Winter 1981, pp. 47–49.

Sorkin, Michael, "The big man on campus: the work of James Stirling and Michael Wilford in America", *The Architectural Review*, Vol. 175, No. 1046, April 1984, pp. 24–28.

Spens, Michael, "James Stirling's Sackler Museum now under threat in the groves of academe", *The Architectural Review*, Vol. 229, No. 1371, May 2011, pp. 20–22.

Stirling, James, "The functional tradition and expression", *Perspecta*, Vol. 6, 1960, pp. 88–97.

Stirling, James, "Stirling Connexions", *The Architectural Review*, Vol. 157, No. 939, May 1975, pp. 273–276.

Stirling, James, Michael Wilford & Associates, "Fogg Bridge", *The Architectural Review*, Vol. 175, No. 1046, April 1984, p. 42.

Stirling, James, Michael Wilford & Associates, "New York houses", *The Architectural Review*, Vol. 175, No. 1046, April 1984, p. 43.

Stirling, James, "AD Profile 85: James Stirling Michael Wilford & Associates", *Architectural Design*, Vol. 60, No. 5/6, 1990, pp. 6–112.

Summerson, John, "Vitruvius Ludens", *The Architectural Review*, March 1983, pp. 18-21

Vidler, Anthony, "James Stirling: an international architect", *Blueprint*, No. 299, February 2011, pp. 48–58.

Warke, Val K, "Stirling: Cornell. Performing Arts Center, Cornell University, Ithaca, New York State", *The Architectural Review*, Vol. 175, No. 1046, April 1984, pp. 28–34.

Wolf, Gary, "The Shock of the Old: Cambridge Architecture Turns to the Past", *New Boston Review*, September/October 1981, pp. 27–28.

Wolf, Gary, "Stirling: Fogg, Extension to Fogg Museum, Harvard University, Cambridge, Mass", *The Architectural Review*, Vol. 175, No. 1046, April 1984, pp. 35–41.

------ "Science Library, Irvine Campus, University of California", *A&U*, No. 10 (301), October 1995, pp. 16–33.

------ "Stirling, Wilford's Science Library at UC Irvine", *Progressive Architecture*, Vol. 75, No. 10, October 1994, p. 24.

------ "Center for the Performing Arts, Cornell University", *GA Document*, No. 26, 1990, pp. 68–79.

------ "Arthur M Sackler Museum", *GA Document*, No. 19, 1988, pp. 82–89.

------ *Casabella*, "Extension to the Chemistry Department at Columbia University", *Casabella*, vol. 47, no. 493, July/August 1983, pp. 26–27.

------ *Casabella*, "October 1990: Manfredo Tafuri talks about James Stirling", *Casabella*, vol. 70, No. 747, September 2006, pp. 68–72, 92–93.

------ *Building Design*, "Arts for Cornell. Performing arts center for Cornell University" *Building Design*, no. 658, 23 September 1983, p. 10.

------ *Architectural Design*, "Chandler North. The extension of the chemistry department at Columbia University, New York", *Architectural Design*, vol. 53, no. 3/4, 1983, pp. 10–15.

------ *Architectural Design*, "AD profile 144: James Stirling- acceptance of the Royal Gold Medal in Architecture 1980", *Architectural Design*, vol. 50, no. 7/8, 1980, pp. 2–58.

------ "Two US projects by Pritzker Prize winner James Stirling: An addition to Harvard University's Fogg Art Museum; and a renovation and expansion of Rice University's School of Architecture", *Architectural Record*, Vol. 169, No. 9, July 1981, pp. 42–43.

------ "School of Architecture in Houston", *Baumeister*, Vol. 79, No. 4, April 1982, pp. 347–351.

Artifice books on architecture
10a Acton Street
London WC1X 9NG
United Kingdom

Tel: +44 (0)20 7713 5097
Fax: +44 (0)20 7713 8682
sales@artificebooksonline.com
www.artificebooksonline.com

Designed by Sylvia Ugga at Artifice books on architecture

Cover image:
James Stirling, Michael Wilford, and Associates
Perry, Dean, Stahl & Rogers
Arthur M Sackler Museum, Harvard University, Cambridge,
Massachusetts: cut away axonmetric, 1979–1985.
James Stirling/Michael Wilford fonds
Collection Centre Canadien d'Architecture/
Canadian Centre for Architecture, Montréal © CCA

British Library Cataloguing-in-Publication Data. A CIP record for
this book is available from the British Library.

ISBN 9781908967343

Artifice books on architecture is an environmentally responsible
company. Stirling+Wilford American Buildings is printed on
sustainably sourced paper.